THE WAR AGAINST THE VETS

The War Against the Vets

the World War I Bonus Army during the Great Depression

JEROME TUCCILLE

Potomac Books

AN IMPRINT OF THE UNIVERSITY OF NEBRASKA PRESS

Library of Congress Cataloging-in-Publication Data
Names: Tuccille, Jerome, author.
Title: The war against the vets: the World War I Bonus
Army during the great Depression / Jerome Tuccille.
Description: Lincoln: Potomac Books, an imprint of
the University of Nebraska Press, 2018. |
Includes bibliographical references and index.
Identifiers: LCCN 2017043080
ISBN 9781612349336 (cloth: alk. paper)
ISBN 9781640120662 (epub)
ISBN 9781640120679 (mobi)
ISBN 9781640120686 (pdf)
Subjects: LCSH: Bonus Expeditionary Forces. |
World War, 1914–1918—Veterans—Washington (D.C.) |
Protest movements—Washington (D.C.)—History—
20th century. | Washington (D.C.)—History—20th
century. | Veterans—Political activity—United States—
History—20th century. | Veterans—United States—
Economic conditions—20th century.
Classification: LCC F199 .T83 2018 |
DDC 973.91/6—dc23
LC record available at https://lccn.loc.gov/2017043080

Set in Scala OT by Mikala R Kolander.

This book is dedicated to the American
veterans who risked their lives for their country,
only to return to an uncaring public and a
government that paid them only lip
service for their sacrifice.

CONTENTS

List of Illustrations   ix

Prologue   1

PART 1. THE GREAT MARCH

1. Making the World Safe for Democracy—and for Wall Street   13

2. From a Roar to a Whimper   23

3. A Motorcycle Cop Rides to the Rescue   35

4. American-Style Fascism Descends on Washington   47

5. An Unholy Alliance   57

6. The Smell of Revolution in the Air   67

7. Glassford's Frankenstein Monster Rears His Ugly Head   76

8. The Death March Upstages the BEF   87

9. Khaki Shirts Take on the Reds   96

PART 2. BLITZKRIEG

10. An American Caesar Crosses the Anacostia   111

11. Flames Light Up the Night   121

12. Hoover Pays the Price for His Incompetence   131

13. The Vets March Once Again   141

PART 3. THE BIG BLOW

14. The Island of Bones   151

15. Paradise Lost   160

16. The Hurricane Makes a Direct Hit on the Camps   168

17. The Struggle for Survival   179

18. The Cover-Up   188

19. The Vets Finally Get Their Money   197
20. The Battle Continues   206

Acknowledgments   215
Notes   217
Bibliography   229
Index   233

ILLUSTRATIONS

Following page 100

1. Coxey's Army on the march

2. The stock market crash of 1929

3. Bonus Army marches to the Capitol

4. Bonus Army demonstration at the Capitol

5. Bonus Army on the Capitol Lawn

6. Ford Hunger March funeral

7. Ford Hunger March funeral procession

8. Herbert Hoover and Mrs. Hoover

9. Calvin Coolidge, Andrew Mellon, and Herbert Hoover

10. Franklin Delano Roosevelt and Herbert Hoover

11. Franklin Delano Roosevelt

12. Pelham Glassford

13. Gen. Douglas MacArthur

14. Congressmen gathered to fight for the bonus bill

15. Bonus Army marchers in a camp in Anacostia

16. Hurricane damage in Florida Keys

THE WAR AGAINST THE VETS

Prologue

Two great American writers bookended the long, tragic story of the World War I bonus marchers in the early years of the Great Depression. At the beginning of the saga a seven-year-old boy named Gore Vidal sat in the back seat of a car beside his blind grandfather, Sen. Thomas P. Gore, one of Oklahoma's first two senators. The boy stared out the window, searching diligently for signs of the "Boners" he had been hearing about for weeks on end. In his mind's eye he envisioned the Boners as looking like preternatural freaks, "white skeletons like those jointed cardboard ones displayed at Halloween." "Bony figures filled my nightmares until it was explained to me that these Boners were not from slaughterhouses but from poorhouses," he wrote later.

What Vidal saw instead was a long stream of "shabby-looking men holding up signs and shouting at occasional cars." Moments later a stone hurled by one of the demonstrators flew through the open window of the car and crashed on the floorboard between the boy and his grandfather. "Shut the window!" the senator shouted, a command the boy obeyed immediately. The chants of the ragged, homeless, and penniless men filled the future author's ears as the chauffeur maneuvered the vehicle through the encroaching mob. "The Yanks are starving! The Yanks are starving!" they sang to the tune of a popular war song of the era.

Three years later the thirty-six-year-old world-famous author Ernest Hemingway decried the deaths of several hundred World War I vets and their families, whose lives were literally blown away during the most devastating hurricane ever to blast the Florida Keys. "Who Murdered the Vets?" Hemingway asked in the most impassioned piece of writing he had yet composed after he boated north from Key West to survey the carnage. In a separate letter to his editor Maxwell Perkins he described his rage at seeing naked women—the wives of vets and some local residents—"tossed up into trees by the water, swollen and stinking, their breasts as big as balloons, flies between their legs." "Who left you there? And what's the punishment for manslaughter now?" Hemingway wrote. He put the blame on the Franklin D. Roosevelt administration, which was responsible for shipping the vets out of the nation's capital, where they had regrouped to demand their unpaid bonuses as they had done in 1932, when Herbert Hoover was still in the White House.

In between Vidal's and Hemingway's moving eyewitness accounts, one of the sorriest chapters in American history unfolded in the makeshift campsites the vets had erected along Pennsylvania Avenue, which linked the executive and legislative branches of the federal government. The drama that played out exploded like a bombshell at the very focal point of American political life.

Before there was the Bonus Army there was Coxey's Army. Before there was the Great Depression there was the Panic of 1893, when the unemployment rate in America soared to a staggering 18 percent. And before Gore Vidal and Ernest Hemingway emerged to describe the travesty of justice that befell the Bonus Army of the 1930s, an earlier American writer named Jack London wrote about his own experiences marching with Kelly's Army, a group affiliated with Coxey, to demand work for unemployed "stiffs," as he called them.

"Underwood, Leola, Menden, Avoca, Walnut, Marno, Atlantic, Wyoto, Anita, Adair, Adam, Casey, Stuart, Dexter, Carlham, De Soto, Van Meter, Booneville, Commerce, Valley junction—how the names of the towns come back to me as I con the map and trace our route through the fat Iowa country!" London wrote. "And the hospitable Iowa farmer-folk! They turned out with their wagons and carried our baggage; gave us hot lunches at noon by the wayside; mayors of comfortable little towns made speeches of welcome and hastened us on our way; deputations of little girls and maidens came out to meet us, and the good citizens turned out by hundreds, locked arms, and marched with us down their main streets."

The march took shape when an Ohio businessman and thoroughbred racehorse breeder named Jacob Coxey staggered to the brink of bankruptcy in the wake of the financial panic of 1893. The American economy had been prone to a series of boom-and-bust cycles throughout its century-long history, and this latest bust hobbled Coxey, undermined his local fiefdom, and sent him into a boiling rage. Virtually overnight as it were, his once prosperous limestone quarries lost most of their value, and Coxey was forced to fire about forty of the workers he employed in his family enterprise. Coxey switched sides, abandoning his role as the employer of dozens of local laborers and setting himself up as a firebrand leader of America's growing army of the downtrodden and unemployed.

His timing could not have been better. The country was ready for just such a leader, a strong man championing people's rights to a job that paid them enough to clothe, feed, and shelter themselves and their families. Coxey called for an army of the disenfranchised to march to the nation's capital to demonstrate in favor of a national public works project that would be financed by government bonds and an infusion of capital into the system. If he got his way Coxey's Army would be put to work rebuilding the infrastructure, particularly the roads, projects dear to the hearts of midwestern farmers, who demanded serviceable roads to get their produce to the markets. Coxey's Army began its march from Massillon, Ohio, on March 25, 1894, with an initial contingent of one hundred men. Other armies quickly joined his cause in different regions of the country, including one from the West headed by self-styled "General" Charles T. Kelly. Kelly's Army, the one that claimed Jack London among its ranks, lost most of its members by the time it reached the Ohio River, and London seemed to have treated it more as a lark—fodder for his stories—than anything else.

Coxey and many of his imitators, however, were determined to get their voices heard in Washington DC. Their plan was to arrive there with ten thousand or more men by May Day. May 1 was a traditional day for organized labor to vent its economic frustrations, and the timing would add drama to the occasion. But by the time they assembled on April 29 and set up campsites along Pennsylvania Avenue, their numbers had dwindled to about six hundred adamant souls; the most generous estimates put the figure at two thousand. As serious as their cause was, and as desperate as the men were who fleshed out the impromptu armies, the entire adventure was not without its comic opera overtones. Coxey appointed as his majordomo a flamboyant westerner named Carl "Old Greasy" Browne, who considered several exotic ideas to be Gospel Truth.

The foremost idea in his head was that a man should never bathe or change his clothing. Attired as he was in an outfit modeled after that of "Buffalo Bill" Cody and sporting a shock of filthy, tangled hair, Browne presented an image that was nothing short of exotic, to say the least, and he exuded a pungent odor that announced his presence before he entered a room. A second idea he held to be sacred was a belief in reincarnation. He thought that everyone was born over and over again with a dash of Jesus Christ nestled in his genes. And a third notion, which underscored and compounded the second idea, was that Jacob Coxey had a dollop more of Jesus in him than most mere mortals did. Indeed, Browne told Coxey that he was the "Cerebrum of Christ." Coxey, a committed agnostic until this point, allowed Browne's canonization to stroke his ego. He accepted his sainthood without giving it much thought and renamed his army the "Commonweal of Christ" at Browne's suggestion. Unfortunately, if there had ever been a chance that Coxey would succeed in attaining his goals in Washington, he managed only to turn his crusade into a circus sideshow with Browne marching beside him.

Coxey's arrival in Washington DC just added to the atmosphere of buffoonery. Coxey and Browne rode in style down Pennsylvania Avenue—Coxey and his family in a horse-drawn carriage, and Browne mounted in his soiled Buffalo Bill costume on one of Coxey's thoroughbreds. Sadly, most of the estimated ten thousand who had begun the long trek from various locations across America never completed their journey. Trains that never got going sidelined many of them; others dropped out because of disillusionment with their cause. The handful of ragtag stalwarts who did make it to Washington shuffled behind the two leaders, looking more forlorn than rebellious. The entire escapade ended ignobly on May Day when the Cerebrum of Christ and his acolyte Browne were arrested for what amounted to "stepping on the grass" in a swampy lot near the Capitol, sentenced to twenty days in jail, and fined five dollars apiece.

As badly as it all ended, with none of the mission's goals coming to fruition, Coxey's Army nevertheless inspired other agitators for justice in later generations. The vision of Coxey's band of foot soldiers taking their grievances directly to the nation's citadel and confronting their elected officials directly struck a romantic chord in American folklore. When all else was lost and hopes of reform seemed to be a distant dream, there was little left to do but thrust a sword into the belly of the beast.

The march of the Bonus Army on Washington in 1932 had its roots in the unpaid bonus promised to the vets of World War I, who had risked their lives on the battlefields of Europe. In 1924, six long years after the combatants signed the armistice and the vets returned home to an uncaring public, the U.S. Congress passed a law granting them "adjusted universal compensation"—a bonus in plain English—for their service to the country. President Calvin Coolidge vetoed the bill, and Congress overrode his veto and passed it into law. There was a catch to the bill, however; the money was not immediately payable except for amounts accruing to fifty dollars or less. Instead the government issued IOUs to the vets—so-called certificates—not redeemable until 1945, by which time many of the vets could be expected to have passed on to their eternal rewards.

The good times roared on in America over the next five years, with the stock market booming and the nightclubs humming with frenzied activity. Meanwhile the vets struggled to find their footing like most returning warriors from foreign wars, wondering if they would ever get their hands on the money promised by their government. They called out now and then for new legislation to get their bonus money early, with their entreaties falling on deaf ears. And then, on a grim Black Tuesday in October 1929, it all came unglued. The stock market, which had plunged almost 13 percent five months earlier—a precursor for what lay in store—crashed like a bombshell over the excesses of the decade, wiping out the fortunes of the country's most privileged classes virtually overnight. The Great Depression was about to begin, and everyone would be maimed by the devastation, not just the vets who had been given the royal runaround by politicians at the helm of power.

The vets had a couple of friends in the House of Representatives, the main one being a Texas Democrat and a vet himself named Wright Patman. The freshman congressman called the bonus "an honest debt" owed the vets by the government, and he co-sponsored legislation designed to immediately pay the vets the money they had been promised. The bill never made it out of committee, and in any event Coolidge's successor in the White House, Herbert Hoover, was also opposed to paying the bonus. The Great Depression was beginning to bite hard, decimating the government's coffers along with the incomes and net worth of most Americans. The harsh reality was that there simply were not enough votes to override Hoover's threatened veto. Adding to the drama was the ugly face of racism hovering over the issue like a malignant black cloud. The overwhelming majority of vets were white, but there was a substantial contingent of "Buffalo Soldiers"—troops in all-black units—who had taken up arms in various wars for the country after Lincoln ended slavery. The prospect of the offspring of former slaves getting their hands on a lump sum of cash for any reason did not sit well with their white brethren.

"The half million Negroes in the South, who probably would receive five hundred or six hundred dollars each, would immediately quit work until the money was spent," the august U.S. Chamber of Commerce had stated at a 1920 convention in Atlantic City, New Jersey, the first time the question of a bonus surfaced.

An African American newspaper, the *Cleveland Advocate*, understandably took issue with that position, reporting that to deprive one black veteran of his bonus meant denying four white veterans *their* bonuses, which was "a most reprehensible injustice to the white world war veteran," as well as to his black comrades in arms.

Friction between black and white veterans had bubbled to the surface of American life as soon as the war ended. White society had long denied blacks access to the job market, which was the reason why so many had gravitated to the army after the Civil War when the government needed warm bodies to flesh out its various battlefields. While blacks and whites had fought beside one another—albeit in segregated units—in wartime, whites resented blacks competing for hard-to-get jobs when the wars ended, and armed clashes had broken out between black and white vets during the interregnum periods. During the summer of 1920 alone, black vets took up arms to defend themselves against marauding bands of white troops in front of the Capitol in Washington DC, and the rioting spread to twenty-five cities across the country before it was contained. The *New York Times*, hardly a beacon of racial equality at the time, blamed the violence on "Bolshevik agitation."

But the Great Depression overrode even the racial hostilities as the economy plummeted over a steep financial cliff. Everyone suffered, including the privileged classes, and there was hardly a groundswell of support anywhere to accelerate the payment of the bonuses promised to the vets—white or black for that matter. Wright Patman remained the lone voice in the wilderness who championed their cause, arguing that the vets deserved a "square deal" after risking their lives for the country. But he was fighting a lost cause. When it became apparent that the vets were not about to get their money anytime soon, they descended en masse on the nation's capital and set up makeshift campsites, which the press called "Hoovervilles," across from the White House. There they clustered in ever-growing numbers, grizzled and aging vets, their wives and children and family pets, demanding that the government pay them their money now instead of distributing IOUs payable in the distant future.

The vets would not go away as the Hoover administration urged them to do. Their ringing voices and cries for justice grew louder, serving as a constant source of embarrassment for a beleaguered president campaigning for reelection in 1932 as the national economy sank further into the abyss. Hoover decided to take action as the November elections loomed closer on the horizon. He unleashed the full force of the U.S. military under the command of Gen. Douglas MacArthur on the campsites— tanks, cavalry with sabers drawn, soldiers against their fellow soldiers, burning down tents and leveling the campsites in a savage effort to disperse the vets. The sabers drew blood and shots were fired, resulting in several deaths. The demoralized vets scattered in the face of the onslaught before the toll of dead and injured could mount higher.

But that was not the end of the story. The vets would return to fight another day. Their struggle for justice continued after the new administration took office. Hoover's problem soon became Roosevelt's problem, with World War I vets camping out in full view of the White House as the Great Depression took hold and jobs across America vanished into the ether. The solution was to ship the vets down to work camps in the Florida Keys and house them in flimsy tent cities that offered little protection against the violent storms that whipped from time to time across the southernmost tip of the country. It all came to a head over the Labor Day weekend in 1935, when the most brutal hurricane in a century roared through the Keys and leveled everything in its path. What MacArthur had tried to accomplish three years earlier had been achieved by a force of nature—hundreds of vets lost their lives, their campsites blown away into the ocean and their bodies blasted over the dunes and into the handful of trees that were left standing.

To understand what happened then, how American soldiers fought older American vets in the worst domestic bloodletting since the Civil War, we have to travel back in time, more than eighty years into the past and one hundred years since the armistice was signed ending "the war to end all wars" and to make the world safe for democracy. This is the saga, now relegated to a footnote in history, of one of the sorriest episodes in the history of the American republic.

1

The Great March

ONE

Making the World Safe for Democracy—and for Wall Street

A century ago Johnny came marching home again, to paraphrase a popular Civil War song penned by Patrick Gilmore. American troops returned to their homeland following a war their country had entered reluctantly, a war to make the world safe for democracy and a war to end all wars, according to President Woodrow Wilson. Would that it had been so; sadly, those sentiments have devolved into terms of derision as the world erupted in a series of devastating conflicts during the ensuing decades and has been gripped in a state of permanent warfare since September 11, 2001. But in 1918 the country took Wilson's words seriously after the armistice was signed on November 11, officially ending the First World War. American servicemen debarked by the thousands from transport ships that had carried them across the vast expanse of ocean from European battlefields to the safety of their own shores.

"We are provincials no longer," President Wilson declared. "The tragic events of the thirty months of vital turmoil through which we have just passed have made us citizens of the world. There can be no turning back."

The war had exacted a heavy toll on those who fought in it and on others uprooted from their homes. France had lost three-quarters of its mobilized men between the ages of twenty and thirty-two. It was one of the deadliest conflicts in human history, with more than 3 million killed, 8.3 million wounded, and 3.6 million taken as prisoners of war or missing in action, exacting a toll of 15 million casualties in all, not counting civilians. The U.S. count amounted to 360,000 casualties, including 126,000 dead and 234,000 wounded.

The country the American vets returned to was mired in a nasty recession—by some definitions a depression—that hit much of the world in the wake of the war. After the war ended the global economy began to decline as a severe downturn took hold. It was a prelude to the Great Depression of the 1930s, with sharp deflationary forces bringing the country and the global economy to their knees from January 1920 to July 1921. The vets faced few job prospects as they created a surge in the civilian labor force that triggered racial warfare between white and black soldiers who suddenly found themselves competing for whatever jobs were available.

But the mini-depression was short-lived compared to the one that battered the nation and the world a decade later. The economy started to grow from the middle of 1921 until 1929, although it had not yet made all the adjustments in shifting from wartime to peacetime conditions. As the economic life of the country recovered, the quality of life of most Americans improved with it, sparking a nonstop party that lasted throughout the rest of the decade romanticized in history as the Roaring Twenties. Middle-class Americans soon forgot about the war, eager to put all that unpleasantness behind them. But the vets—many jobless and desperate—remembered it all too well, still carrying with them the scars of battle and the nightmares of fallen comrades blasted into oblivion by enemy shells. Many of the vets were financially strapped and others suffered from horrors of war that would later be classified as post-traumatic stress disorder, while the rest of their countrymen danced and drank and partied throughout the night.

The plight of the vets caught the attention of a wealthy Virginia farmer named W. Bruce Shafer Jr., who had helped prevent wartime food shortages by encouraging the planting of potatoes to replace wheat and other grains, which had lower yields per acre. During a party that his father threw for local vets right after the war ended, Shafer learned that most of the vets had risked their lives for a pittance amounting to a dollar a day, and that many could not find work when they mustered out of the service. "I thought it was a darn shame that these fellows didn't have enough money to take a girl to the moving pictures," Shafer said. "They won the war that everyone else thought was going to take twice as long."

To acknowledge their service to the nation Shafer went to Washington to lobby for a doubling of servicemen's pay for those still in the military, and for a bonus of an extra year's pay for the ones who had been discharged. Shafer received a good reception at first. Within a few months following his lobbying blitz on Washington, bolstered by his support from the recently founded American Legion, hundreds of bills were introduced on the federal and state levels to increase veterans' benefits. Congress authorized a bonus of sixty dollars, amounting to an extra two months' pay instead of the year requested by Shafer. But it was a step in the right direction, with the promise of further debate on the subject in future sessions of Congress. The Veterans of Foreign Wars joined forces with Shafer and the American Legion. Together they petitioned for a package of benefits that included a bonus of a dollar a day for each month of service, a one-time payment of one hundred dollars for overseas service, and help in buying a farm or house with a federal mortgage guarantee up to one thousand dollars.

Various states followed suit with proposals to introduce an assortment of their own bonus packages. On October 16, 1920, New York asked voters to approve a measure to float bonds to cover the cost of bonus payments for its in-state vets. In support of the pending legislation fifty thousand vets, cheered on by one hundred thousand spectators, marched in solidarity up Fifth Avenue past viewing stands lined with politicians and other officials. Five hundred cars and trucks carried two thousand wounded vets up the avenue, their march resonating with the blare of dozens of brass bands and fife and drum and bugle corps, and the blast of cannons that shot pro-bonus literature over the heads of the crowd, raining the pamphlets down on the thousands lining the sidewalks. It was a glorious parade in grand New York style, heavy on bombast and drama but with little follow-through in its aftermath, as subsequent events would pan out.

Immediately resistance to the bonus as something the government could not afford began to emerge in the nation's capital, slowing down progress on the state level as well. Warren Harding had campaigned in favor of a bonus bill during the 1920 elections, but he abruptly did an about-face as soon as he was voted into office. "To float bonds . . . or to meet such an additional expenditure out of taxes would present grave problems and might result in disaster," warned Treasury Secretary David E. Houston while the campaign was still in full swing. Once elected to the presidency, with the steep recession not yet over, Harding took Houston's dire comment to heart and later reversed himself on the issue.

Compounding the problem for the vets was the isolationist sentiment prevailing in the country at the time. Isolationism— resistance to getting involved in other countries' wars—had been ingrained in the American psyche since the days of our Founding Fathers, with both Washington and Jefferson voicing opposition to foreign entanglements. "Our detached and distant situation invites and enables us to pursue a different course," Washington had said in his 1796 farewell address to the nation, while Jefferson warned against "entangling alliances." All that changed during the Spanish-American War of 1898, with American jingoism spurred on by a saber-rattling press, but when the war ended the U.S. populace returned to its isolationist roots. A significant majority of Americans believed that sending U.S. troops over to European battlefields had been a monumental mistake and that British propaganda, working in concert with U.S. bankers and arms merchants looking to profit from the engagement, had duped us into it. A Gallup poll at the time revealed that 70 percent of the American people believed that it had been a mistake for the United States to enter the war. So public opinion was not on the side of the vets in the aftermath of the Great War, leaving them to battle for themselves with the aid of a handful of their congressional allies.

Racial bigotry also reared its ugly head during the presidential campaign of 1920. Many of the returning vets were black "Buffalo Soldiers," a term bestowed on them by the Cheyenne and Comanche tribes whom the all-black regiments had fought in the plains in the early 1890s. The Indians had never seen black troops before, and they were in awe of their fighting ability and their dark skin and curly hair, which gave them the appearance of the wild buffalo that the Indians hunted across the vast sweep of the American plains. The name Buffalo Soldiers became a point of pride that the blacks wore with distinction over the decades until President Harry S. Truman desegregated the military in 1948.

Now that the Great War in Europe was over, however, white America had little use for its black warriors and resented their competing with white men for jobs at a time when work was in scant supply as America transitioned into a peacetime economy. Blacks, according to prevailing white attitudes at the time, were ill-equipped to handle lump-sum payments of cash and were likely to quit working until the money was gone, an argument that made little sense since most of the black vets—and white vets, for that matter—were out of work in the first place. The *Cleveland Advocate* fought back by noting that blacks who had been freed from slavery little more than a half century before had cultivated millions of acres of farmland and had demonstrated a strong work ethic while under the lash of white slave owners. Even if the money were ill-spent, the paper reasoned, it was likely to benefit white merchants who sold their goods and services to blacks at elevated prices.

But the main concern of both major political parties was the cost of the bonus at a time when the country was still reeling beneath the burden of its massive war debt. Woodrow Wilson's assistant secretary of the treasury, R. C. Leffingwell, figured the bonus would cost more than $2 billion, a staggering sum at the time. The money "is not in the treasury and available for distribution," Leffingwell was quoted in the *Washington Post*. The bill pending before Congress, which had been passed in the House but shelved in the Senate, was laid to rest. And Warren Harding was content to let it lie there when he assumed office in 1921, notwithstanding his rhetoric in favor of the bill during his presidential campaign.

Harding had powerful friends in the business world who were also worried about the federal government's bottom line. A bonus would make "mercenaries out of our patriotic boys," intoned George Eastman of Eastman Kodak. In response a popular humorist of the time, Will Rogers, retorted, "That old alibi about the country not being able to pay is all applesauce." "This country is not broke," Rogers wrote. "Automobile manufacturers are three months behind in their orders, and whiskey was never as high in its life. If we owed it to some Foreign Nation you would talk about honor and then pay it. . . . I think the best Insurance in the World against another War is to take care of the Boys who fought in the last one. YOU MAY WANT TO USE THEM AGAIN."

The squabble continued over the next few years, with various veterans' organizations and sympathetic individuals like Rogers on the pro-bonus side of the issue, and big business and their flunkies in government posturing against it. Some corporations compelled their employees to flood their representatives with letters arguing against the passage of a bonus package, and Thomas Edison celebrated his seventy-fifth birthday by declaring, "I think we should postpone the bonus. The country is in no condition for it." The Congress was in no mood to march in lockstep with the anti-bonus lobby, however. On March 23, 1922, the House passed a bonus bill by an overwhelming margin, with 242 Republicans and 90 Democrats voting in favor. The Senate followed with an equally lopsided majority voting for passage. It then fell on the desk of President Harding, who had first been in favor, then against, and seemed to be tilting back in favor of it again. But once more he flip-flopped and vetoed the bill on September 19. The House mustered enough votes to override his veto, but the Senate came up four votes short of overturning it.

When the economy was in recession, there was some justification to deny passage on financial grounds, but the recession was well over by 1922 and the good times were starting to roll again. The argument that the country could not afford to pay the vets sounded hollower than ever at a time of renewed prosperity. But Harding was in no position to focus on the vets as his first term in office wore on. One scandal after another crippled his administration. He had fleshed out his cabinet with an assortment of cronies who appeared to be in competition to see which was the most corrupt. They raided the public till, sold the naval oil reserve at Teapot Dome and Elk Hills, stole money from the Veterans Bureau, seized confiscated liquor and sold it for personal profit, and otherwise engaged in an orgy of unfettered governmental brigandage that Harding proved incapable of reining in. The hapless Harding, whose presidency would go down as one of the most corrupt in history, was destroyed by his hand-picked advisors. He died on August 2, 1923, following a trip to Alaska.

Next up was Vice President Calvin Coolidge, who was sworn in as president in the wake of Harding's demise. No one expected Coolidge, who firmly believed that "the chief business of the American people is business," to be more favorable to a veterans bonus than his predecessor had been.

Coolidge had been an outsider within Harding's administration, a vice president whom the president and his larcenous cronies had shunted off to the sidelines. He had remained above all the wheeling and dealing that had taken place under Harding's nose, a fiscal conservative by nature who seemed to have been born with a green eyeshade affixed to his brow. He believed passionately in balanced budgets and federal government frugality, and was ideologically opposed to any expenditures that he deemed nonessential to the government's wellbeing. The veterans' bonus was a nonstarter for him. "Patriotism which is bought and paid for is not patriotism," he believed. "To attempt to make a money payment out of the earnings of the people to those who are physically well and financially able is to abandon one of our most cherished American ideals."

His sentiments, honest as they were, hardly endeared him to the thousands of impatient vets who had been clamoring for their bonuses for the past five years. In the early months of 1924 their demands reached a crescendo. Armies of protestors demonstrated for the bonus all over the country, but their entreaties engendered counter-protestors, many of them organized by big business, which denounced the bonus as a giveaway the country could not afford. Employers threatened their labor forces with the loss of their jobs if they failed to join the anti-bonus brigades in the streets of America. To his credit President Coolidge denounced the heavy-handed tactics of the business community as "utterly un-American," even though he maintained his principled stand against the bonus itself.

In an effort to defuse the explosive atmosphere New York representative Hamilton Fish III, a cousin of the Rough Rider who had been killed in action fighting with Teddy Roosevelt in Cuba during the Spanish-American War, rode to the rescue with a new bonus bill that he introduced in Congress on February 26, 1924. Fish crafted the bill in a way that he believed would make it acceptable to both sides of the dispute. The vets would receive a bonus, but it would not be payable until 1945 with interest accruing over the next twenty years. The vets could borrow against their policies but could not cash them in before the due date—or when they died, in which case their families would get the money. Realizing that this was the best they were likely to get from a tight-fisted Congress and president, the American Legion and the vfw organized marches in New York and other cities urging Congress to pass the bill into law. The House and Senate did exactly that and passed the legislation by overwhelming margins. But even the stretched-out payment dates were not enough to mollify the man in the White House, who was loath to saddle future generations with the ultimate cost of the bill. Coolidge was nothing if not consistent; he vetoed the bill, but this time Congress had enough votes to override the president's veto.

Media wags quickly labeled the bill "the Tombstone Bonus" for obvious reasons. But in reality it was not truly a bonus at all but rather an insurance policy, payable on death or on the due date twenty-one years in the future. Fish's bill, designed to pacify agitators on both sides of the issue, satisfied no one. These types of compromises normally leave a bitter taste in the mouths of everyone involved, who feel that opposing forces have short-changed them. Fish's legislation hardly put the issue to rest. It lay there smoldering, a campfire whose glowing embers were not fully extinguished. It was just a question of time before it flared back up into roaring flames again.

Wright Patman was among those who refused to let Fish's bonus bill stand as the final word on the controversy. John William Wright Patman was a self-styled populist hailing from Hughes Springs in Cass County, Texas, whose cherubic appearance stood in contrast to the fiery passions burning beneath his surface. He had joined the army as a private during the Great War and quickly risen to the rank of first lieutenant and machine-gun officer. When the war ended Patman ran for public office and was elected to the Texas House of Representatives in 1920. He left that post in 1924 when he was appointed district attorney of the fifth judicial district. But he had set his sights on the national scene, and in 1928 he successfully ran for Congress in the first congressional district. As a veteran himself who regarded the Tombstone Bonus as nothing short of a mockery, he embraced the bonus issue like a dog in pursuit of his favorite bone.

Patman's political enemies described him as possessing the "convictions of a Baptist crusader." He thought of himself as a "champion of plain people" and an enemy of big banks and the rich "few who already own and control a majority of the wealth." He refused to let the issue rest where it was following the stretched-out bill enacted into law four years earlier. The vets deserved a "square deal," said Patman, particularly since the big corporations that had profited from the war had all been paid in full before the ink on the armistice agreement was completely dry. The country was still prospering with a near-decade-long party while the vets stood on the sidelines with their hands out, waiting for money that should have been paid to them after putting their lives on the line for their country ten years earlier.

Patman's first order of business after taking his seat in Congress was to introduce a bill calling for the immediate payment of the bonus to the vets. "They got only twenty-one dollars a month," Patman reasoned, "and had to pay their own laundry bills. If they made an allotment to a wife or child they had nothing left." By contrast shipyard workers made twenty dollars a day during the war, three thousand miles removed from the action overseas. It was time to get the balance right. Senator Smith Wildman Brookhart, an "insurgent Republican" from Iowa who lived up to his middle name and labeled himself a "cowboy radical," lent his support to Patman's bill. The veterans organizations also got behind the legislation, but the Patman-Brookhart bill never made it out of committee. Coolidge's successor in the White House, Herbert Hoover, was no more inclined than his predecessor was to breathe life into the moribund bill. And so it died a quiet death there, like Lazarus in his crypt, until Patman returned at a more propitious moment to bring it back to life.

But that moment would have to wait a bit longer before it came to pass. Five months after Patman arrived in Washington a monumental event rocked the financial world and sent shockwaves of hysteria reverberating throughout the country and across most of the civilized world. It would go down in history as the Crash of 1929, and the damage it inflicted on the nation's economy would impair the lifestyles of rich and poor alike for the coming decade. Patman had to take a bleacher seat in the political arena while the country reeled beneath the wreckage of an economy that had soared to unprecedented heights throughout most of the decade and appeared as though it would never descend to earth again. But he would not lose sight of his ultimate goal as he waited for the opportunity to strike again in the struggle to secure a square deal for the vets.

TWO

From a Roar to a Whimper

The Roaring Twenties had roared loudest on the New York Stock Exchange as the Dow Jones Industrial Average blasted its way to unprecedented heights over an eight-year period. Between August 1921 and September 1929 the Dow increased six-fold from a base of 63 to 381. To put that gain in a modern context, it was equivalent to the DJIA rocketing from 6,443, where it bottomed on March 6, 2009, following the meltdown of 2008 in the midst of the Great Recession, to more than 36,000 eight years later. The DJIA merely tripled to an all-time high of 20,000 in 2016. Most investors who hopped aboard for the later ride were happy to have seen their net worth recover after the 2008 drubbing, but we can imagine the euphoria that gripped the investment world in the 1920s when stocks soared to such giddy altitudes.

Why did the stock market fall apart in October 1929? Some blame it on the impending passage of the Smoot-Hawley Tariff Act of 1930, which would eventually raise tariffs on more than twenty thousand imported goods into the United States to their highest levels in more than one hundred years. "Economists still agree that Smoot-Hawley and the ensuing tariff wars were highly counterproductive and contributed to the depth and length of the global Depression," said former chairman of the Federal Reserve Ben Bernanke during a speech he delivered at the London School of Economics on March 25, 2013. Others blame the 1929 collapse on the excesses associated with rampaging stock speculation itself. The cataclysmic bust began on Black Monday, October 28, 1929, when the Dow collapsed about 13 percent. On Black Tuesday, the following day, stocks shed another 12 percent. The selling frenzy continued almost nonstop for another couple of years, until the

Dow cratered at 41, its lowest level of the century, 89 percent below its 1929 peak.

The crash occurred during a period of unbridled optimism and prosperity for the country at large. No less an authority than Irving Fisher, widely regarded as one of America's greatest mathematical economists and one of the world's clearest economics writers, weighed in on the subject. He was a man with the intellect to use mathematics in most of his theories and the good sense to present them only after he had clearly explained his central principles in plain English. Fisher proclaimed on October 16, 1929, "Stock prices have reached what looks like a permanently high plateau." A lesser-known eminence, Roger Babson, challenged Fisher's prognostication and warned, "Sooner or later a crash is coming, and it may be terrific." Fisher reiterated his faith in the stock market on October 23 in a speech before the District of Columbia's Bankers Association, five days before stocks began the tailspin that Wall Street analysts labeled "the Babson Break." Not even Fisher's carefully honed mathematical models foretold the dangers lurking ahead in investors' mania to buy more and more stocks at higher and higher prices.

What Babson saw in his crystal ball that Fisher failed to discern in his was that ordinary, unsophisticated investors were buying stocks with larger and larger amounts of borrowed money. While the vets waited in the wings for the government to pay them the promised bonuses, their fellow countrymen—savvy stock traders, waiters and waitresses, cabdrivers, speculators from every segment of society—took on rising levels of debt to fund their stock purchases. Brokerage houses dropped their margin requirements to as low as 10 percent to allow rich and poor people alike to take on greater risk. It was possible to buy one hundred dollars' worth of stock with only ten dollars down, and it seemed as though the good times could last forever as long as stock prices were rising. If stocks appreciated another 10 percent, speculators could double their money, whereas they had only a 10 percent gain if they paid full price for the shares.

As we saw during the housing crisis of the first decade of the twenty-first century, that strategy worked well as long as the bull market was in full swing. But when homeowners took on no-income-verification mortgages worth more than the market value of their abodes, the prescription for a market meltdown was writ large upon the wall. In 1929 all it took was a 10 percent decline in stock prices to wipe out the entire net worth of a margin investor with only 10 percent down. When the Babson Break commenced in earnest, the brokerage houses came calling again, this time with margin calls demanding that their highly leveraged customers put up more money, ordering them in effect to throw good money after bad money to cover their losses on their stock portfolios.

The banks stepped in to buy stocks in an attempt to instill some confidence in the market, but it was a case of too little too late. The strategy was little more than a stopgap measure that failed to stem the wave of panic selling that engulfed the nation from coast to coast. Fear and greed have always ruled the marketplace, bringing to mind the old adage that "bulls and bears make money, but pigs get slaughtered." There is no ceiling on the prices investors are willing to pay for stocks when greed is rising. Then, when fear and panic set in, a stock that looked attractive at fifty dollars a share fails to attract any buyers when the price plummets to five dollars. Overnight, as it were, vast fortunes of the rich and powerful evaporated into the ether, and the life savings of ordinary Americans were obliterated. The collapse took a devastating toll on the overall economy as people fell behind on their bills, banks and brokerage houses tottered on the precipice of bankruptcy under an avalanche of bad loans, and jobs disappeared, plunging a growing army of unemployed deeper into a black hole of misery and despair.

President Herbert Hoover, elected in 1928, got into the act by stating in a radio address to the nation, "The fundamental business of the country . . . is on a sound and prosperous basis." Still the carnage continued. No reassurances from the president and from the country's major financial institutions proved adequate to stanch the financial hemorrhaging. In just a few days of selling, a total of $25 billion—about $345 billion in current dollars—sank into the void. And the worst was not yet over. The next few years would see many more billions of the nation's collective wealth lost to the graveyards of financial ruin.

Hoover's administration was bedeviled from the start. The thirty-first president had a distinguished enough background before he ran for public office. A Quaker who began his career as a mining engineer, he was drawn to humanitarian efforts during World War I, serving as head of the U.S. Food Administration, which provided relief services to the war-ravaged countries of Europe. His work caught the attention of President Harding, who appointed Hoover to his cabinet as secretary of commerce. In that role Hoover escaped being tainted by the scandals that brought Harding to ruin, and when Calvin Coolidge succeeded Harding after the latter's death the new president kept Hoover on in the same position.

Lurking in the recesses of Hoover's mind, however, was an odd juxtaposition of ideas that did not quite gel in the real world. He subscribed to a philosophy he called the "Efficiency Movement," which held that inefficiencies in both government and in the private sector could be pinpointed by panels of central planners who could analyze and resolve them. This theory was at odds with Coolidge's faith in the efficacies of the marketplace and his belief that fair and honest competition was the best medicine for reining in economic excesses. For this reason Hoover kept his own ideas under wraps while serving in Coolidge's cabinet. But when the 1928 elections rolled around and Hoover stormed to victory over Democrat Al Smith—one of only two presidents along with William Howard Taft to achieve the highest office in the land with no previous electoral experience—Hoover was free to experiment with his own notions about the presumed efficiency of central planning experts.

The hapless Hoover could not have taken the oath of office at a worse time. He came in under a cloud of sorts, since the curmudgeonly Coolidge had been fond of giving him advice he never asked for. "I was particularly offended by his comment 'to shit or get off the pot,'" Hoover complained. Hoover had a way of procrastinating when it came to making decisions that exasperated his self-confident predecessor.

The crash on Wall Street swept like a tornado across the country less than eight months after Hoover was sworn in, through no fault of his own. But it occurred on his watch, making him the wrong man in the wrong place during the worst catastrophe the nation had experienced in decades. Hoover's response was to spend more federal money on public works projects, most notably plans for the construction of the Hoover dam across the Black Canyon on the border between Arizona and Nevada to tame the Colorado River. Thousands of men and their families traveled out west to work on what would become the largest dam of its time. It was an engineering marvel, a towering monument presided over by the former mining engineer who was now the country's president. But the dam, massive as it was, represented only a drop in the bucket in light of the massive problems gripping the country, and it was not the medicine the country needed to resurrect the citizenry from the dark pit of despair and to put most of the unemployed back on the payrolls.

When Smoot-Hawley kicked in the year after Hoover assumed the highest office in the land, another sucker punch staggered the new president with record high tariffs and hefty increases in both corporate taxes and personal income taxes that drove the top bracket rate from 25 percent to 63 percent. The combination of barriers to free trade and higher taxes at a time when a growing army of Americans was out of work was the opposite of what was required. Hoover's policies ran counter to the advice he would have received from John Maynard Keynes on the left wing of the political spectrum and Milton Friedman on the right. Hoover consulted with his central planning experts to fix what was wrong with America, but they failed to serve the president well.

As though Hoover didn't have enough to occupy his attention, the question of the bonus payment to the World War I veterans rose to the surface of the country's consciousness just as the midterm elections of 1930 began in earnest. Hoover compounded his dilemma by trying to reassure the voting public that the future of the country was "bright with hope" and the Republicans represented the "Party of Prosperity." That message carried some weight in the years and months before the crash, but it rang hollow in the weeks leading up to the 1930 election. The voters rejected Hoover's assessment of the country's future, a hopelessly Pollyannaish view that bore little resemblance to the reality of life in the streets. Hoover's failure to understand the distinction cost the Republicans control of the House in the November elections, as the Democrats picked up fifty-three seats and control of the lower chamber for the first time since 1916. The electorate also whittled the Republicans down to a single vote advantage in the Senate.

Hoover largely relied for advice on his Quaker upbringing rather than on sound economic reasoning. He rose religiously each morning at six, fell to his knees, and implored his heavenly father to guide him through the day. "Our loving heavenly Father," he prayed. "I have tried to hide these fears and worries. I don't know if others can see through my smiles, but I believe you can know my heart. I come to you for help. Please show me what to do and give me the strength to do it. In Jesus's loving name I pray, Amen."

When Franklin D. Roosevelt ran against Hoover in 1932 he said, "There is nothing inside that man but jelly."

Wright Patman had not lost sight of the cause that had initially driven him to win his seat in Congress. The bonus question had remained his top priority since he first introduced his legislation after being elected to the House in 1928. And now that the economy had deteriorated drastically, reducing the vets and most other Americans to dire circumstances in the months following the crash, Patman seized the opportunity to agitate for the immediate payment of the bonus owed to the World War I veterans. He proved to be a master at organizing parades, public demonstrations replete with marching bands and martial music, and in eliciting favorable articles from the powerful Hearst newspapers, which always backed the military and those who served in it.

For many of the vets the IOU the government had given them in lieu of cash represented their only real asset. Once again Patman enlisted the support of the VFW and organized a coalition of other pro-bonus colleagues in Congress. They presented a new bill to Hoover, who had an ally in a powerful former American Legion commander named Hanford "Jack" MacNider. He was a highly decorated army general during the First World War and assistant secretary of war from 1925 to 1928. Appointed ambassador to Canada in 1930, he succeeded in shocking his hosts when he showed up in his civilian role decked out in full military regalia—a total breach of protocol.

MacNider, who hoped to become Hoover's running mate in 1932 and president of the United States one day, sided with the president, saying that the country was in no condition to spend any more money on veterans' benefits. Hoover spoke before a divided American Legion convention in Boston in October 1930, telling the legionnaires that while the country couldn't afford to assume any additional outlays for the vets, he would definitely give them "a sympathetic ear" when the nation's fiscal situation improved. The pro-Hoover forces prevailed and again succeeded in tabling Patman's legislation. MacNider, for all his efforts on Hoover's behalf, grew bitter afterward when his political aspirations evaporated into thin air, stymieing him with the first major defeat in a life otherwise filled with victories. "I am not a politician and never was," he had said earlier in his career. His words turned out to be prescient in ways that he had never anticipated.

And there the issue stood, unresolved and more contentious than ever as the vets and millions of other Americans scrambled to put food on the table and keep a roof over their heads. The unemployment lines grew longer, and the army of out-of-work Americans took on a grim and shabby aspect as the black cloud of despair descended like a plague from the heavens. But Patman was determined to keep the bonus issue front and center on the country's political agenda. He believed that political expediency would force Hoover to change his position when he ran for reelection in 1932, but Hoover remained adamant in his conviction that a stepped-up payment of the bonus was not an efficient way to run the nation's fiscal policies. He criticized the vets' demands for a $4.5 billion handout "under the guise of giving relief of some kind or another" as an expenditure the government could not afford.

The estimated five hundred to a thousand unemployed vets who marched along Pennsylvania Avenue on the way to the Capitol on January 21, 1931, was a harbinger of what was to follow shortly afterward. Patman and more than one hundred of his like-minded congressional colleagues greeted them on the steps of the Capitol, welcoming the vets to the center of America's political arena. The show of force was impressive, and it appeared for a brief moment that the pro-bonus forces would prevail. The House Ways and Means Committee began hearings on the issue a week later, but there was opposition in the Senate, which threatened to derail any legislation calling for a stepped-up payment of the bonus.

The powerful banker Andrew Mellon sided with Hoover and claimed that the vets "would not seem to be a class which, as such, is in particular need. . . . Their careers would be blighted for years by such ill-advised, reckless, and needless spending." He also claimed that the bonus would lead to a $650 million federal budget deficit at a time when the government actually ran a surplus of $350 million—a billion-dollar error from a man who was sometimes touted as "the greatest secretary of the treasury since Alexander Hamilton." Other bankers and business moguls joined ranks with Mellon and maintained that the government should hold the line on any further expenditures. Most hypocritical of all was a statement made by Pierre S. Du Pont, whose chemical company was a major beneficiary of the war. The veterans were "the most favored class in the United States," said Du Pont, "having health, youth, and opportunity."

The Ex-Servicemen's Anti-Bonus League, which was little more than a rump organization with a mailbox and a letterhead, called the bonus "a disgraceful display of inordinate greed." Able-bodied vets were still "in the years of their strong young manhood."

The Patman forces presented opposing arguments in favor of the vets, stating that the bonus was "not a dole, a handout," but rather "an adjustment in a very small degree of the soldier's pay while he served his country." He was joined by a freshman Democratic congressman from Massachusetts named William Connery, who railed against "a well-organized, concerted conspiracy, concocted by the big moneyed interests" to defeat the bonus.

"The war contractors" all got theirs, said Congressman John J. Cochran, a Missouri Democrat, and now it was time for the men who did the actual fighting to get the money owed to them.

The most dramatic moment of the proceedings occurred on February 4, 1931, when an emaciated vet named Joseph T. Angelo took center stage at the hearings. Angelo looked the very personification of the Great Depression itself. He was a short slip of a man who weighed barely one hundred pounds. Despite his diminutive stature, which had almost gotten him disqualified from military service, Angelo earned the accolades of future general George S. Patton after he saved Patton's life during the Meuse-Argonne offensive on September 26, 1918. Patton was standing tall during the battle when enemy machine-gun fire cut him down, nearly ending his life. Angelo raced to Patton's side and pulled him to safety, preserving the life of a man who would go on to become a military legend during World War II.

Angelo was "without doubt the bravest man in the American Army," Patton said after the First World War ended. "I have never seen his equal."

After the war Angelo gave his own account of the incident. "We had a hundred and fifty tanks on the move and were plowing through a dense fog. As I was the Colonel's [Patton's] orderly I accompanied him in the advance. We had fifteen men and two first lieutenants in our party. The tanks followed us. I was walking by the side of the Colonel, but when we came to a crossroad the Colonel told me to remain there and be on the watch for Germans. . . . The Colonel, who was ahead of me, appeared on top of a knoll and shouted: 'Joe, is that you shooting down there?' Then I thought sure hell had broken loose. Bullets from machine guns just naturally rained all around. 'Come on, we'll clean out those nests,' shouted the Colonel, and I followed him up the hill. The Colonel was sore and couldn't understand why our boys couldn't break up those nests. Then he saw the tanks were not moving and sent me to see Captain English to find out the cause. The tanks were stuck in the mud."

Patton ordered Angelo to follow him, and when he reached the tanks, almost hub-deep in the mud, he grabbed a shovel and began digging the tanks free. Angelo and a few other men followed the colonel's example and got busy digging. The Germans were sending over heavy artillery fire, but finally they got the tanks moving and drove them over the hill. Later Patton told Angelo to get around to the side and wipe out the machine-gun nests. "Take fifteen men with you," he ordered. "I'm sorry," Angelo told him. "But they have all been killed." "My God! They are not all gone?" the colonel cried out. When Angelo told Patton that the machine-gun fire had killed the infantrymen, Patton ordered Angelo to accompany him, declaring that he would clear them out himself. Angelo thought Patton had gone mad and grabbed him in an effort to restrain him. Patton grabbed Angelo by the hair and began to shake him, ordering Angelo to follow him.

"We went about thirty yards and the Colonel fell with a bullet in his thigh," Angelo testified. "I assisted the Colonel into a shell hole, bandaged his wounds, and took observations of our surroundings. Shells flew all about us." Patton then ordered Angelo to get out on top of their shell hole and prevent any oncoming tanks from getting below them, as the firepower from the Germans was almost overwhelming. Then Patton said, "Joe, the Germans have been making this shell hole a living hell since you left. Get a tank and wipe out those nests." Angelo did as ordered, and he learned later that four infantrymen had moved in and carried Patton to the rear.

Angelo had left his home in Camden, New Jersey, on foot a few days before the hearings. He and a buddy walked all the way to the nation's capital in the dead of winter to testify before Congress. The very appearance of the gaunt, cadaverous vet mesmerized the assembled politicians, who could not believe he had made the journey under his own power. "I done it all by my feet—shoe leather," Angelo told the dignitaries. "I was not picked up by any machine. I come to show you people that we need our bonus. I represent one thousand eight hundred from New Jersey. They are men just like myself—men out of work. I have got a little home back there that I built with my own two hands after I came home from France. Now I expect to lose that little place. Why? My taxes are not paid. I have not worked for two years and a half. Last week I went to our town committee and they gave me four dollars for rations."

Before the war Angelo had worked for DuPont Powder Works, where he earned $1.25 an hour. When the war broke out he left his job and enlisted in the army for soldier's pay of $1 a day. "You took ten percent of the amount you were making in civil life to take a position to go over and be shot?" asked Wisconsin Republican representative James A. Frear.

"Yes, sir," Angelo replied. "Absolutely. And I was proud of it." He pulled a pocket watch that Patton's wife had given him and a stickpin, a gift from Patton's mother, out of his pocket and showed them to the committee. "So, folks," Angelo added after making a pitch for the bonus, "don't forget me for a job. That is all I care for."

The appearance of Jacob Coxey added a more bizarre note to the proceedings. Seventy-seven years old now, he followed Joe Angelo on the witness stand. Coxey had kept a low profile since he marched to Washington with Carl "Old Greasy" Browne in 1894 following the depression of 1893. But there he was again, this time without his disheveled sidekick, arguing in favor of the immediate bonus payment to the vets.

Angelo's testimony, which stirred the committee and earned him glowing reviews in the press, failed to resonate with the president and his major allies. On February 26, 1931, Hoover vetoed the bill, stating, "The number of veterans in need of such relief is a minor percentage of the whole." He added that the vets were likely to spend any money they received on "wasteful expenditures." A lump sum cash payment would "break the barriers of self-reliance and self-support in our people."

As Hoover spoke the lines of the unemployed continued to lengthen, with the percentage of jobless rising above 25 percent. The vets did receive some relief thanks to the efforts of a South Dakota Republican congressman named Royal C. Johnson, a veteran himself, who was able to engineer legislation allowing the vets to borrow up to 50 percent of the maturity value of their bonuses at a compound interest rate of 3 percent a year. The bill passed through the House and Senate with veto-proof majorities, forcing Hoover to sign the bill into law in early March. Patman, however, recognized the compromise legislation for what it was: a new version of Hamilton Fish's 1924 bill, which also permitted the vets to borrow against their promised bonuses. The 3 percent compound interest rate charged to the vets would rob them of the remaining amount owed to them before the certificates came due in 1945, Patman argued, while the government fattened its coffers at the vets' expense. He was not satisfied to settle for half measures this time around. He vowed to continue the fight on behalf of the vets.

THREE

A Motorcycle Cop Rides to the Rescue

Patman continued to enjoy the support of the vfw, whose allies included former brigadier general Pelham Davis Glassford. Glassford entered the world on August 8, 1883, in Las Vegas, New Mexico. From the time he was a boy he set out to follow his father's footsteps and pursue a military career. His father had fought Geronimo and had been a chief signal officer in the Spanish-American War. Glassford's brother William graduated from the U.S. Naval Academy. Glassford opted for the army and went to West Point, where he graduated eighteenth out of 124 cadets in 1904. He rose quickly through the ranks, following early tours of duty in Hawaii, in the Philippines, and along the Mexican border.

When World War I broke out Glassford shipped across the Atlantic to France as commander of the 103rd Field Artillery Brigade. With that assignment he became the youngest brigadier general in the U.S. Army. He stayed in the army until 1931 after twenty-seven years of active duty, teaching painting at West Point toward the end. After his retirement he relocated to his adopted state of Arizona, where he established a reputation as a painter of watercolors and murals.

Painting was his main love, but on a visit to Washington DC for a vfw rally Glassford was asked by local authorities to take over the police force, which was in disarray because of a host of internal corruption scandals. Reluctantly, on October 21, 1931, he accepted the job of superintendent of police, equivalent to the current post of chief of police. He took the job with the stipulation that the Washington establishment give him a free hand in reforming the department. Pelham Glassford was a colorful figure of a man, six-foot-three and well-muscled, who enjoyed careening through the streets of the nation's capital on his signature blue police motorcycle. The press loved him for the headline copy he provided, lauding him as "the artist who became a cop."

"What do you know about police work?" a reporter asked him.

"Well, I've been arrested," Glassford answered with a grin. "Once for driving through a red light and once for speeding on a motorcycle."

Glassford had sympathized with the plight of the vets since the war ended, and he adamantly disagreed with the government's refusal to pay them their bonus upfront instead of fobbing them off for more than two decades, when many of them would likely be dead, with a promise that was little more than a worthless IOU. He also believed that charging the veterans interest for any of the money they borrowed was tantamount to rubbing salt in the wounds the men had received in combat and then in civilian life at the hands of their own elected officials. A staunch ally of Patman, Glassford was no friend of the buttoned-down Hoover administration. He spent a good deal of his time helping the vets find food and shelter, particularly when their circumstances deteriorated further as the Great Depression exacted its horrific toll.

Glassford's first major test as the head of the police department took place a mere six weeks after he took office. On December 6, 1931, a small army of hunger marchers, nearly four thousand strong, stormed into Washington under Communist banners singing "The Internationale," the Soviet hymn and battle song. Glassford himself was no Red, but he had his own ideas on how to deal with the demonstrators.

While keeping a wary eye on their activities, particularly any attempts to provoke the police into clamping down on their First Amendment guarantees, Glassford welcomed them as tourists and supplied them with hot meals straight from the kitchen of the Mayflower Hotel and shelter in some of the city's public buildings. He arranged for the federal government to provide them with tents, blanket rolls, cots, mobile kitchens, and other equipment to make their stay in Washington as comfortable as possible. Glassford gave their leader, the son of Lithuanian immigrants and a Communist Party organizer named Herbert Benjamin, permission to drive through town with his followers. Glassford even went so far as to lead this procession of self-styled revolutionaries down Pennsylvania Avenue on his big blue motorcycle, thereby coopting much of their radical appeal. But Glassford drew the line at allowing them onto the floor of the Senate to voice their grievances.

Glassford further disarmed Benjamin and his legions by showing up dressed in non-threatening civilian attire at a rally the Reds sponsored at the Washington Auditorium, the same site where the vfw had held its own gala. Benjamin fired up his followers with revolutionary rhetoric, his voice bellowing through loudspeakers with a call to arms, telling the masses that "workers of this country must defend their Fatherland, Soviet Russia, the country that has done away with unemployment." He denounced "the thugs of the ruling class." Glassford took it all in without rising to the bait. He restrained the police from overreacting and triggering the physical confrontation that Benjamin hoped to provoke.

The army's military intelligence division was also on hand to assist Glassford. Its leader, Capt. Charles H. Titus, an expert at sizing up the mood of various demonstrators, assured Glassford that most of Benjamin's minions were not known Communists but rather down-and-out workers anxious to support anyone who could provide them with their next square meal. Benjamin was a revolutionary, a political opportunist, who was using the economic crisis gripping the nation to advance his own agenda. Near the end of World War II Benjamin softened his hard political stance and renounced Communism in favor of a more moderate version of Socialism. He actually became a member of the *petite bourgeoisie* himself when he opened a pottery shop called Pottery Fair in Washington dc's upscale Georgetown section and moved to upper-middle-class Chevy Chase, Maryland.

The year 1932 would prove to be the cruelest to date since the Crash of '29. Breadlines lengthened in towns and cities across the country, and the nation's financial institutions began an ominous slide into the black hole of total collapse. Three thousand banks had failed the year before, and the pace accelerated as the new year began. The foreclosure rate on homes and farms picked up throughout the Midwest and in the major cities that bookended the nation on both coasts. President Hoover assured his fellow citizens that "nobody is actually starving" even as reports reached the White House that hundreds of children and the elderly in New York and San Francisco were dying of malnutrition. Hoover was up for reelection that year, and he could hardly have been running in a more toxic atmosphere for a political incumbent, particularly one at the center of the country's economic crisis. Compounding Hoover's predicament were the hundreds of squalid tarpaper slums for the penniless that sprang up like poisonous mushrooms in communities across the length and breadth of the land. The press lost no time in portraying these so-called Hoovervilles as the very face of the administration itself.

Hoover's prospects looked even bleaker when a new threat descended on the nation's citadel of power during the first month of the year. A Roman Catholic priest named James Renshaw Cox, inspired by Coxey's Army two generations earlier, organized a legion of twenty-five thousand unemployed for his own invasion of Washington—the largest demonstration ever in the capital. Cox was a firebrand preacher, all thunder and lightning, unencumbered by the presence of comic opera figures like Carl "Old Greasy" Browne to detract from his mission. "Our president is still trying to give money to the bankers, but none to the people!" Cox roared. "There is plenty of money in this country, but try and get it. . . . The government sent Al Capone to jail for cheating it out of one hundred thousand dollars, yet John D. Rockefeller is giving four million dollars to his son to escape the inheritance tax."

Cox tried to set up a meeting with Hoover, but the president not only refused—"We will not see this man. If he has a petition we will be glad to receive it," his secretary said—he reacted in the most tone-deaf manner possible by asking Glassford to investigate whether the priest was just another Communist looking to promote his Red agenda. Glassford's investigators informed

Hoover that a large percentage of Cox's followers were vets who had fought in the Great War and many of them in the Spanish-American War as well. Hoover was temporarily mollified and invited Cox to the White House, where the priest accused him of acting like "an ostrich that sticks its head in the sand, believing that if he cannot see the hunter pursuing him or the trouble that is nearby, that the hunter or the trouble does not exist." Hoover countered with his assertion that the Great Depression had run its course and that he had a plan to put the economy back on its footing after the fall election.

Cox was unconvinced. He left the White House with the same doubts and grievances that he had brought into the Oval Office, only to discover that Hoover was not finished with him. Cox's demonstration on his doorstep embarrassed the president to the point where he launched a full-scale investigation of the priest to determine whether the Vatican funded the march on Washington and bought the gasoline to fuel his trip. Hoover's investigation came to naught, however, when he learned that his Pittsburgh buddy Andrew Mellon, his own treasury secretary, had ordered his Gulf Oil stations to provide the marchers with free gasoline for two thousand cars and trucks for their drive from Pennsylvania to Washington. Hoover was furious about Mellon's apparent betrayal, but the celebrated banker was as well known for his independence and his philanthropy as he was for his miserly grip on the public purse.

Then it was Cox's turn to exact his revenge on the foundering president. The priest, who had begun his career as a cabdriver and steelworker in Pittsburgh, decided to embark on a crusade to weaken Hoover further by running against him in the fall. It was bad enough that the president had a popular Democrat opposing him in the person of Franklin Delano Roosevelt, a distant cousin of the iconic Teddy Roosevelt whose larger-than-life presence had dominated American politics thirty years earlier, but now he had a firebrand priest to contend with who stirred up the electorate under the banner of his Jobless Party. Cox lambasted Hoover and his policies for most of the campaign season, but in September he abandoned his effort, fearing that he would siphon votes from the Democrats, and threw his support behind FDR.

Cox was not the president's only distraction as the 1932 campaign heated up in earnest. Mellon came under fire and planted Hoover in the center of a firestorm at a time when he could least afford it. Patman's fury intensified over the president's refusal to pay the vets the bonus the government had promised, and it reached the boiling point before the first month of the year passed into the annals of history. Patman and his congressional colleagues initiated impeachment proceedings against Mellon, charging him with "high crimes and misdemeanors" for failing to separate his business interests from his role as treasury secretary. Mellon presided over a network of investments that spanned an array of industries, from banking to cargo ships to liquor to gas and energy consortia and more. Most critically, he had long advocated changes in the tax code that would benefit his financial empire at the expense of what Patman and other house members considered to be in the interests of the country's poor.

Mellon had told Hoover that if he wanted to end the Depression he needed to "liquidate labor, liquidate stocks, liquidate farmers, liquidate real estate—it will purge the rottenness out of the system. High costs of living and high living will come down. People will work harder, live a more moral life. Values will be adjusted, and enterprising people will pick up from less competent people." He also advocated weeding out "weak banks," which did not include his own, as a harsh but necessary measure that would lead to the recovery of the banking system. Mellon advocated deep spending cuts to balance the federal budget, which precluded making stepped-up bonus payments to the World War I veterans.

Hoover was already miffed with Mellon for helping to finance Cox's hunger march on Washington, and now he had impeachment hearings before the House Judiciary Committee to complicate his precarious grip on the presidency. If Hoover and Patman had one goal in common, it was to get Mellon out of Washington, as far away from the debates affecting public policy as possible. Hoover resolved his dilemma by appointing Mellon ambassador to the United Kingdom, an assignment Mellon accepted with some reluctance. Once Hoover had removed Mellon from the turmoil besetting the seat of American politics, Patman dropped his charges against Mellon. Patman understood the futility of impeaching a cabinet member who no longer held that post—which was the whole point of impeaching him in the first place—but he was determined to weigh in one more time on the controversy.

"Mr. Mellon has violated more laws, caused more human suffering, and illegally acquired more property to satisfy his personal greed than any other person on earth," he said. He called Hoover's exile of Mellon to England as nothing less than a "presidential pardon."

With Mellon out of the way Hoover turned his attention back to the business of running for reelection in the midst of the country's insurmountable economic woes. Mellon had barely packed his bags for the voyage across the Atlantic when the president announced the creation of the Reconstruction Finance Corporation, whose business it was to lend money to banks and various corporations in the hope that they would put the money to work creating jobs and boosting economic activity. The RFC was a precursor to the "trickle down" economic theory of later years, which held that vast sums lavished on the institutions at the top of the economic ladder would eventually work their way down to benefit people on the lowest rungs. The problem was that the "big boys," as Patman called them, tended to hoard the cash in their own rainy-day funds before they spent it in an unstable economic environment—precisely what happened during the Great Recession of 2008.

"The millions released by the Reconstruction Finance Corporation went to the big boys by way of New York," Patman charged. In any event, such a plan requires some time before its effects take root in the real world, and there simply was not enough time remaining in the campaign to do Hoover any good.

"If the government can pay two billion dollars to the bankers and railroads, having had no obligation toward them," thundered Father Charles E. Coughlin on his popular weekly radio show, "why cannot it pay the two billion dollars to the soldiers, already recognized as an obligation?"

That humorist with a bite, Will Rogers, also took the opportunity to castigate the RFC. "Every hotel [in Washington] is jammed to the doors with bankers from all over America to get their 'hand out' from the Reconstruction Finance Corporation," Rogers wrote in his syndicated column. "[They] have the honor of being the first group to go on the 'dole' in America."

Hoover came under attack from all quarters, except from his Wall Street buddies and CEOs from corporate America, and vitriolic letters containing threats of assassination poured into the White House from all corners of the nation. Hoover and his minions were mostly concerned about the Red Scare making inroads throughout the country, and with it came the fear that a Bolshevik-style revolution with the ability to undermine the foundations of the shaky American republic was lurking on the horizon. The president's guardians went on full security alert, checking mail and packages before they reached the president's office. And then, on March 7, 1932, a violent confrontation erupted between demonstrators marching for better working conditions and top management attempting to hold the line around the Ford plant in Dearborn, Michigan.

After the stock market crash of 1929 unemployment had skyrocketed at the once-prosperous plant at the River Rouge Complex. The average wage for workers at the plant had plummeted from $1,639 a year in 1929 to $757 two years later. Automobile production declined by 75 percent to 1.3 million vehicles in 1931 from more than 5 million in 1929. With 4,000 laborers out of work the number of suicides in Detroit soared from 113 in 1927 to 568 in 1931. A tsunami of bank failures decimated the life savings of the unemployed, with every local bank in Detroit shuttering its doors in an age before the Federal Deposit Insurance

Corporation was ushered into existence. A wave of foreclosures, evictions, repossessions, and bankruptcies forced the already desperate legion of autoworkers at the Ford plant to take more desperate actions to redress their grievances.

On March 7, 1932, a cold and gloomy day that reflected the mood of the demonstrators, about four thousand men and women marched from Detroit to Dearborn to present a list of grievances. It was "one of the coldest days of the winter, with a frigid gale whooping out of the northwest," according to the *Detroit Times*. Detroit mayor Frank Murphy, who later became governor of Michigan and an associate justice of the Supreme Court, gave the green light to the march even though the demonstrators had not yet secured a permit. Unfortunately the Communist Party USA was the main sponsor of the event, lending credence to the charge that the Red Menace was fomenting disturbances across the nation to promote its own revolutionary agenda. There was no question that the Communists had indeed rushed in to fill a power vacuum created by the weak Auto Workers Union, which had not yet attained its clout of later years. For the average rank-and-file workers, however, it made little difference who championed their cause, since all they wanted were jobs that provided them with a decent living.

The marchers brought with them a list of demands that included the rehiring of laid-off workers, company-paid health care benefits, an end to racial discrimination at the plant, the right to unionize, and the elimination of company spies and private police who beat up workers agitating for better working conditions. When the four-thousand-strong throng of laborers crossed the line into Dearborn, the local police responded by firing tear gas canisters into their midst, then wading in with gas masks and pummeling the marchers with clubs. One cop shot his gun into the crowd. The marchers retreated temporarily to a nearby field, where they regrouped, picked up stones and hurled them at the police, then continued their march toward the Ford plant. Before they could reach it, however, the fire department and private cops hired by the automaker joined the cops on an overpass and showered the marchers with jet streams of icy water. Then the private and public cops opened up with live ammunition and fired randomly into the crowd of protesters. Four of the marchers fell to the ground dead, and dozens more twisted in pain from their gunshot wounds.

"I would guess that hundreds of shots were fired into the mob," wrote a reporter for the *Detroit News*. "I saw their leaders drop, writhing with their wounds, and the mob dropped back, leaving their casualties on the road." Many others hit by machine-gun fire pitched forward onto the ground and lay in agony where they fell. The Ford Massacre, as the press promptly labeled it, turned into a public relations nightmare for Henry Ford and the company that bore his name. The unemployed workers "wanted bread and Ford gave them bullets" became the rallying cry for out-of-work Americans throughout the nation. The company and the police attempted to defend themselves by claiming that a known Communist agitator who fired shots while "hiding behind a parked car" started the massacre, but the charge fooled no one. The image that resonated across the nation was the one painted by the *New York Times*, which reported, "Dearborn streets were stained with blood, streets were littered with broken glass and the wreckage of bullet-riddled automobiles, and nearly every window in the Ford plant's employment building had been broken."

In the aftermath of the melee, as many as sixty thousand workers joined in a funeral procession for the four dead marchers, who were laid to rest in Detroit's Woodmere Cemetery. The solemn affair prompted the nation's press to castigate Ford directly. "The killing of obscure workmen, innocent of crime, was a blow directed at the very heart of American institutions," claimed the *Detroit Times*. Its sister newspaper, the *Detroit News*, lamented the murders and reported, "Insofar as the demonstration itself had leaders present in the march, they appear to have warned the participants against a fight."

The massacre jolted the president. It had occurred on his watch, during an election year no less. Given Hoover's mindset, he blamed

Communist agitators for instigating the demonstration rather than the economic conditions besetting the nation for creating an environment that galvanized jobless workers into taking action. It is true that the Communists were hell-bent on overthrowing the government in favor of a Soviet-style model. Indeed, the Communist Party had seized control of City Hall in St. Louis for a few hours, and it threatened to topple the established order in cities across the nation from Boston, New York, and Philadelphia to Cleveland, Chicago, and Dayton, and as far west as Seattle and San Francisco. The military was on alert to put down any threat of wide-scale insurrection, and the army's Tank School at Fort Benning, Georgia, offered special training on the use of tanks to suppress anti-American revolutionaries. An anti-radical task force spearheaded by J. Edgar Hoover rounded up more than six thousand known revolutionaries and had about a tenth of them deported. But there was no denying that the parlous economic conditions afflicting the great majority of Americans made the Red call for better working conditions more appealing and attracted many to the cause. It was not a question of ideology to those looking to feed and shelter their families. In the absence of any strong support from the traditional labor unions, the professional Communists represented the only viable alternative.

The vets, most of them out of work themselves, had been shunted to the sidelines of the country's political and fiscal affairs. Nevertheless they were never far from view or too far removed from the action. The immediate payment of their bonuses was more important to them than ever as the Great Depression became more and more critical. As the grim winter of 1932 evolved into an uneasy spring, a new threat emerged that would occupy the attention of the Hoover administration throughout the remaining months of his presidency. This time, however, the threat came from the right wing of the political spectrum in the person of a self-appointed bonus march leader with Fascistic political views named Walter W. Waters. All decked out in brown-shirt regalia, Waters led the way from the western rim of the country deeper into the American heartland, flying the banner of the Bonus Expeditionary Force. The president of the United States, preoccupied until now with agitation on the left, now found himself caught in a radical pincer movement as both extremes of the political spectrum zeroed in on the focal point of American power. Radicals on the left and the right wanted nothing less than Hoover's head on a platter, a latter-day Nero driven to the point of humiliating suicide when the Roman Senate threatened to parade him through the streets naked so that the citizenry could line up on both sides of the street and beat him to death with heavy rods.

FOUR

American-Style Fascism Descends on Washington

Walter W. Waters was an oddity out of central casting, which made him the right man in the right place at the right time. If he had not already existed the toxic atmosphere of the period would have had to create him. In retrospect he appears almost buffoon-like with his khaki uniform and knee-high leather boots. But given the temper of the times, with so many families striving to survive on the edge of destitution, a legion of World War I veterans flocked beneath Waters's banner as he marched across the nation to demand the immediate payment of their bonuses—and his as well.

The self-appointed commander in chief of the Bonus Expeditionary Force hailed from Burns, Oregon, where he was born in 1898. He experienced his first taste of combat in Mexico in 1916, where he served under Gen. John "Black Jack" Pershing during the United States' futile effort to hunt down Mexican revolutionary Pancho Villa, whose band had killed a number of Americans in a raid across the New Mexico border. President Woodrow Wilson put an end to the operation early the next year, turning his attention to more pressing concerns in Europe as the Great War blazed out of control. Waters shipped over to France the following year as a medic—although he later portrayed himself as a combat soldier—in the 41st Infantry, which became part of the Army of Occupation when the war ended.

Waters got his honorable discharge in June 1919 with the rank of sergeant and returned to the West, where jobs were in scant supply. The work he managed to get was menial: auto mechanic, used-car salesman, helper in a bakery, anything he could find to generate some money at the bottom of the economic totem pole.

Hoping that a change of name would result in a reversal of fortune, Waters adopted the moniker Bill Kincaid and in 1925 hitchhiked from Idaho to Washington State where he found work, first as a fruit picker in the state's apple, peach, and cherry orchards. His luck improved when he landed a job in a fruit cannery in Wenatchee, situated in the north-central region of the state at the confluence of the Columbia and Wenatchee Rivers.

There he found the woman who would become his wife. Still using the name of Bill Kincaid, Waters met a young worker at the cannery named Wilma Anderson. Their jobs brought them closer together, but again his luck ran out when the economy headed further south and forced the cannery to shut down. They traveled down to Portland, Oregon, where they lined up work at another cannery in the area. With both of them marginally employed again Waters married Wilma under his assumed identity, and they moved into a shabby two-room apartment in a poor area of the city. But their attempt to climb the economic ladder to a more respectable level was woefully short-lived. By 1930 Waters and Wilma were jobless again, with two young kids to support, victims of the crisis that spread across the nation like a metastasizing cancer. Out of work and penniless, Waters was desperate to find some way to keep body and soul together. His attention turned to Washington DC, where Wright Patman and his allies were still fighting to get a creditable bonus bill through Congress and onto the desk of President Hoover. Waters was beyond desperate. Getting his hands on that bonus now rather than later was a critical necessity, a matter of survival.

As the spring of 1932 budded into bloom, Waters—reverting to his legal name by this time—conceived the notion of positioning himself as the leader of an army of equally desperate vets who would trek across the nation and take their case to the citadel of power. He wrote out a speech, committed it to memory, and on March 15, 1932, attended a meeting of a few hundred veterans organized by a rough-and-tumble lumberjack named George Alman. Alman spoke first, trying to stir the vets to take action on their own behalf by lobbying their representatives, then asked if anyone else in the crowd wanted to come up to the podium to speak. Waters rose to his feet and stepped forward. His demeanor was unimpressive. Skinny to the point of emaciation, with a tight mat of blond curls plastered across his head, dressed in threadbare clothes and sporting a clip-on bowtie, he looked like anything but the dynamic, radical leader of a bunch of grizzled vets looking to put an end to their own misery.

The crowd was silent as Waters delivered his memorized, uninspired speech. He told the assemblage that he and his wife and kids had nothing to eat but fried potatoes for Christmas dinner. He asked them to join him by hopping a freight train that would carry them eastward, then marching as an army of forgotten warriors to Washington DC to present their case to the political establishment. The silence was deafening. There were no takers as the vets sat unmoved in their seats. "My speech fell flat," Waters admitted later. But he emerged from the experience even more determined to sharpen his speaking skills and launch a new and more glamorous career as a political leader on center stage. He was tired of struggling in the shadows with nothing to show for his efforts in a life filled with misery and disappointment.

"My interest in all this was not inspired through pure curiosity or altruistic benevolence," Waters admitted in a book he wrote a year later. "I was broke, and was unable to pay the rent on the two small rooms we were occupying in one of the poorer sections of the city. The man who managed the building was a veteran and only his kindness and sympathy prevented our being moved out on the street. For food we were forced to depend solely on friends or on the municipal charity organizations."

Burning a hole in his pocket was a note obligating the federal government to pay the vets a bonus, a sum of money that the authorities claimed they could not disburse for another thirteen years. It was clear to Waters that he and a hundred thousand like him needed that money now rather than later. Waters could not help but notice that "highly organized lobbies in Washington for special industries were producing results; loans were being granted to their special interests and those lobbies seemed to justify their existence. Personal lobbying paid, regardless of the justice or injustice of the demand." At the same time, in Portland alone, about two thousand veterans who were the so-called breadwinners for their families languished on the unemployment lines. Hundreds of others without dependents fleshed out their ranks. Most of them were clad in patchwork clothing and paced the streets in rundown shoes looking for any kind of work they could get, and in lieu of that a sympathetic audience for their tale of misery. Waters and his family had little in the way of possessions outside of a scant wardrobe of their own. He refused to let the poor reception to his speech stand as his final word on the subject.

He went back to the drawing board and learned how other successful leaders managed to attract an army of follows to their own causes—fewer details, more appeal to the emotions with some select catchphrases. Before too much time had elapsed he noticed that he was striking a chord among more people in his audiences. While Waters was struggling in Portland the vfw had already spun plans to stage a demonstration in Washington, joined by large contingents of renegades from American Legion posts throughout the country. They were furious about the anti-bonus posture of their national commander, a South Carolina lawyer named Henry L. Stevens Jr. Stevens told President Hoover that the American legion stood "solidly behind him" on the bonus issue. He promised the president that the organization would keep all bonus matters off the floor of the Republican convention to avoid further embarrassment—a pledge that ran counter to the interests of the rank-and-file vets.

The first contingent of veterans arrived in the nation's capital on April 8. They numbered more than 1,200 in all, with flags flying and martial music stirring the crowds as they marched to the steps of the U.S. Capitol. They presented Patman and his congressional allies with petitions containing more than two million names demanding the immediate payment of the bonus. The demonstration attracted media attention across the nation, and Father Coughlin declared on his popular radio show that two and a half million letters in support of the vets from a broad variety of Americans had overwhelmed him, with more on the way. So far Congress had steeled itself against the demonstrators. The numbers in the streets were still relatively small, and the signatures on the petitions carried less weight than warm bodies threatening to storm the Capitol and take the building by force. Even such stalwart defenders of the poor as future New York mayor Fiorello La Guardia argued against the bonus in favor of a more comprehensive antipoverty program that would benefit all working-class Americans—although La Guardia would later attack Hoover for evicting the bonus demonstrators from their encampment in the city.

"Soup is cheaper than tear bombs and bread better than bullets," the fiery New Yorker, a vet himself, would lament.

Waters read about the demonstration at his home in Oregon and was itching to travel east with a contingent of his own. The main event was getting under way and he was still out there in the wings while others basked in the spotlight. His speaking skills had improved somewhat, but he was a long way from being the spellbinding orator he envisioned who could inspire legions to follow him into battle. But other West Coast veterans read the same newspapers that Waters did, and they closely followed the reports about the efforts of Wright Patman and his political allies to get an acceptable bonus bill through Congress. All ears tuned into the radio on May 1, when the Associated Press broke the news that the House Ways and Means Committee had defeated Patman's latest bill to pay the vets the money now. It was nothing short of a declaration of war against the vets, a call to arms that galvanized them into taking action. It was clear that the system was rigged against them—a prescient insight into the 2016 political atmosphere. All hope of democratic reform was lost.

Waters had been waiting for this moment. As the crowds grew and the mood of the Oregon veterans became more militant, Waters's rhetoric took on a more fiery tone. He announced the formation of an organization he called the Bonus Expeditionary Force, which would travel east across the American heartland and join fellow vets from all over the country in Washington. On May 10, at an outdoor rally near Portland City Hall, about three hundred frustrated vets with nothing to lose agreed on some semblance of a structure for their fledgling army.

Waters was not alone in his desire to lead the vets eastward. Drifters hopped freight trains, hitchhiked, and trekked into town on foot from various corners of the Pacific Northwest to join the BEF and assume leadership roles. Chester A. Hazen, a gruff ex-sergeant wracked with asthma, shouldered Waters aside and appointed himself commander in chief of the outfit. George Alman, the lumberjack who introduced Waters to the vets' group in March, became a field marshal. Waters asserted himself by declaring that he was an assistant field marshal. Others, many of them out-of-work vagabonds and roustabouts with no permanent addresses, called themselves captains, lieutenants, and sergeants. No one quibbled about rank or supremacy. The BEF, in the beginning at least, was a loose assemblage of hard-boiled, unmanageable rebels. Trying to lead them was like trying to herd a bunch of alley cats.

As the BEF made an effort to create its own structure, hundreds of thousands of disparate souls throughout the nation, some organized and others shuffling along under no particular banner, were already on the move. The great march on Washington DC had begun. The spontaneous, hydra-headed uprising assumed a life of its own. Vets in one state heard about others on the march. They gathered their families, packed up their meager belongings, and hit the road themselves. From the South, from the West, from the Midwest, from the farthest reaches of New England, they hit the main streets and back roads of America and shuffled toward the capital of the nation. Townspeople welcomed them for the most part as they passed through, fed them, showered them with hand-me-down clothes, and made room in public parks so they could pitch tents, spread their bedrolls, and spend the night before they continued on their way in the morning. Some opened their doors for a night or two so the vets could bathe and wash the dirt from their tattered clothing. In May 1932 a roving army of tens of thousands of vets and their families were on the move, snaking over the land, many headed for Washington, others hoping to find work and sink new roots in a hospitable new environment.

Hazen, the self-appointed commander in chief of the BEF, rode ahead of the pack in a battered automobile with the organization's meager supply of funds totaling about thirty dollars. He pulled a gun on some of the foot soldiers trekking along behind him before he stepped on the gas and disappeared over the horizon. That was the last that the BEF saw of their commander and their funds—although the authorities captured him later and charged him with larceny. In the power vacuum that followed, with the marchers growing demoralized before they had barely started on their historic journey, Waters found himself in his element at last. He borrowed a drum and beat it loudly as he marched at the head of the army, which numbered about three hundred vets from Oregon. He took charge of the logistics of locating enough food to feed his troops. Food was paramount.

"A few of us realized that unless something was done to secure food for the morrow," he wrote, "the final break-up was only being postponed. For the first time the problem that faced the Bonus Army through its whole existence faced us—how to feed the men. . . . We canvassed whatever nearby restaurants and bakeries we found open and . . . learned that much popular sympathy, expressed in donations of food, was with us." He also arranged for transportation. Railroad officials told the men that under no circumstances could they ride free in empty boxcars. But when the vets forced a freight train to slow down as it clambered into the yard, the men began to climb up the outside ladders and the railroad crew relented.

"If you men will climb into some empty stock cars on that track over there," the engineer told them, "we'll hook them on the train for you. That's the best we can do!"

As the putrid cars, stinking with stale dung, rocked and swayed over the mountains to Pocatello, Idaho, Waters grasped the fact that the men "would reach no destination other than local jails" unless someone established an atmosphere of law and order over the loose assembly of marchers. He climbed to the top of a boxcar and instructed the bugler to sound the alarm for an immediate assembly. "If we can't go to Washington like a group of gentlemen and decent citizens," Waters declaimed, "then I don't want to go at all." He called for a new election of officers, and the men favored him with the title of "Regimental Commander," with total control over the organization.

Waters lost no time in creating a tight new structure with himself at the pinnacle of power. He selected a former boxer named Mickey Dolan, a man known to be quick with his fists, as the head of military police in charge of discipline. Waters put together an outfit for himself complete with a khaki shirt and jodhpurs, a bowtie, and riding boots that rose to his knees. He dressed his enforcers in khaki and armed them with clubs, with strict orders to crack down on drinking, gambling, dissension in the ranks, and panhandling, and to enforce other rules he put in place. Waters's transformation was complete, from a nonentity who had failed to elicit an enthusiastic response from the vets two months earlier, to the leader of an organization that would grow in size and influence during the coming weeks. As the sheer number of veterans descending on Washington approached twenty-five thousand by July, Waters's efforts at recruiting them under the BEF banner elevated his profile to a level that had not seemed possible as recently as March.

They were ready to roll again, hitting the road toward Washington, parading through small towns along the way, picking up new recruits who journeyed without leadership on foot and in broken-down jalopies that soon littered the landscape when their engines conked out. Whole fleets of Hudsons, Fords, LaSalles, and other cars of the era that had expired en route sat steaming and rusting on the side of the road, some of them serving as temporary shelters for derelict families. Waters's BEF offered the solo marchers some hot coffee and food and a chance to march as part of a group. Some hopped aboard boxcars, and others wore out their shoes as they limped across the country on swollen and blistered feet. Some men dropped out when they could go no farther, but new recruits maintained the ranks of the BEF at about three hundred penniless men. The numbers were small compared with other groups of marchers that had already arrived in the nation's capital. The BEF trekked on largely unnoticed until an incident in East St. Louis, Illinois, earned Waters and his minions some unexpected national publicity that brought them to the attention of the authorities in Washington.

The newspapers headlined the incident "The Battle of East St. Louis," focusing the spotlight on Waters and the BEF and stirring the imagination of citizens across the land. After receiving word that an army of marchers was coming to town with the intention of occupying the freight yards, officials of the Baltimore and Ohio Railroad greeted the BEF with a contingent of well-armed local police and their own security force. They presented the vets with an injunction barring them from uncoupling boxcars to block the tracks. Both sides faced off against each other for three days, with the marchers and the railroad refusing to back down. The unemployment rate in town was a staggering 60 percent, and no one from the mayor on down wanted three hundred more mouths to feed, even if they belonged to hungry vets who elicited the sympathy of the locals.

"I don't know when we'll get to Washington but we're going to stay there until the bonus bill is passed if it takes until 1945," Waters told the railroad executives. "We're going to Washington. Nothing can stop us but bullets."

"To Washington they may go," replied P. J. Young, superintendent of the railroad's security force. "But they're not going on the B&O."

Finally local union leaders defused the potentially explosive standoff by arranging for trucks to transport the BEF marchers across state lines to Indiana. Now they were no longer Illinois's problem but Indiana's. There the Waters group faced the same situation, with railroad and local cops cordoning off the marchers behind a screen of barbed wire. Indiana's governor stepped in at this point and ordered state trucks to carry the marchers farther east across the border to Ohio. And so the saga continued, with each state trucking Waters and his marchers farther east, to Pennsylvania, to Maryland, until they were scarcely a day's march from their final destination, Washington DC. The country followed the story with great interest and amusement. In the blink of an eye, as it were, Waters transformed himself from just one of many thousands of obscure vets marching for their bonuses into a national celebrity. From late May on, the bonus march ranked as one of the five biggest domestic stories of 1932, along with the Great Depression, the election, the Lindbergh kidnapping, and a marathon bridge match.

While the story titillated the country at large, officials in Washington were anything but amused. The Hoover administration lived in fear of an assassination attempt on the president's life by militant radicals on the left. Memories of McKinley's assassination had faded into the background, but the assassination of the president of France and of two of Japan's most prominent political leaders in the spring of 1932 heightened fears of similar attempts against Hoover. Even Wright Patman tried to distance himself from the swelling hordes of protesters flocking into Washington. Patman was "very nervous lest he be credited in any way with having inspired the march," Waters wrote.

Waters traveled ahead of his men by train and arrived in Washington on Sunday, May 29, at two o'clock in the morning. He considered it essential that he lay the groundwork for his army before they all assembled there a few days later. The men needed to know where they would be camping, who would feed them, what facilities would be available for bathing, and how they would experience some semblance of a civilized existence while they presented the government with their grievances. Aside from Hoover the man most alarmed about the reenergized vets swarming into Washington was the one responsible for maintaining safety and order in the streets. Pelham Glassford had acquitted himself well during the earlier demonstrations, mainly by providing food and shelter and honoring the demonstrators' constitutional right to press for political reforms. But the logistics of feeding and housing thousands upon thousands of angry vets camping out on the streets of the nation's capital would require superhuman skills of biblical proportions.

FIVE

An Unholy Alliance

Waters's first order of business was to meet with Glassford, who was anxious to find out whom and what he was dealing with before a deluge of homeless men overwhelmed him and the city he was responsible for safeguarding. But before Waters even arrived, Glassford ran into a stone wall when he appealed to Secretary of War Patrick J. Hurley for the same type of assistance he had received during the earlier demonstrations. The government had provided the Communist agitators with tents, cots, blankets, food, and other amenities that had been successful in ameliorating the potentially tense confrontation with radicals hell-bent on overthrowing the U.S. political and economic system. Glassford was stunned when Hurley turned him down.

"The federal government could not recognize the invasion," Hurley said, reflecting the position of the president himself.

Glassford had no better luck with the navy, the marine corps, various army posts, and the Anacostia Naval Air Station, all of which Hoover had charged with taking a hard line against this latest onslaught of dissidents. His own government had backed him into a corner and refused to give him the basic equipment he needed to maneuver when new contingents of vets ambled into town. Perhaps the most vociferous opponent of accommodating the vets was Maj. Gen. George Van Horn Moseley, deputy army chief of staff, who was tight with Hurley.

"Intensive investigations of the past months," Moseley told Glassford, revealed that "we are harboring a very large group of drifters, dope fiends, unfortunates, and degenerates of all kinds."

Glassford was at a loss to understand the attitude. Food, shelter, and cots for Red revolutionaries who wanted to overthrow the

U.S. government, but not even a glass of water for veterans who had served their country and risked their lives in a devastating war across the Atlantic. He went over to Capitol Hill to see his immediate boss, Maj. Gen. Harold B. Crosby, the commissioner overseeing police and fire matters. Crosby told Glassford that the president did not want to treat the vets like a special group but rather like any other "floaters" coming to town. "If you feed and house them, others will come by the thousands."

"It would be far better to have ten thousand orderly veterans under control than five thousand hungry, desperate men breaking into stores and committing other depredations," Glassford reasoned.

"What are the police for?" Crosby sneered.

"Are you making a suggestion or issuing an order?"

"In the army, it has been my experience that a suggestion is obeyed just the same as an order."

"We're not in the army now," Glassford snapped, his frustration mounting. "I cannot follow suggestions. If you desire to take the responsibility yourself for such a policy all you have to do is issue written orders and they will be carried out. In the absence of such orders I shall take what I consider the correct course."

Glassford knew what he was up against before he even agreed to sit down with Waters. It was clear that his approach to dealing with the vets ran counter to the interests of the Hoover administration. In fact Sen. James E. Watson, a friend and ally of Hoover, went so far as to spell it out for Glassford in case there was the slightest doubt about the matter. "The president has taken a great dislike to you," Watson informed Glassford during Glassford's initial meeting with Waters at nine o'clock in the morning, just seven hours after Waters made it to the capital. Glassford listened carefully to Waters and sized up the man and his bizarre outfit, trying to determine if was dealing with a visionary or a certifiable lunatic.

Waters sat across from Glassford, impressed by the respectful treatment he received from the superintendent of police. "He was friendly, courteous, and above all humanly considerate," Waters wrote. "I found it difficult to realize myself in the presence of an ex-Brigadier General of the Army."

Glassford wanted information from Waters more than anything else. The city's top cop needed to know what kind of onslaught he was dealing with, and the kind of resources he would need to maintain order in the streets of the nation's capital. "How many veterans will come here, do you think?" he asked Waters.

"There will be twenty thousand here within the next two weeks," Waters answered.

It is hard to know how Waters, who still had only a few hundred protestors under his own control, came up with that figure. But his estimate proved to be on the low side. In fact over the next two weeks more than twenty thousand would stream into the city, with others on the way. Glassford would have to reconsider the plans he had made to accommodate the men. He had temporarily arranged for them to be billeted in an abandoned wooden building that had once been a department store, located at Eighth and I Streets in the southeast quadrant of Washington. The vets would be spilling out onto the streets if anywhere near the number that Waters talked about invaded the city. Glassford arranged for Waters to be driven to the facility, and after inspecting it Waters returned and asked Glassford if there was somewhere he could lie down and sleep for a couple of hours before his men arrived.

"If you want to, stretch out over there," Glassford said, pointing to the courthouse lawn across from police headquarters. Waters found a shady spot and joined a couple of other stragglers who were already lying down nearby. "It will be hell if we have to sleep here until 1945," one of them said.

"We ain't ever gonna get a bonus," the other one said. "What the hell use is a veteran to the government after the war's over, buddy?"

The Hoover administration's main fear was that Communists, whose primary goal was launching a Soviet-style revolution in the United States, would infiltrate the bonus marchers. It was a gen-

59

uine concern since the Communist Party was anxious to exploit the discontent among the vets and recruit them to its own cause. The CP formed a front organization for exactly that purpose and named it the Workers' Ex-Servicemen's League (WESL, or Weasel as it came to be known among the vets, who were mostly anti-Communist themselves). WESL promoted black-white solidarity, which the vets had no problem with; except for a few deep-South contingents, the vets were already racially integrated in a common cause to secure their bonuses and find suitable employment. Civil rights activist Roy Wilkins checked out the racial mix for the NAACP and was surprised to find that Jim Crow was "absent with leave" in most of the groups he encountered. Only a handful on the fringes had any interest in replacing their own government with a dictatorship of any variety.

The CP functionary in charge of stirring up the masses was a former marine named Emanuel Levin, who had spent most of the years after the war organizing demonstrations in cities across the United States. "We fought the last war for the capitalists; the next war for the working class!" was the slogan that characterized his street uprisings in New York, Chicago, Cleveland, Toledo, and other towns. Levin had worked his way up through the CP hierarchy and evolved into a dedicated Stalinist, intent on organizing "a tightly disciplined, quasi-military party . . . in which every member would function as an obedient soldier."

Another CP firebrand named John T. Pace emerged as the public face of the WESL bonus marchers in Washington. Pace had a genuine war record to back up his claim for an immediate bonus payment for him and his men, but he was a dedicated Marxist-Leninist to the marrow of his bones. The threat he posed was the possibility that he might replace Waters as the driving force behind the entire legion of vets swarming into the District of Columbia and subvert the vets to his radical left-wing agenda.

After studying the clash of ideologies some years later, historian Arthur Schlesinger Jr. wrote: "It may be said definitely that (a) the bonus march originated spontaneously and the Communists were latecomers in their effort to exploit it, (b) the BEF leaders were openly and militantly anti-Communist, (c) the Communists represented at no time more than a minuscule and beleaguered minority, and (d) there would have been a Bonus March if there had been no Communist Party in existence."

Colonel Edmund W. Starling, the supervisor of presidential security for the Secret Service, had gone so far as to plant undercover agents into the BEF, and he concluded, "Generally speaking, there were few Communists, and they had little effect on the men's thinking. The veterans were Americans, down on their luck, but by no means ready to overthrow their government."

Glassford was well aware of the dangers posed by the left. While he was sympathetic to the plight of the vets and supportive of their right to congregate and demonstrate for a redress of grievances, he was as anxious as anyone else in Washington to make sure that the protest was orderly and free of radical subversion. Indeed, his superiors in the Hoover administration were happy enough to advise him about the threat of assassination and general turmoil in the streets. It fell to Glassford to play the role of kingmaker. He needed to establish someone as the de facto leader of all the vets descending on the city, someone he could keep a close eye on and control from his own perch at the top of the police pyramid. By Glassford's count twenty-two separate groups of marchers were heading toward Washington from various parts of the country, and he needed someone to organize them once they arrived.

Waters was certainly a shadowy figure, not someone Glassford would have selected from a lineup of serious alternatives. But, considering what he had to work with, it made sense to entrust Waters with the responsibility of organizing and directing the thousands of vets who would be arriving in the weeks ahead. Glassford had no way of knowing then the extent of Waters's anti-Semitism and anti-Communist fervor, nor his favorable disposition toward Fascism. But even if he had known, Glassford had little choice but to set Waters up as the leader of most of the vets pouring into Washington.

Glassford called Maryland governor Albert C. Ritchie before the rest of Waters's Portland contingent made it through the state and asked him to direct the traveling armada to the abandoned building he had set up on the corner of Eighth and I Streets. In the meantime he put pressure on the Hoover administration by taking his case directly to the press, complaining about the lack of basic services awaiting the vets when they came to town. Hoover, already perceived to be a heartless flunky of his rich supporters, did an about-face and ordered his commissioners to supply cots, mobile kitchens, and other basic equipment to accommodate the influx of men who would shortly be heading into the district. Before long the commissioners miraculously freed up thousands of cots, tents, bedrolls, and army rations; surplus clothing; and several field kitchens for Glassford's use. Later in the day after Waters's arrival eighteen Maryland National Guard trucks rumbled across the border of the District of Columbia on their way to the empty former department store. American flags hung from the windows of the buses, along with hand-scrawled signs proclaiming that the vets would "stay 'til we get our bonus" or "stay 'til 1945," if they had to. The men on the buses were tired, hungry, filthy, close to emaciated, and disoriented after having spent nearly twenty days traveling three thousand miles across the country.

The precise number of veterans who would be converging on Washington in the weeks ahead was open to speculation at this point. Historians have debated the actual count over the past eighty years. Estimates ranged from as few as six thousand to as many as sixty thousand, but figures put together afterward by Glassford are closer to the mark. Judging by the number of mouths he had to feed and bodies to shelter, Glassford concluded that there were more than twenty thousand in the city at the height of the occupation in July. Waters claimed that his own roster contained 28,540 names, addresses, and service numbers, amounting to about half of those who marched. Many vets drifted in and out of the city periodically without taking up residence. Others started out but never completed the journey. The most accurate assumption is that about forty thousand vets began to march on Washington in 1932, and about twenty-five thousand vets and their families were actually encamped in Washington during the siege that lasted until the end of July.

Further complicating the issue was the effort by the government to get rid of as many bonus marchers as possible by issuing them travel vouchers for railroad tickets out of Washington. But this turned out not to be a gift at all. The 5,109 vets who accepted the offer were actually borrowing the money against their future bonuses and paying interest on the loans, which would eat up some of the money due them in 1945. It was a lousy deal for the vets and a good one for the government, which benefited by getting the demonstrators out of the city and collecting interest on the IOUs due in thirteen years. Most of the vets who accepted the travel vouchers were from distant states and, presumably, were more interested in getting back home than they were in scrambling for food and shelter in a strange and hostile city so far from home.

The eighteen trucks containing the three hundred BEF vets from Oregon came to a stop in front of the building Glassford had secured for them. The weary men piled out onto the street and shuffled into the abandoned structure, where Glassford treated them to a meal of vegetable soup, bread, and milk, which he paid for himself with $120 that he contributed to their cause. Glassford arranged for the vets to receive two meals a day, usually oatmeal, coffee, milk, and bread for breakfast, and some sort of a stew in the evening. After they ate, Patrolman J. E. Bennett, one of Glassford's aides, addressed the vets and established some ground rules.

"You're welcome here," he said, "but the minute you start mixing with Reds and Socialists, out you go. If you get mixed up with that gang, you're through here. The marine barracks are across the street, the navy yard is a couple of blocks away, and there's lots of army posts around. We don't want to call them, and we won't call them as long as you fellows act like gentlemen."

"If we find any Red agitators," one of the men yelled, "we'll take care of them ourselves. We came here under the same flag we fought for."

A flood of dirty, hungry, angry, and disheveled men began to stream into Washington starting on Monday, May 30, wondering where they could find a hot meal and a place to rest their aching bones. Glassford needed a broad network of campsites to house them all, and within a few days he had established twenty-seven sites in all, many of them in the northeast quadrant not far from Capitol Plaza and the downtown shopping neighborhoods. The largest settlement by far was a pestilential sprawl of mud-flats across the bridge spanning the Anacostia River, 2,500 acres of swampland that often overflowed with raw sewage and river debris after a storm. The land had once belonged to the Anacostan Indians, from whom the sprawl of mudflats had gotten its name. The vets labeled the campsite Camp Marks in honor of a friendly police captain at the nearby eleventh precinct. It was spacious enough to accommodate 15,000 residents, including 1,100 of the vets' wives and children. They were all crowded into a half-mile semicircle bordering the filthy river, either baking under a relentless sun, choking on clouds of dust, or sloshing around in a sea of mud after a summer rainstorm.

The other sites were considerably smaller, ranging from Camp Sims with a housing capacity of 200 to Camp Bartlett's 2,100. Camp Bartlett sat on private land owned by former postmaster general John H. Bartlett, high up on a wooded plot, a long walk away from the Capitol. Camp Meigs near the Columbia Institute for the Deaf was also within walking distance of the Capitol, but it was far enough away for the vets to complain about trekking there on blistered feet in busted-out shoes. Many protestors occupied empty government office buildings on Pennsylvania Avenue near the Washington Monument and farther up the avenue close to the Capitol Building itself. These buildings, earmarked by the federal government for eventual demolition, were the most desirable campsites of all because of their close proximity to the Capitol. The fifteen thousand vets and their families at Anacostia had a view of the Capitol dome, but it was a long hike from there to the center of action along Pennsylvania Avenue.

Lumber for construction was virtually nonexistent despite Glassford's efforts to provide it. The men at Anacostia, in particular, found themselves erecting a profusion of shelters with anything they could lay their hands on. From the nearby dumps they hauled away large pieces of corrugated metal, packing crates, mattresses, cardboard boxes of every description, large wooden piano and furniture boxes, oilcloth, canvas, loose bricks and whatever lumber they could find. They found makeshift tools to hammer together this motley collection of junk into enclosed shelters or lean-tos. The more ingenious among them cut holes in packing crates for doors and windows and secured enough space to furnish their abodes with cots and small boxes for use as a table and chairs. Others made do with pitched tents or bedrolls stacked on makeshift straw mattresses.

The mudflats at Anacostia became a virtual city within a city—albeit a city straight from the imagination of dystopian geniuses like Franz Kafka, Jerzy Kosinski, and Dante Alighieri. Glassford appointed Waters as the commander of the Anacostia compound, his man in charge of keeping order among the largest settlement of vets in the nation's capital. Waters relished the role, which was the most recognition he had ever received in a lifetime of failure. He was well on his way to becoming Glassford's creature, more than just a vet demanding his bonus. In Waters's own mind, at least, he had become a political leader, the driving force behind a full-blown movement that he hoped to launch in the weeks and months ahead.

"I chose one Oregon man, George Alman, as my aide," Waters crowed, referring to the lumberjack who had introduced him to the assembly of vets in Portland. "He also became the 'Billeting Officer,' to take care of sheltering the men as they came in. Mickey Dolan, ex-pugilist, was my bodyguard and through the next weeks was never more than ten feet away from me."

Waters established his own intelligence network, which would total about three hundred agents over time, with only Waters and three trusted aides privy to who they all were. Their job was to inform Waters about any Communists infiltrating the BEF, and about any infraction of the tight strictures he had established about drinking and radical dissension within the ranks. He was especially concerned about Jewish radicals, whom he considered the most dangerous instigators of all. Mickey Dolan was in charge of the goon squads, cadres of a kind of Gestapo who were not beyond bashing a few heads whenever someone stepped seriously across the line Waters had established in camp. Campsites at Anacostia were partitioned by states so the vets and their families knew which commanders and their subordinates to report to. As men poured into town from freight yards or in sputtering automobiles, they marched in military formation to the mudflats, where Waters and his men checked their discharge papers and other credentials.

"We wanted only veterans," Waters wrote. "The food supply was too slim to permit us to feed any nonveterans, sympathetic as they might be, who may have been attracted by our presence to Washington. . . . A few Communists sneaked in the first week but they were kicked out during the second."

Glassford had entrusted Waters with the leading role that Waters felt he had been born to play. He did not intend to allow it to slip from his grasp now that he was occupying center stage.

SIX

The Smell of Revolution in the Air

More and more vets began to criticize Waters's concentration on military structure within the ranks instead of on quick passage of a new bonus bill, which is what had drawn them all to Washington in the first place. Many chafed at Waters's strict rules and regulations and the dictatorial role he had adopted since arriving in Washington. They also thought that Waters had allowed his chumminess with Glassford to go to his head and undermine his effectiveness as a leader in their struggle to get their hands on the bonuses now. By Waters's own admission, "Many of the members of the BEF believed that I was 'selling them out to Glassford.' That rumor was as common in the camps as weather reports. . . . I strove to impress the men with the fact that [Glassford] was our friend, that we could trust him, and that we must do so if we wanted to prevent riot and bloodshed in the city . . . although he failed me . . . at the most critical moment."

Other reports about Waters's increasing infatuation with power were much harsher than the criticism emanating from the ranks of the vets. The *New York Times* and other newspapers called Waters a "Hitlerite," a charge that Waters openly welcomed. His own news organ quoted him as saying that his "organization brings up comparisons with the Fascisti of Italy and the NAZI of Germany. . . . For five years Hitler was lampooned and derided, but today he controls Germany. Mussolini, before the war was a tramp printer driven from Italy because of his political views. But today he is a world figure." The Catholic magazine *Commonweal* pointed out that the BEF's insistence on "soldier's superiority" was the same line taken by Adolf Hitler, and that the bonus issue had dropped to second place in Waters's political agenda. Waters's views were unequivocal; his political views had evolved as far to the right as the Communists had veered to the left. He left no doubt in anyone's mind that he had become, if he had not already been one before he left Oregon, a dedicated Fascist and Nazi sympathizer.

The great majority of veterans who descended on Washington, hoping for quick passage of the bonus that the government had been promising them for years past, found themselves sidelined to the role of innocent bystanders while the struggle for power continued at the top. The press had described their march as a "pilgrimage," but the men discovered when they reached their final destination that they had trooped into the middle of a political dance orchestrated by their own leaders. In addition the Hoover administration was far more concerned about the Red menace threatening the country's political stability than it was about any danger from the right. This anti-Communist fever burning at the highest levels of government played right into Waters's hands. No one was in a better position than Waters to claim, justifiably, that the primary goal of the BEF and his khaki-clad minions was to prevent Communists from gaining a foothold among the bonus marchers. They staked out that position even as the adjutant general of the VFW assured the government that Communists were "trying to create the impression that thousands of veterans are falling in behind the red flag. Nothing could be further from the truth."

But government officials refused to let go of their fear that a Communist revolution, punctuated by an assassination attempt on the president, was a constant menace in their midst. For a solid week, from June 1 through June 7, a series of incidents involving the Communist Party rattled the composure of the most level heads in Washington. Party leader Emanuel Levin intensified the already explosive atmosphere by issuing a statement that the CP had originated the bonus march, not Waters or other "Fascist leaders" who claimed to speak for the veterans. He threatened to organize street demonstrations across the nation and a huge parade in Washington on June 8, the very date that the BEF planned a parade along Pennsylvania Avenue under its own banner. The prospect of street fighting among various contingents of vets alarmed Glassford to the point that he briefly entertained the idea of declaring a state of emergency in the district.

"Although no disorders have occurred," Glassford wrote in a secret report, "the plan of the Police Department is to assemble all disaffected groups at Anacostia Park and should emergency arise to hold the Eleventh Street Bridge against a riotous invasion across the Anacostia River. Plans and preparations are being made to this end, including plans for the use of tear gas: at the same time a force of police will be held in readiness . . . to localize any riot that may occur. . . . Recommendation: That preparations be made by the Commissioners to declare an emergency, and to provide for the use of the National Guard."

In the end Levin's plans for street riots and a provocative parade in Washington never materialized. He and Pace failed to generate much enthusiasm for their agenda among the rank-and-file vets, and Glassford called off his contingency plans. With the threat of a Stalinist uprising now behind them, several senators who had been less than enthusiastic about the legions of vets pouring into town began to rally to their cause. Sen. James Hamilton Lewis, a flamboyant Democrat from Illinois who sported an ill-fitting wig and a Van Dyke beard dyed a "pinkish" color, had at one time told the veterans to "go to hell." Following a visit to the Anacostia camps, however, Lewis was convinced that the men and their families were asking for no more than the government had promised them after their service in the Great War. Addressing the veterans from the roof of his car, Lewis told them to make a list of the things they needed the most.

"A great number of men are without shoes," reported the Illinois delegation. "There are practically no blankets; the food is not near enough; soldiers are sleeping on the ground on ticks filled with hay; we have no tents, just a barracks which leaks . . . the rest are scattered around on the ground. . . . The boys would also like facilities for writing home and procuring tobacco for chewing and smoking."

While the War Department was less than helpful in supplying enough tents to shelter the men, whose numbers increased daily as they swarmed into town, Glassford succeeded in convincing several restaurants to send more food out to Anacostia and to the other sites he had established—large turtles for making soup, hundreds of pounds of pork, beans, and other provisions. Evalyn Walsh McLean, the wife of *Washington Post* owner Ned McLean, joined Glassford in his effort to feed the thousands filtering into the camps throughout the city. She had turned over her seventy-five-acre estate to the Red Cross during the war and had established a reputation as a champion of the poor when the Great Depression took hold. She was especially sympathetic to the plight of the vets, whom she observed in a truck rumbling past her Massachusetts Avenue mansion on Embassy Row.

"I saw the unshaven, tired faces of the men who were riding in it standing up," she observed. Truckload after truckload of starving, unkempt, ragged men passed by silently, some peering resentfully at the opulence around them that was in stark contrast to their own circumstances. McLean drove to a neighborhood Childs Restaurant with Glassford and ordered a thousand sandwiches and a thousand packs of cigarettes. "I haven't got a nickel with me, but you can trust me," she told the startled counterman. "I am Mrs. McLean." Her word was her bond. Childs delivered the sandwiches and cigarettes that night to grateful veterans throughout the city. "Nothing I had seen before in my whole life touched me as deeply as what I had seen in the faces of the Bonus Army," McLean said later.

As Waters solidified his power over the BEF, attracting larger donations of money and equipment for the vets, it seemed almost inevitable that charges of misappropriation of funds would rise up from the ranks. Waters denied that he had directly handled any of the money, and he tried to deflect the mounting criticism of his leadership about his using the vets "to make money" for himself. Nevertheless complaints about his larcenous and self-serving behavior put him at odds with his men and refused to fade away. On June 5 Waters put his aide George Alman temporarily in charge of the BEF, claiming that he was at the point of collapse and needed to get away for a few days. Some of the men maintained that he was hiding out in the Washington home of Don Zelaya, a Central American politician who was a West Point graduate and a close friend of Glassford. Others said that Waters had gone up to Philadelphia and New York City on foraging trips to raise money and garner more publicity for his own role as leader of the BEF.

No one could deny that Waters lived considerably better than the men whom he claimed to serve. While traveling on his sporadic trips, he slept indoors on a real bed and had enough money to pay for commercial transportation and decent hotels, and his clothes were always clean and pressed in contrast to the other veterans who grew shabbier from day to day. The only logical conclusion was that Waters had tapped into a private source of contributions that enabled him to pay his expenses and visibly improve his lifestyle. Waters was also shrewd enough to know that a power vacuum would emerge in his absence, since Alman and his other top lieutenants lacked the leadership skills necessary to control the vast hordes of veterans flooding into the camps at Anacostia and the other locations that Glassford had established. Waters returned to the district on June 8 after an absence of three days and assumed his role as BEF commander with the support of an executive committee that his aides had organized while he was away. He made a big show of turning more than $5,000 and food over to Glassford, who became the unofficial treasurer of the BEF in an effort to appease the men who distrusted Waters. Waters knew that time and Glassford's continuing support were critical if he was going to reach his goal of becoming virtual dictator of the BEF.

Waters's extreme political views put Glassford in the awkward position of losing control of the Frankenstein monster he had created for his own benefit. His handpicked inmate was now in charge of the asylum, and Glassford had little choice but to accede to Waters's insistence on establishing squads of military police to enforce the rules he had imposed at Anacostia in particular. Glassford appointed police officers to oversee what Waters was up to and rein in his excesses, but the effort was only marginally successful.

"When we get in here," one of the CP members complained, "the stool pigeons point us out to the MPS and they took us to the commander of the camp. He says, 'You're a damned Red. All right, men, give him the works.' The strong-arm squad takes you in a car and beats you before turning you loose."

Glassford had to step in on several occasions to protect the Communists' constitutional rights. As wary as he was of the CP's penchant for stirring up trouble, Glassford was a civil libertarian who disdained Waters's style of administering vigilante justice to those who opposed his agenda. "The Communist Party is not outlawed," Glassford wrote in the fall of 1932. "It is running candidates for President and Vice President and for other offices. . . . It has constitutional rights that must be protected until those rights are withdrawn by due process of law. It is a curious thing that while the avowed purpose of the Communist Party is the overthrow of our present social structure, the law confers upon it the protection of the Constitution it seeks to destroy and guarantees it the fundamental rights of free speech, free press, and free assembly."

Glassford's was one of the lone voices expressing concern for the constitutional rights of revolutionary Marxist-Leninists in Washington. The prevailing attitude within the Hoover administration and the military was that the establishment had to use all possible measures to crush the Red menace before it overwhelmed an increasingly fragile democracy that threatened to crumble under the weight of the economic misery weighing on the country. The pressure on Glassford became so intense that he tried to alleviate it by convincing the vets that they would all be better off leaving town and waiting for due process to run its course. Toward that end he offered them free truck rides out of the district up to fifty miles in the direction of their homes.

"I want your cooperation and the cooperation of your men

toward getting all of you out of town," he said to Alman during one of Waters's sudden absences. "If you won't go, I'm not making any threats. I shall simply close up these quarters and discontinue furnishing food. The people of the District no longer feel they should feed your men."

"Well, I don't feel they should either," said Alman.

"And you understand, I hope, that there is no feeling of antagonism on my part, that what I am telling you comes in a friendly vein."

"I shall give you the answer of the men as soon as I can," Alman replied.

He lost no time, however, giving the press a different story. "We came here to stay until the bonus bill is passed," he said defiantly. "And neither General Glassford nor anybody else is going to run us out of town."

Waters backed up his top aide as soon as he returned to Washington. "Whenever the bonus is voted, we will be very glad to accept the police offer of free truckage out of the city," he told the press.

Glassford was realistic enough to anticipate this outcome. He was not inclined toward a physical confrontation with the vets who refused to leave, which put him in the unenviable position of finding a way to supply them with enough food to prevent them from panhandling in the streets or, worse, from breaking into stores and shops to assuage their nagging hunger pangs. The solution Glassford came up with was ingenious; he needed to raise money for food and other necessities, and he could think of no better way of doing it than arranging for a marine corps major to set up a fight night, consisting of a minimum of fifteen boxing matches. The BEF supplied several fighters from its own ranks, and other boxers from different weight divisions came from the police and military. Dozens of professional fighters fleshed out the card for the evening. Glassford enlisted the services of legendary promoter Jimmy Lake to stage the event. Lake was perhaps the leading entertainment impresario of the era, the owner of the Gayety Burlesque Theater at 513 Ninth Street, NW, where he featured a Who's Who of entertainers, including W. C. Fields, Abbott and Costello, Will Rogers, Bert Lahr, Mickey Rooney, and strip tease queens Ann Corio and Gypsy Rose Lee.

Since his theater held only about 1,500 people, enough to fill the place for a burlesque act but not large enough to accommodate the huge crowd he and Glassford expected, Lake went to see Clark Griffith, a former baseball player who owned the Washington Senators and a much larger venue, Griffith Stadium, with a seating capacity of 50,000. Lake got Griffith's attention with an enticing sales pitch: "Clark, how would you like to have the opportunity to sell fifty thousand bottles of pop, fifty thousand bags of peanuts, as many packages of Cracker Jacks, and probably ten thousand cups of coffee? And cigars and cigarettes, too?"

Lake told Griffith about his plans to raise money for the legions of vets flooding into town, preceded by a huge twilight parade through the streets of Washington on June 7, the evening before the big event. Griffith needed no further convincing. More than one hundred thousand citizens lined up to view the "strangest military parade the Capital has ever witnessed," according to the *Washington Post*. The Hearst newspapers described the march in bleaker language, calling it a "ghost parade," while the *Star* said it was "the saddest parade Washington has ever known," with gaunt and ragged veterans shuffling along at a subdued pace. Even Waters had to admit that the spectacle was less than inspiring. "In silent ranks . . . marched coal miners from Pennsylvania and cotton pickers from Alabama," he wrote. "Men from New York 'flop houses' walked beside fruit pickers from Miami, Tennessee mountaineers, and even one light-house keeper from South Carolina." Waters had hoped to parade eight thousand vets down Pennsylvania Avenue in front of the White House, but Glassford altered that route in favor of a less confrontational path along Constitution Avenue from Seventeenth Street, then down to Pennsylvania Avenue to the Peace Monument near Capitol Hill.

The boxing matches themselves turned out to be hugely successful. More than fifteen thousand fans turned out to see fifty fights in a ring set up over the infield diamond. "Sitting side by side," wrote sportswriter Jack Espey in the *Washington Post*, "were overalled laborers and daintily clad ladies, men in tattered sweaters and young fashion plates." Lake and some volunteers passed the proverbial hat between bouts and collected about $3,000, most of it spent on food and various essentials that Glassford distributed to the vets at Anacostia and the other campsites.

The vets had dug in for the duration. The Hoover administration blamed Glassford for not doing more to usher the vets out of town, but it was too late now as thousands more arrived in Washington by the carload and under their own power every day. Eight thousand were already on hand and their numbers increased from day to day as stories about the great march on Washington captured headlines all over the country. Men and their families with nothing to lose, and little or no prospects for viable employment, figured they could get at least a couple of square meals a day and some shelter from the weather while they waited for Congress and the president to pass a bill granting them the immediate payment of their bonuses. Little did they know that they were entering a battle zone that would end in a bloody confrontation with a younger generation of soldiers under the command of an American Caesar who regarded the bonus marchers as an invading army of Communist agitators.

SEVEN

Glassford's Frankenstein Monster Rears His Ugly Head

H oover's chief of staff, Maj. Gen. Douglas MacArthur, had been on a mission to beef up America's military might well before the bonus army descended on the capital. In the wake of the Great War the military deteriorated to a point where there were only 132,000 soldiers in the army, ranking it sixteenth in the world behind Portugal and Greece, with outdated weapons and generally appalling equipment. MacArthur spent much of his time fighting to preserve the remnants of his dwindling forces. He feuded with an apathetic Congress and its meager military appropriations and a reduction in the ranks of officers; he launched a campaign to restructure the army and convince Congress that a powerful military was essential for national defense.

"Further reductions would be calamitous," he argued. Though he was a veteran who had distinguished himself on the battlefields of France, he had little patience with a bunch of grumbling protesters, as he viewed them. They only served to distract the nation's attention from his primary goals: strengthening the army's manpower reserves, artillery capabilities, tank corps, and cavalry regiments, and creating an impregnable bastion of defense against the encroaching Red menace intent on world domination. Bolshevik sympathizers riddled the bonus army, MacArthur believed, despite various reports to the contrary. A Veteran's Administration survey showed that 94 percent of the bonus marchers had served during wartime in the army or navy, 67 percent had seen combat overseas, and one out of five had returned home with disabling injuries. But MacArthur would have none of it. He believed that 90 percent of the marching vets were fakes, and he clung to that view throughout his life.

On June 8, during his commencement speech at the University of Pittsburgh, MacArthur announced, "Pacifism and its bedfellow, Communism, are all around us. In the theatre, newspapers and magazines, pulpits and lecture halls, schools and colleges . . . this canker eats deeper into the body politic." The bonus marchers passing through Pittsburgh on their way to Washington were representative of this canker, MacArthur emphasized. Three hundred students jeered his performance, and the police arrested and fined three of their leaders. MacArthur lobbied for incoming freshmen to sign a loyalty oath, which never passed muster, and his victory proved to be only temporary. An appeals court reversed the conviction of the three student leaders, leaving MacArthur with a bitter taste in his mouth. "It was bitter as gall," he said, "and I knew something of that gall would always be with me."

MacArthur and his allies in the Hoover administration kept a wary eye on the hordes of veterans who kept pouring into the city and joining the ranks of those who had arrived before them. MacArthur instructed officers commanding the country's nine corps areas to send him information on any agitators posing as veterans. The numbers of vets kept growing from day to day, reaching twenty-five thousand as they eagerly anticipated the outcome of new legislation that Patman and others had introduced for a final congressional showdown on the bonus question. Waters prepared the vets for the looming battle in a broadside he ordered to be read at all the campsites in the city.

"There is going to be a determined effort on the part of the bonus enemies to bring about the evacuation of Washington by the BEF," his message stated. "They are particularly hoping to start this disbanding of the veterans immediately after adjournment of the House and Senate. National General Headquarters will be in accord with the evacuation provided the bonus bill is passed. However, if the bill is pigeonholed or if any reason it fails to pass, National General Headquarters will not officially countenance the return home of the groups at present in Washington DC. General Headquarters BEF has from the beginning emphatically stated that if necessary we will stay on the job until 1945. That attitude is unchanged."

On June 16 Sen. Reed Smoot, co-architect of the disastrous Smoot-Hawley legislation that many blamed for triggering the Great Depression, brought the new bonus bill to the floor for a debate scheduled for the following day. Smoot was an ardent conservative who chaired the Senate Finance Committee, and he believed that Congress should levy stiff tariffs on all foreign goods entering the United States. A staunch Republican who backed Hoover to the hilt, he made it clear that he strongly opposed the new bill calling for the immediate payment of the bonus. Underlining the shibboleth that politics often makes for strange bedfellows, a number of so-called leftist progressives joined Smoot in his opposition to Patman's bill, arguing that treating the vets as a special class would undermine their own efforts to provide relief for everyone.

Sen. Burton K. Wheeler, a liberal Democrat who ran for vice president on the Progressive Party ticket headed by Robert La Follette, agonized over the dilemma before deciding to cast his lot with Patman and the vets. "We ought to provide work rather than give money to these ex-soldiers," he reasoned. "If . . . I felt sure that we could pass such legislation and give employment to the men on the streets tonight, and to the veterans, I would not vote for this legislation. . . . I have sat here waiting month after month and week after week and day after day in vain for the great engineer on the other end of Pennsylvania Avenue to come forward with some proposal for taking care not only of these ex-soldiers, not only of these veterans, but of the other thousands and millions of men and women of this country who are anxious and willing to work, but nothing has been done and nothing will be done." Under the circumstances Wheeler believed that he had little choice but to support the vets in their need, at least until after the November elections, in the hope that a more sympathetic administration would occupy the White House.

Rep. Fred Vinson of Kentucky, a Democrat, argued that the immediate payment of the bonus would put billions of dollars in circulation, but two of his Republican colleagues called the bonus march "a foolish trip and one which should not have been undertaken." Rep. James Frear of Wisconsin, who had served in the army from 1879 to 1884, told his colleagues, "Those who here enjoy thirty dollars a day or more should not denounce these wet, ragged, bedraggled men soaked for days in the rain, who only ask for a dollar a day. They ask for bread for themselves and their families . . . from the wealthiest country in the world, for which they fought."

One of the major American novelists of the day, John Dos Passos, compared what he observed to some of the more harrowing scenes he had witnessed in France during the Great War. "There is the same goulash of faces and dialects, foreigners' pidgin English, lingoes from industrial towns and farming towns, East, Northeast, Middle West, Southwest, South," he wrote. But these men were older, which made their plight even more sympathetic. They had "sunken eyes, hollow cheeks off breadlines," reminding the author that the lean years quickly consume the fat years. "The cops and the ex-servicemen play baseball games in the afternoon," he continued. "They are buddies together."

Evening Star reporter Thomas R. Henry called the changing face of Washington a "rag and tin-can city" that appeared to have doubled in size virtually overnight. "New streets with their nicely aligned junk-pile shelters appeared as if by magic as more and more veterans seemed to get the knack of making themselves comfortable." The vets' self-discipline particularly impressed Henry, since they had gathered in this strange, alien environment and established their dilapidated homesteads with "no crime, no dissension, no rebellion." Both Dos Passos and Henry noted that "white men and colored men crowded together under the same shelters," which was virtually unheard of at the time. Hoover gave lip service to ending discrimination in federal agencies, and he went so far as to appoint some blacks to federal commissions, but he wobbled in the face of political opposition and refused to support legislation that would have prohibited the lynchings that still took place throughout the South.

As the numbers of vets continued to grow, with more on the way, the camp at Anacostia easily claimed the title of the largest Hooverville in the country. More than 1,100 wives and children joined their husbands there and at the other campsites that Glassford had established, and they all waited patiently for Congress to get on with the job of passing the latest legislation to pay their bonuses now.

The battle lines, muddy as they were, were drawn. On June 15, while the legions of vets mounted in the streets, their numbers climbing each hour as the rain fell, the House voted in favor of the Patman bill 211 to 176. Fifty-seven Republicans broke ranks with their party and joined the Democrats and a representative of the Farmer-Labor Party in support of the legislation. One supporter, Rep. Edward Eslick of Tennessee, worked himself into a frenzy, chastising his colleagues for giving "two billion dollars for the great corporations, but when the American soldier comes you are unwilling . . . to pay a hungry and needy man." A coughing fit seized Eslick when he finished his peroration, and he dropped dead of a heart attack moments later. The margin of victory, however, was too narrow to override an expected veto from President Hoover in the unlikely event that it passed in the Senate, which was where the real battle was about to commence. It appeared certain that opposition in the Senate would be too stiff to overcome. Republican senator Hiram Johnson described the atmosphere in a letter to his son.

"Those men ought not to have come here in the first instance, they should not have swarmed down upon the Capitol, and no legislator should respond to their mere numbers or their veiled threats. . . . If I could have seen any way in which they could have been afforded relief without jeopardizing the whole financial fabric of the nation I would have voted with them. Their presence, although in my opinion it threatens no particular ill, is ominous." Johnson maintained that if other downtrodden men had joined ranks with the vets and marched with them, it would "not be difficult for a real revolution to start in this country."

Fear of a Bolshevik-style revolution engulfing the streets of America was very much on the minds of the president and his supporters in the Senate as it got ready to vote on the bonus bill. Only twenty-eight senators cast their votes in favor, while sixty-eight voted against it. Waters and the other vets had anticipated a defeat, but the lopsided results shocked even the most optimistic among them. Waters addressed the throngs, who stood helplessly on the steps of the Capitol, with the grim news. "The bonus has been defeated," he announced. "This is only a temporary setback. We are going to get more and more men, and we are going to stay here until we change the minds of these guys. You're ten times better Americans than the senators who voted against the bill."

The men stood glued to the steps, unsure how to react to this latest humiliation or to Waters's stoic reaction to it, which many of his followers found even more infuriating than their defeat in the Senate. Had someone yelled, "Charge!" most of the vets would have swarmed past the police lines into the Capitol and taken out their frustration on any politicians they could have laid their hands on. The atmosphere had become so charged that one journalist said the vets reminded him of "the mobs of the French revolution; the crash of the Kerensky government in Russia; the Spanish uprising." The vets could have, he contended, "had they wished, by sheer force of numbers swept away every obstruction."

Waters urged restraint, however, and after conferring with Glassford he told the vets to return to their campsites and regroup for the battles that lay ahead. Despite Waters's comforting words, there was a lot of grumbling among the men who wanted the politicians to take more decisive action. It took a woman to defuse the situation, a columnist with the Hearst newspapers named Elsie Robinson, who whispered in Waters's ear, "Tell the men to sing 'America,'" figuring that would dispel the tension from the air. She started to sing the hymn, and soon thousands of vets jointed in, bellowing the lyrics ". . . sweet land of liberty, of thee I sing." The men shuffled aimlessly when the song ended and began to disperse.

The men were only temporarily silenced, however, their fury and frustration only subdued for the moment. Among themselves the vets began to grumble once more about the quality of Waters's leadership, whether he was more interested in basking in the spotlight and currying favor with Glassford and the authorities than he was in achieving concrete results so they could all go home with some money in their pockets. One of Waters's more vocal critics was the cadaverous vet from New Jersey, Joe Angelo, who had saved Patton's life during the Meuse-Argonne offensive in September 1918 and walked all the way to Washington to testify before Congress in February 1931. Angelo made it clear that Waters's act had not impressed him.

"Waters swore to us when we made him boss," Angelo said, "that we would all stay here until 1945 if we did not get our bonus. Is he trying to sell out to the cops? Well, he won't get away with it."

As far as Glassford and some of the vets' most ardent allies were concerned, their greatest hope was that the vets would leave town now that the Senate had had its say. Sen. Elmer Thomas of Oklahoma, a major supporter of the vets, expressed his desire that the vets "would commence immediately to make their plans for evacuation of this so-called camp." The friendly *Washington Star* urged the vets to leave, editorializing that "if they go now every hand will be turned to help them. Their return will be likened to the return of an army from battle, where honor has been won."

This was all wishful thinking, of course. The sad fact was that most of the vets had nowhere to go and no jobs or money to sustain them if they did abandon their camps. At least they had a place to sleep and a couple of meals a day in their Hooverville homes courtesy of Glassford. Washington's top cop had anticipated the outcome of the Senate vote and moved quickly to head off any rebellion by the vets. "You men have as much right to be here as anyone else," he reassured them during a visit to Anacostia. "I'll admit I've been trying to get some of you to go home to make room for others who are coming in. At eleven o'clock every morning, we have trucks available with sufficient rations for those who want to go. But I want to tell you boys who want to stay here we'll keep on feeding you as long as a cent remains, and we'll do the best we can for you."

Privately Glassford was miffed at Waters for continuing his fiery rhetoric about staying until 1945. In discussions he had with the BEF leader, Waters admitted that this scenario was unrealistic and that the men could not endure without the resources to carry them through the cold fall and winter months that loomed over the horizon. Glassford talked about the ongoing "chess game" he was playing with Waters, but he also knew that he needed his Fascistic Frankenstein monster to maintain order at the camps. Glassford sent military bands into the camps to serenade the vets with patriotic music as a way of appealing to their sense of duty, and he instructed Waters to march the men in drill formation to create a feeling of quasi-military discipline among them. But when Waters balked at distributing fliers to the men, urging them to pick up stakes and leave town, Glassford went over his head literally and dropped three thousand leaflets from an airplane over the encampments. By June 25, as Waters became more defiant, skirting a fine line between his authority over the vets and his dependence on Glassford's good will and forbearance, Glassford resigned himself to the fact that the vets were going to remain until after the November elections.

"It is a fact that these efforts will bring scant results," Glassford reported to the commissioners, "and we will have on our hands for many weeks, if not months, several thousands of veterans." He proposed that the administration should erect barracks at the various camps to house them more comfortably as their numbers grew during the coming months with the weather taking a turn for the worse. Glassford's superiors balked at the prospect of accommodating a semi-permanent army of occupation on the government's doorstep, however, and they blamed Glassford during a stormy session on June 27 for allowing the situation to continue. Glassford contended that it would require the National Guard to quell any disturbances that would erupt from an attempt to evict the vets forcefully, escalating the standoff from a police procedure to a military confrontation.

The commissioners advising the president had already discussed the inevitability of a greater show of force to get the vets to leave, and talk of violence began to fill the airwaves, the news-papers, the halls of Congress, and the campsites themselves as the vets grew more rebellious and settled in for the long haul. When Glassford pleaded with the vets that it would be better for everyone if they left town peacefully, they grew increasingly defi-ant. "There's a lot of warehouses and stores in this town that are stuffed full of food," one vet told Glassford, "and we're not going to starve." More and more vets criticized Waters openly, but when he called for a new election for a BEF commander, the men reelected him by a wide margin, figuring he was the only one with a direct pipeline to Glassford, their only hope of salvation. "I have made many mistakes," Waters said to the men, "but I hardly believe my sincerity is open to question."

Waters's victory encouraged him to assume more power than before. He surrounded himself with larger squads of enforcers, amounting to five hundred "shock troops" in all, and he declared he would continue to command the BEF only if the vets were will-ing to give him "complete dictatorial powers." The men must obey his orders without complaint, he told them. He would drive any-one who disobeyed his orders out of Washington, Waters told the vets. "To hell with civil law and General Glassford!" Waters bel-lowed, desperate to repudiate the charge that he was nothing more than Glassford's flunky. "I'm going to have *my* orders carried out!"

At the same time he sent his goon squads into the ranks, crack-ing the heads of potential troublemakers, primarily those spouting Marxist rhetoric. Offering a deeper insight into his own politi-cal leanings, Waters created a subgroup of his most loyal follow-ers and named it the "Khaki Shirts," leaving little doubt—if any remained—that he was determined to launch a new economic and political order modeled on those that Hitler with his brownshirts and Mussolini with his blackshirts were establishing in Europe. If cooler heads in the government had prevailed, it would have been realized that the threat of revolution was more likely to emerge from the right than from the disorganized and fragmented left.

Most of the vets, however, were not buying any of Waters's rhetoric and ideological inclinations. All they knew was that they were hungry, miserable, and despairing of a sympathetic Congress to pay them the money that was due them. Hoover came up with a final proposal to encourage the men to leave town, well before the fall election cycle heated up in earnest. On July 9 the president signed a transportation bill, offering the vets low-cost government loans to abandon their camps and return home. Even Patman and the supportive Hearst newspapers decided it was time for the vets to end their occupation. Newspaper editorials speculated that if the vets left peacefully, the federal government would likely cancel the loan provision of the bill and treat the transportation money as an outright grant. But Waters dug in his heels, realizing that if a sizable percentage of vets took advantage of the offer, he was going to lose his power base and resume the life of a nonentity without a bona fide career or job to go back to.

This is just "an effort to send us back to our home towns so we can starve again," he thundered.

Again Waters launched his Khaki Shirts among the vets, where they terrorized various groups who were not 100 percent loyal to his regime. He believed that by doing so he could convince the authorities that he was serious about cleaning Commie sympathizers out of the ranks. But even Waters's political allies were disgusted by his heavy-handed tactics. The BEF's chief lobbyist, Harold B. Foulkrod, turned against Waters, saying that he could no longer "contaminate" himself "by pretending to agree with the stupid slogan: 'We Stay Here Until 1945.'" This was just one more example of Waters's "false, ignorant, inefficient leadership [which] has already cost the BEF the support of its best friends," said Foulkrod. It was time "to end this farce."

When about five thousand bonus marchers opted to take the government's transportation money, Waters flew into a panic. He could have spared himself needless anxiety since it turned out that many of the vets sold their travel vouchers at discounts to travelers and returned to the camps with some money in their pockets. In an effort to stanch the apparent exodus out of Washington and shore up his base, Waters embarked on a recruitment campaign to lure more veterans into town. He sent teams of recruiters out to key cities across the country and bragged that he would have 150,000 new vets in town by the fall—an absurd estimate considering that there were barely enough resources available to accommodate the estimated 40,000 who already occupied the city. Besides, there was little reason for thousands more to flock into Washington since Congress was now in recess and Hoover was not inclined to call it back into session to vote on another bill. Waters turned his attention to the political arena and urged the vets "to defeat every last man that voted against the bonus." His primary target was the president, the man who promised to veto any new bonus legislation that crossed his desk. But the vets hardly needed Waters's directives on how to cast their votes. They were already inclined to toss out those who had abandoned them and to support the pols who had championed their cause.

EIGHT

The Death March Upstages the BEF

Waters was not the only colorful figure leading a procession of vets to Washington from diverse corners of the nation. Aside from Pace, the leader of the Communists who never did gain any traction with the great majority of veterans, there was a Texas delegation headed by a woman dressed in men's clothing whom the press called "Joan of Arc in Overalls." She paraded her vets into town with two mascots in tow, a donkey named "Patman" and a goat named "Hoover." The most flamboyant figure of all was a former navy man from Los Angeles, Royal W. Robertson, who led more than a thousand vets across the country in an epic journey that left dozens of dilapidated, broken-down automobiles strewn in their path as they forged their way eastward.

Robertson wore an elaborate neck brace made of leather, supported by a steel column that extended almost a foot above his shoulders, a result of a broken neck he had suffered in the navy. He looked like a man whose head was perpetually in a noose. Most people assumed he had injured his neck in combat, but a later investigation revealed that he had hurt himself falling out of a hammock while in training. Nevertheless he received a pension for a bona fide service injury. Army intelligence reports described him as cunning and unscrupulous, a man with Communist leanings who was "very anti-government, anti-Congress, and anti-Hoover." Robertson was a political independent, definitely not a Communist despite the government's paranoia on the subject.

Rail-thin, with a dynamic speaking voice, Robertson attracted to his cause a large group of vets who had been camping out in vacant lots and public parks in Los Angeles. One of his followers described him as "a very articulate fellow, rather slight, but alive, tense, a flaming little guy" with "a rapier-like wit." By the middle of June about 2,500 of them had "registered and pledged to travel," according to Robertson. The mayor of Los Angeles sponsored a parade for them before their departure, no doubt happy to see the last of so many homeless, disgruntled citizens camped out on public property.

They headed east to Phoenix, Arizona, in a caravan of 350 cars and trucks of dubious reliability. The mayor of Phoenix prepared for their arrival by making the fairgrounds available for their stay and arranging for some local merchants to provide them with a meal. Robertson was able to call upon the support of veterans' organizations and local civic groups, who donated cash, food, and gasoline, allowing him to build up a treasury of about $2,500 to feed and clothe his men. From Phoenix Robertson led his vets back on the road again toward Texas, but by the time they arrived in El Paso most of their vehicles had broken down and sat lifeless where they had expired. Robertson was not to be discouraged. Feisty and strong-willed, he herded his men to the freight yards, where they hopped aboard boxcars without too much resistance from the railroad authorities. Pushing ahead eastward, the Robertson contingent, totaling about 1,500 vets, crossed into the district on July 9 after an adventurous six-week journey.

The press had publicized their struggle to reach the nation's capital in advance, since Robertson made for good copy and quickly became a media favorite. But the attention he received did not sit well with Waters, who immediately regarded Robertson as his main rival for the spotlight. Like others who enjoyed a taste of power and celebrity for the first time in their lives, Waters guarded his own measure of recognition like a mother bear protecting her cubs. No sooner did Robertson and his vets set foot in the capital than Waters rode in from the mudflats at Anacostia in his unreliable, broken-down jalopy to greet him.

"Would you like to join the BEF and move to our camps?" Waters asked Robertson.

Robertson's response was less than cordial. He turned a critical eye on Waters, dressed in his khaki regalia, jodhpurs, and riding boots. "Well, I'm going to wait a few days until I see what it is all about," said Robertson. "We came to Washington to petition Congress, not to picnic."

Robertson was totally put off by what he saw as Waters's grandstanding and his infatuation with operating a tightly knit paramilitary organization. "I had already had enough of all this military stuff," he fumed. He was more interested in getting results. "We naturally believed that [Waters] had some business ability and a definite legislative program [and that] we might strengthen the organization and force Congress to pass the bonus bill at once." Robertson told the press, "My men will refuse to follow Waters as long as he continues with his stew-and-beans mooching policy. The public is supporting these men here and my men feel they should try to do something constructive instead of sitting in a puddle and whittling a stick until 1945."

Robertson's excoriating words were the last thing Waters wanted to hear.

Robertson quickly established himself as Glassford's new main source of concern. He made it clear that he was not going to direct his men to any of the established campsites Instead, he instructed them to picket the Capitol, and he told Glassford that his vets would sleep on the Capitol grounds until the government addressed their grievances. Glassford was powerless to do anything to stop him since his metropolitan police force did not have jurisdiction over federal property, which was the bailiwick of the Capitol Police Board and its own separate police force under the command of Capt. S. J. Gnash. Glassford and Gnash had long been at loggerheads, with Gnash favoring a tougher stand against the vets, for whom he had little sympathy. Gnash's skeletal police force, however, was unable to protect the Capitol from such a large group of demonstrators, so he reluctantly turned over that responsibility to Glassford. Glassford immediately arranged for Vice President Charles Curtis to allow Robertson's men to parade to the Capitol on July 12 to present a petition, but he drew the line at permitting them to carry their bedrolls with them for a planned "sleep-in" on the Capitol grounds. The vets were determined to sleep out in any event, with or without their bedrolls, and they spent the night sleeping on lawns and sidewalks under the watchful eyes of both Gnash and Glassford.

As the press focused its attention on Robertson and his defiant brigades, Waters found himself shunted off to the sidelines for the first time since his arrival in Washington. Robertson, as Waters had feared, had positioned himself as his main rival for the attention of the media and the political authorities. In a blatant attempt to recapture the spotlight, Waters led a contingent of his BEF vets to the Capitol and addressed the press from the steps. He had decked himself out in his now familiar riding breeches, knee-high boots, and khaki shirt, flanked on both sides by four of his shock troops. Waters made the startling announcement that he had secured a meeting during the following week with Democratic presidential candidate Franklin D. Roosevelt. "When I see him," Waters told the crowd, "I will get a statement which I will bring back to you and repeat word for word."

Even if Waters's forthcoming meeting with FDR was an established fact rather than a ploy to recapture center stage, Waters was not likely to hear words of encouragement to bring back to the vets. Roosevelt had already stated his own position on the bonus in unequivocal language. "I do not see how, as a practical business sense," he had said, "a government running behind two billion dollars annually can consider the anticipation of the bonus payment until it has a balanced budget, not only on paper but with a surplus of cash in the Treasury."

Roosevelt stuck to this position through the rest of the campaign despite pressure from Sen. Huey "Kingfish" Long of Louisiana, who told the Democratic nominee that he was a "gone goose" unless he changed his mind. With the leaders of both major political parties lined up against the immediate payment of the bonus, Waters's claim that any meeting with FDR could produce positive results was fanciful at best. After observing Robertson and Waters in action for a while, reporter Thomas R. Henry of the *Evening Star* wrote that Robertson was "one of those natural-born leaders with a confidence inspiring positiveness who arise suddenly out of obscurity in times of crisis and whom men will follow to the death." In contrast Henry dismissed Waters as a "tin-soldier sort."

On the morning of July 13, the day after the impromptu sleep-in on the Capitol grounds, Glassford informed Robertson that he could not permit his vets to loiter there another day. Glassford was under a tremendous load of pressure from the highest levels of government to take a tougher stance against the vets and their occupation of the nation's capital. When word got out that Glassford had actually laid out $600 of his own money to buy food for them, the commissioners accused him of divided loyalties and shirking his duty to impose law and order throughout the city. Robertson responded to Glassford's warning by asking him if there was any law against citizens walking along the Capitol grounds. Glassford told Robertson that there was no such restriction, whereupon Robertson told his men to line up in single file and to start walking slowly in a circle around the grounds. To assure that they would not stop to rest on the grass the maintenance crews left the sprinklers on all night and into the next day to keep the vets on the sidewalks.

The spectacle of more than 350 beat-up veterans—their numbers growing as some of Waters's BEF vets joined the Robertson demonstration—shuffling in slow motion in front of the Capitol captured the attention of the national press, which promptly labeled the grim procession the "Death March." One account called it "one of the grittiest demonstrations of the Depression." The vets' "supreme dramatic gesture" captured Thomas Henry's sympathies as he described the unspeakable horror of "men in bare feet, in stocking feet, with toes sticking though their shoes . . . most with faces fixed on the ground."

Waters chose the occasion of the Death March to leave town on one of his mysterious absences, ostensibly to raise more money and food supplies from allies in New York City. He later admitted, however, that his scheduled appearances in various theaters and on the radio did not come off as planned. "When I went to the studio," he wrote, "I found that pressure from higher up had canceled my appointment." The same was true for his ostensible theater appeals, which also vanished mysteriously into the ether. When he returned to Washington with his wife Wilma in tow, only to find Robertson stealing his thunder at the center of all the activity, he departed with Wilma to Evalyn McLean's mansion. The camp at Anacostia was clearly not what Wilma had in mind when she arrived from Portland to join her husband. "I could have lived in Anacostia," she said, "but things were bad there—there were always upheavals."

Wilma's diminutive appearance struck a chord within McLean, one of Waters' chief benefactors. Wilma was "a little ninety-three pounder, dressed as a man," McLean said, "her legs and feet in shiny boots. Her yellow hair was freshly marcelled." Waters's main priority was to reassert his own relevance in the battle for the bonus and to divert press attention away from Robertson, whose Death March dragged on for three days and four nights while Waters and the BEF faded from the headlines. McLean was Waters's main link to the Washington political establishment, and he decided to leverage his relationship with her to further his own agenda. "I'm desperate," he told her. "Unless these men are fed, I can't say what won't happen in this town."

As Waters expected, the implied threat of violence alarmed McLean enough that she picked up her phone and called Vice President Curtis, who was a frequent guest at her dinner parties and poker nights. "These men are in a desperate situation," she told the vice president. "Unless something is done for them, unless they are fed, there is bound to be a lot of trouble. They have no money nor any food."

Curtis's reaction was less than she had hoped for. His options were limited by a president who was not inclined to spend a nickel on food or any other relief that would induce the vets to remain in town a second longer than necessary. McLean had long ago sized Curtis up as one of the weakest vice presidents in history, a veritable nonentity whose own president ignored and disdained him. She had a low opinion of Hoover as well and thought wistfully of the days when her old drinking buddy Warren Harding occupied the Oval Office. "Harding would have gone among those men and talked in such a manner as to make them cheer him and cheer their flag," she wrote. "If Hoover had done that, I think, not even troublemakers in the swarm could have caused any harm."

But that was not Hoover's style. McLean resigned herself to the inevitable play of events as they unfolded. She directed Waters and Wilma to an apartment she had taken for them at her own expense, where they could at least live in comfort while Robertson and his own vets continued their Death March, hobbled by misery and despair.

The plight of the vets became even more intractable when an intelligence report claimed that a BEF splinter group armed with machine guns, led by one Charles M. Bundell, was on its way to Washington from upstate New York, determined to start a revolution. Allegedly this offshoot of the BEF had the support of some active-duty marines, who were ready to launch a revolution to overthrow the government. The report, which turned out to be bogus, stoked the worst fears of the administration, that Communists were determined to take over the bonus march and use it to incite the vets to adopt a more radical posture against the entire capitalist system. Incendiary incidents at Anacostia only served to convince the Hoover administration that a Communist uprising was imminent. Taking advantage of Waters's absence, a group of card-carrying Communists led by Pace descended on Anacostia and denounced "Mussolini Waters" as a tool of the establishment. When several BEF shock troops closed in on them with clubs and truncheons, Glassford's quick thinking kept the confrontation from becoming bloody.

"There is not to be a fight among the veterans," Glassford told the men. "Pace has a right to speak. If you don't want to listen, go back and play baseball."

The truth was that just about everyone in the city was growing weary of the seemingly endless demonstrations that had continued nonstop for days and weeks. Even the friendly *Washington Post* editorialized that "to urge [the vets] to stay here is to keep them in deeper and deeper distress and perhaps to bring them to face utter disaster." Other newspapers chimed in with their own editorials, prompting Glassford to state, "It is futile to expect favorable bonus legislation at this session. No political advantage can be gained by remaining longer in this city." The situation worsened on July 14, Bastille Day, when Vice President Curtis panicked at the thought of imminent revolution and uncharacteristically took it upon himself to call in a contingent of marines to defend the Capitol building. Sixty of them arrived in full battle regalia and fixed bayonets, only to find themselves cheered on by the vets, who welcomed them as comrades in arms who were there to lend support.

Glassford flew into a rage when he heard about "The Curtis Blunder," as the *Washington Daily News* called it, saying that Curtis's actions could have produced "bloody and tragic" results. "I'm fed up with hysterical meddlers," Glassford fumed, referring to Curtis, whose unilateral decision to bring in the marines marked the first time since the Civil War that the government called in troops to defend the nation's capital. Curtis's foolhardy interference served only to attract even more vets and onlookers to the Capitol area, as more and more vets left their camps and joined the Death March. The numbers mounted steadily, and at dawn on July 16 Robertson called off his march to make room for the estimated seventeen thousand vets and their supporters who swarmed onto the steps and around the grounds in front of the Capitol.

With Robertson still the center of attention from the media and the new de facto leader of the reenergized vets, Waters decided to make his move to recapture the spotlight. In his own words, "When I was ten feet from the front line I turned and without a word, but signaling with my arm, I started towards the Capitol. I heard a roar behind me and saw that the men were quickening their pace after me." Waters led the charge up the steps and escalated what had been a peaceful demonstration, with men shuffling around hoping for some news to break in their favor, into something approaching a near riot. Glassford was infuriated by what he regarded as Waters's betrayal. Until now the BEF commander had remained sympathetic to the police chief's precarious balancing act between his need to mollify the top echelons in the Hoover administration and his desire to protect the vets in their struggle for the bonus. And now Waters had taken it upon himself to turn up the fire beneath an already volatile cauldron of frustration, despair, and seething anger. Waters left Glassford no choice but to have him arrested and taken down to the basement of the Capitol. When he emerged moments later the voices of the vets grew louder and more belligerent, and Waters became even more defiant, prompting Glassford to have him arrested a second time to prevent the demonstration from exploding into violence.

"It looked for a moment like stark riot ahead," said reporter Bess Furman. But bloodshed was averted when Waters made another one of his false, self-serving announcements. He declared that he had secured a meeting with Speaker of the House John Nance Garner and that he planned to meet with President Hoover afterward. Waters's claims came as news to both men. Hoover's secretary said the president was "too occupied" to meet with anyone and was planning instead to preside over the closing of Congress— shutting down Garner along with it. With Waters's bluff quickly revealed for what it was—so much hot air—the vets started to drift away more disheartened than before. Waters became desperate and told the milling throngs that they could either follow him back to Anacostia and the other camps, or else "join that outfit over there," pointing to Robertson and his growing army of vets who were observing Waters's histrionics from the grounds in front of the Capitol. Many of Waters's former BEF followers peeled off and joined the Robertson brigade, which now marched toward the opposite end of Pennsylvania Avenue to continue their protest in front of the White House.

NINE

Khaki Shirts Take on the Reds

With the ranks of the BEF declining from a high of more than twenty-two thousand to less than fifteen thousand by Waters's count, Waters attempted to broaden his base by saying that his BEF now represented all of the nation's unemployed. In addition to the bonus Waters demanded federal relief for all the poor and destitute. His recharged rhetoric attracted the attention of Pace and the Communists, who regarded Waters as a fraud and a Fascistic opportunist. Once again the Reds attempted to stir up the vets with renewed attacks on Waters and an appeal for them to join other groups who were taking their fight down Pennsylvania Avenue to the White House. Glassford grew increasingly alarmed about reenergized Communists who "would take advantage of the situation" and complicate his efforts to maintain order in the camps. On July 20 Pace made his move, marching at the head of a contingent of two hundred men toward the White House, chanting Communist slogans as they closed in on their destination. Before they could get there, however, police inspector Albert Headley and his force of forty cops intercepted the marchers and told Pace they could not proceed any further without a permit.

"We are not marching," Pace replied. "This is not a parade. We are walking on the public streets as individuals."

Headley was not in a mood to make such fine distinctions. He lunged forward, grabbed Pace by the throat, and threw him back at the men behind him. When Pace tried to regroup Headley arrested him, and his vets scattered off in different directions. The incident attracted the attention of the press, which blamed the Hoover administration for letting the situation get out of control.

Police cordoned off the streets around the White House, blocking all traffic. Secret Service agents chained and locked the gates and stationed themselves at thirty-foot intervals around the perimeter. "Hoover Locks Self in the White House!" blared a front-page headline in the *New York Daily News*. The imagery of the president of the United States hunkered down in his bunker while starving veterans demonstrated in the streets pushed Hoover and his minions to the tipping point. One way or another he was determined to get the vets out of town, even if it required federal troops to get the job done.

If Hoover had had the patience to wait calmly while events played themselves out, he could have spared the nation much of the grief and tragedy that ensued during the coming weeks. Many of the vets, realizing that there was little to be gained at this point from the political establishment, pulled up stakes and headed out of Washington on their own. By the end of July the ranks of the BEF had dwindled to about one-third of their peak strength, according to more objective estimates than the numbers disseminated by Waters. Police estimates put the count at 11,698 vets scattered among twenty-four separate camps, plus an indeterminate number of women and children, with the ranks thinning out every day. But Hoover was growing increasingly impatient as the campaign season heated up, and he wanted a quick resolution to his precarious grip on the presidency before the vets completely undermined his bid for reelection.

The president directed Assistant Secretary of the Treasury Ferry K. Heath and his colleague Seymour Lowman to revoke permission for the vets to occupy a swath of partially demolished buildings on Pennsylvania Avenue near the Capitol, bounded by C and D Streets and Twelfth and Thirteenth Streets, SW. One of the structures had been the home of poet Walt Whitman during the Civil War. The two thousand vets who lived in the area, along with about five hundred women and children and a couple of hundred Communists, had named their neighborhood Camp Glassford, a tribute to the man who had arranged to house them there. The president's directive, however, ordered construction crews "to proceed immediately with the completion" of the demolition so that construction could begin on more modern buildings in the area.

Glassford had no choice but to comply with the president's order. He sent Waters a memo stating, "It is recommended that the veterans quartered in this area be urged to take advantage of the transportation home available until midnight, July 25, 1932. It will be necessary for those who do not take advantage of this transportation to find accommodations elsewhere. In this connection you are advised that no public buildings or public space will be occupied by veterans unless authority is granted by Police Headquarters, and no private buildings or grounds will be occupied without written authority from the owners." Waters was unnerved by the unexpected turn of events. "They can issue orders, but I don't know how they are going to enforce them," he said. "Wait until they start moving out the women and children. . . . That will make swell pictures."

As for Robertson, he knew when it was time to depart from a losing battle and return to fight another day when the outlook was more encouraging. He told his men that they had accomplished as much as they could reasonably hope for considering the circumstances and that they should all return to California. But when the police brought in trucks to haul them all to the Maryland border, no one hopped in. Robertson climbed into his own wreck of a car with his neck brace riding high over his shoulders and waved goodbye as he headed west by himself.

Subsequent orders from Hoover took on an even more draconian tone. Glassford assumed that the administration would grant him ample time to usher the vets from their temporary lodgings. But new directives passed down through Director of Public Buildings and Public Parks Ulysses S. Grant III, a Hoover loyalist, called for the total evacuation not only of the buildings on Pennsylvania Avenue by midnight July 22, less than thirty-six hours away, but also from the main camp at Anacostia and the other campsites by noon August 4. In addition the orders called for the return of all National Guard equipment, including tents and rolling kitchens, by noon of August 1. Glassford was incensed. The tight deadlines seemed totally arbitrary and counterproductive to him. He told the commissioners that a gradual, peaceful evacuation was already under way, and he warned them about "the great danger inherent" in such an unnecessary ultimatum. His pleas ran into a stone wall, however. There were to be "no exceptions" to the president's orders. The administration had effectively defanged Glassford, stripped him of all decision-making authority, and reduced him to a messenger passing along orders from people higher up the command chain.

Glassford was not one to take it all lying down. He questioned the legality of the orders, claiming that the treasury officials had no authority to use local police to evict the vets from public property. Glassford consulted with Washington's legal counsel, W. W. West, who agreed that the order was unlawful. Glassford needed no further corroboration. The next morning he called for a meeting with the U.S. district attorney, the corporation counsel for the District of Columbia, the U.S. marshal, and a representative of the solicitor of the treasury. After several hours of discussion they emerged unanimous in their opinion that the commissioners did not have the legal authority to order evictions from the buildings, and that they required a court order to evacuate the area. And that even if the commissioners were able to obtain one, they would have to carry out the eviction themselves without relying on the metropolitan police force. Glassford served up the final challenge that brought the episode to a rest, at least for the moment.

The vets were "known to be preparing for passive resistance against forcible ejection," he warned in a memo. "The situation is fraught with potentialities of riot and bloodshed should any attempt be made in an illegal manner to evacuate the buildings in question by midnight this date." And there the matter rested while the Hoover administration backed off and tried to figure out how to proceed.

With Robertson missing in action and his followers milling about without a leader to direct them, Waters moved in to fill the power vacuum. He would have been better off letting Glassford orchestrate the fate of the vets, since the city's top cop had the law on his side and had fought the administration to a stalemate. But Waters was more interested in reestablishing his own relevance than in finding a peaceful resolution to the stand-off. He issued a statement, urging the vets "to stand your ground. I, as your commander in chief, need only to raise my hand above my head and my following of twelve thousand men will either fight or frolic, according to my wishes." His proclamation was nothing less than delusional. The vets had grown more and more frustrated and restless without a viable action plan in place, and Waters offered them nothing but empty, self-serving rhetoric. Glassford, the only authority figure they could rely on, was urging them to go home and avoid further confrontation with the political establishment. It was the worst scenario imaginable, thousands of angry, hungry, homeless men and their families wandering aimlessly around, unsure toward what kind of special hell their steps were leading them.

With the coffers of the BEF reduced to three dollars and change and no prospect of food or additional supplies on the way to tide the vets over, Waters still refused to accept reality. He "declared war" on Hoover and ordered his Khaki Shirts to assault the Communists under Pace by leaping "into the breach between American institutions and threatened anarchy." Pace was quick to respond to the challenge. Defying Waters, he staged a demonstration in front of the White House at noon on July 25, fully expecting not only the vets to flock to his banner but thousands of government workers to join his march as he led about five hundred of his followers in a charge through the police lines. The pending clash played into the worst fears of the administration, which had only to turn to Europe to witness street battles between armed groups of Fascists and Communists contending for dominance. The conflict intensified when the police clubbed the vets with nightsticks and the vets fought back with their fists and feet. Pace's strategy backfired when one of his marchers succeeded in yanking a revolver out of a policeman's holster and waving it overhead while a claque of infuriated cops chased him.

1. Coxey's Army on the march to the Capitol steps in Washington. From
E. Benjamin Andrews, *History of the United States from the Earliest Discovery
of America to the Present Time* (New York: Charles Scribner's Sons, 1912).

2. (*opposite top*) A crowd of people gathers outside the New York Stock Exchange following the crash of 1929. Library of Congress, LC-USZ62-123429.

3. (*opposite bottom*) Bonus Army marches to the Capitol; the Washington Monument is in the background. Library of Congress, LC-USZ62-47831.

4. (*above*) Bonus Army stages a huge demonstration at the empty Capitol, 1932. Library of Congress, LC-USZ62-31111.

5. Bonus Army on the Capitol Lawn, Washington DC, July 13, 1932. Library of Congress, LC-USZ6-525.

6. (*opposite top*) Mourners stand by memorial wreaths during the funerals of Joe York, George Bussell, Coleman Leny, and Joe Blasio, four of the men killed during the Ford Hunger March, at Detroit's Woodmere Cemetery, March 12, 1932. Walter P. Reuther Library, Archives of Labor and Urban Affairs, Wayne State University.

7. (*opposite bottom*) Thousands line Woodward Avenue as the funeral procession for four of the men slain during the Ford Hunger March passes by, Detroit, Michigan, March 12, 1932. Within the crowds, people hold banners and signs denouncing the violence and urging men to join the auto workers' union. Walter P. Reuther Library, Archives of Labor and Urban Affairs, Wayne State University.

8. Herbert Hoover and Mrs. Hoover, full-length portrait, 1929.
Library of Congress, LC-USZ62-131568.

9. Calvin Coolidge, Andrew Mellon, and Herbert Hoover outside
the White House, 1928. Library of Congress, LC-DIG-hec-35070.

10. Franklin Delano Roosevelt and Herbert Hoover in a convertible on the way to the U.S. Capitol for Roosevelt's inauguration, March 4, 1933. Library of Congress, LC-DIG-ppmsca-19179.

11. Franklin Delano Roosevelt, 1938. Library of Congress, LC-DIG-hec-47384.

12. Pelham Glassford, year unknown. Library of Congress, LC-DIG-hec-20930.

13. Gen. Douglas MacArthur, year unknown. Library of Congress, LC-DIG-hec-18381.

14. Ready for bonus fight. This group of
congressmen is organizing for a vigorous fight
to put the soldiers' bonus bill through the
House. From the left: Representatives Clarence
Cannon (D-MO), parliamentarian for the steering
committee; Adolph J. Sabath (D-IL), dean of
the House; Wright Patman (D-TX), chairman;
Abe Murdock (D-UT), secretary; and Arthur
H. Greenwood (D-IN), whip, January 24, 1935.
Library of Congress, LC-DIG-hec-38264.

15. Bonus Army marchers in a camp in Anacostia, Washington DC, 1932. Library of Congress, LC-DIG-hec-36887.

16. Example of damage in Florida Keys after 1935 hurricane. Florida Memory State Library & Archives of Florida, Florida Photographic Collection, PR09314.

At that point a Pace loyalist named Walter Eicker climbed up a tree and urged the vets to fight the police. The march ended when the police took Pace and a half dozen of his followers into custody and charged them with inciting a riot. Eicker supplied a Keystone Kops dimension to the festivities as he yelled from his perch in the trees, "We want our bonus! To hell with Wall Street! Comrades, this is only the beginning of the uprising of the rank and file!" While the gun-snatcher scampered through the throngs trying to avoid the pursuing men in blue, two police officers started to climb the tree, forcing Eicker to climb higher in an effort to elude them. The enraged cops finally grabbed him and dragged him down to earth, where they charged him not only with inciting a riot but also with destroying public property by snapping off some branches when he climbed up the tree.

Waters softened his tone afterwards and tried to buy more time to plan his next move. Glassford had given up hope of depending on Waters to keep the vets in check, but Waters was the only one with any semblance of a following, so Glassford had little choice but to deal with the devil he knew rather than scout around for another authority figure. It was far too late in the game for that, especially since Hoover had already drawn up plans to impose martial law in the district. The army had secretly relocated two combat vehicles from Aberdeen, Maryland, to just outside the district—a truck mounted with a 75-millimeter gun and an armored car with .30- and .50-caliber machine guns. Glassford set up a meeting between Waters and an attorney representing the BEF, Herbert S. Ward, with the commissioners, asking for an extension on the deadline. Also present at the five-hour meeting in the State, War, and Navy Building near the White House was Gen. Douglas MacArthur, who said little but listened intently, keeping his own counsel.

General MacArthur "never once stopped his ceaseless tread around the room," Waters recalled later. In an attempt to engage MacArthur, Waters, perhaps spotting the handwriting on the wall, asked him directly, "If the troops should be called out against us, will the BEF be given the opportunity to form in columns, salvage their belongings, and retreat in orderly fashion?"

"'Yes, my friend, of course,' MacArthur replied," according to Waters. It is hard to believe that MacArthur uttered those words, if indeed he did, since he was convinced—a conviction reinforced by one of his aides, Maj. Gen. Courtney Whitney—that the ranks of the BEF were swollen with "a heavy percentage of criminals, men with prison records for such crimes as murder, manslaughter, rape, robbery, burglary, blackmail, and assault." Whitney claimed that "a secret document which was captured later disclosed that the Communist plan covered even such details as the public trial and hanging in front of the Capitol of high government officials. At the very top of the list was the name of army chief of staff MacArthur." Whitney never was able to come up with this so-called secret document, but MacArthur, who was paranoid to begin with, needed no further convincing. It is unlikely that he would have addressed Waters as "my friend," or would even have acknowledged the presence of the misfit whom he regarded as the leader of a pack of BEF criminals.

Secretary of War Patrick J. Hurley, no friend of the vets, was as blunt as possible, observing Waters as though he were a sub-human life form. "Waters, the War Department has no tentage available, and if it did have we certainly would not place it at your disposal. . . . We are only interested in getting you out of the District. At the first sign of disorder or bloodshed in the BEF, you will all get out. And we have plenty of troops to put you out."

The commissioners granted the vets an extra twenty-four hours to abandon the camps, but even that proved impractical when the contractors refused to proceed with the demolition work on July 27, claiming that their insurance carriers threatened to cancel their coverage if they did. Hoover, however, was not inclined to let an insurance dispute derail him from his goal of getting the vets out of town one way or another. He turned the matter over to the Justice and War Departments, which were not bound by the same legal straitjackets as the Treasury Department. The U.S. marshal was ordered "to cause the [bonus marchers] to be

ejected and removed" from Anacostia and the other public campsites. The authorities put Glassford on a need-to-know basis and
did not fully inform him about the extent of the administration's
directive. His authority was limited to "making arrests for viola-
tions of the law committed in the presence of police officers, and
protecting such property as may be repossessed against unlawful reoccupancy." But he correctly assumed that the situation
would soon spiral out of control and end in disaster if he failed
to take steps to deflect the administration from its hardline, mil-
itaristic stance.

In an effort to head off any unnecessary violence and bloodshed
looming on the horizon, Glassford once again arranged for Waters
to meet with the commissioners, but this time they refused to
engage him face to face. Instead they treated him like a nuisance
who stood in the way of their plans and refused to allow him in
the same room where the deliberations took place. They passed
messages along to him through Glassford, who returned to the
conference room with Waters's responses. The irony of Glassford
serving as the bearer of messages between the BEF commander
and the commissioners, who held his fate in their hands, was not
lost on Waters. "The General would go into the Commissioners'
office," Waters wrote, "get their statement, return to me, then take
back my comments to the gentlemen in the next room. It isn't
every ex-sergeant that can have an ex-General for a messenger boy."

Glassford had little power of his own at this stage, as the Hoover
administration had effectively turned the entire operation over
to the military and reduced the role of the metropolitan police
to a peacekeeping function. Glassford attempted to work out the
best deal he could for Waters and the vets under less-than-ideal
circumstances, and Waters at first agreed to honor the timeta-
ble set by the commissioners. He said that he would evacuate
two hundred vets from the Pennsylvania buildings the next day
but did not think it was possible to move all of them from the
area by 4:00 p.m. on Friday, July 29, as the commissioners had
demanded. He countered with a deadline he thought was more

feasible, the relocation of all the vets to other camps by 7:30 a.m. on Monday, August 1.

Waters's standing with the BEF had fallen sharply, however, and most of them had begun to consider him a laughingstock. When he told the vets camped out in the buildings slated for demolition that two hundred of them had to move, they greeted his remarks with a round of heckling and booing. Waters, unnerved by his reception, decided to revert to the more militant tone he had previously adopted to regain his credibility with the bonus marchers. A police officer assigned to monitor Waters, Private J. O. Patton, described the scene in a report he wrote. Waters arrived at about 8:15 a.m., July 28, the officer reported, and when the vets shouted him down, he told them, "Men, I have not changed my mind about moving. We do not intend to move until they provide us with proper shelter and food, and we can remain here and be locked up, then they will have to provide for us. However if the Army comes they will move us and you can depend on that."

Patton interrupted Waters' garbled speech when an emissary from Glassford arrived and told him that the police chief had a message for Waters. The piecemeal eviction of the vets from the Pennsylvania Avenue buildings would begin at once, whether the vets agreed to it or not. Waters, in a further attempt to regain his stature with the BEF, instructed the vets to assume a posture of "passive resistance" toward the police and force the cops to carry them out bodily. About seventy vets did exactly that, sitting and curling themselves forward, while the others shuffled around unsure of what course to take. Waters, outfitted as usual in his Khaki Shirt regalia, surrounded by similarly attired loyalists, climbed back up on the speaker's platform and tried to command the men's attention.

"Give us our bonus!" the men yelled at him. "Let them come and take us away! We'll fight the whole damn works!"

An increasingly rattled Waters changed his tone again, trying to find a middle ground they could all live with. "Glassford and his police are pretty good fellows," he told the angry vets, "but when you start defying the federal government, which don't take any consideration of the human element, you're going to get licked. We can't lick the United States Government, but when the United States troops are called to escort me out, I'm going out." It was revealing that the vets were so eager to remain in their partially demolished buildings that stood like grotesque skeletons against the sky—the only structures they could call home.

Waters's defeatist message, laced with an undercurrent of half-hearted belligerence, backfired on him. The vets grew even more boisterous, and when Waters asked them, "Will you move or won't you?" they shouted "No!" in a unanimous display of rebellion against their erstwhile leader. At this point Glassford had one of his aides deliver a note to Waters stating that treasury agents, reinforced by the police, would evacuate all the vets in the area, forcefully or peacefully, starting at 10 a.m. Waters read the note to the vets and said, "There you are! You're double-crossed! I'm double-crossed!" Glassford himself was surprised that the government was acting so abruptly, not even waiting until the July 29 deadline he thought he had negotiated. Still the vets refused to abandon the buildings, many of them stunned that the same government that had promised them a bonus for their service in the Great War would snatch their home away from home from them. For the first two hours the eviction proceeded smoothly, with many of the vets leaving under their own power, and others who refused to leave carted out to the street by the cops and federal agents.

The situation took a turn for the worse at noon, however, when Attorney General William D. Mitchell issued a new directive ordering the expulsion of the vets and their families from *all* the veterans' camps on public property in the district. Waters had mysteriously vanished from the area. One minute he was on a soapbox unsuccessfully exhorting the vets to rally around his leadership, and the next moment he was nowhere to be found. It is likely that he and his wife had retreated to the comfort of the apartment supplied by his benefactor Evalyn Walsh McLean. Glassford, entrusted with the distasteful job of enforcing the government's arbitrary edicts, was incensed.

"When I needed his cooperation most, Waters failed me," Glassford fumed.

Private Patton described the melee that followed in his report on the day's activities. "A group of twenty-five bonus marchers led by a white man carrying a flag began forging their way through a crowd of bonus marchers assembled around the building and were met at the police line by Major and Superintendent Glassford who told them that they could not proceed further. One of the men of this group, a white man named McCoy—known as a Communist, tore the Major's police badge from his shirt and struck him. The individual carrying the American flag immediately attacked an officer and bricks and stones began to fly from all directions . . . three or four men were arrested [and] the majority of the assailants made their escape into the crowd."

Glassford stepped forward and got the confrontation under control. "This game is getting dangerous," he shouted to the vets, "and it's time for lunch." The mention of food was all the men needed to calm things down. So far the police superintendent's cool response to the volatile proceedings had headed off the threat of further violence without a shot being fired. But the cauldron of discontent among the vets simmered just beneath the surface. Glassford knew that a single spark was all it would take to incite a riot. The police, whom the vets vastly outnumbered, would be unable to contain a spontaneous uprising in Anacostia and the other camps scattered throughout the city, which could be triggered by the presence of combat-ready regular army units at the camps. Glassford later denied that he asked for such assistance, but the commissioners reported otherwise in a letter to President Hoover.

"It is the opinion of the Major and Superintendent of Police, in which the Commissioners concur," they stated, "that it will be impossible for the Police Department to maintain law and order except by the free use of firearms which will make the situation a dangerous one; it is believed, however, that the presence of Federal troops in some number will obviate the seriousness of the situation and result in far less violence and bloodshed."

It seems unlikely that Glassford would have asked for backup from federal troops when his position all along had been that federal troops would only spur the vets on to greater resistance. And the commissioners' letter to Hoover did not say that Glassford specifically asked for federal forces, only that it would be impossible for the police to contain any violence that erupted. Most likely the commissioners were adopting a rationale to advance the administration's goal of ridding the city of demonstrating veterans as quickly as possible. In any event the finer points of who asked for what would soon be buried by the tragic showdown that was about to occur near the steps of the Capitol.

2

Blitzkrieg

TEN

An American Caesar Crosses the Anacostia

G lassford's own account of what happened next paints a vivid portrait of the traumatic events of July 28. After lunch, at around 1:45 in the afternoon, a brawl broke out on the side-walk near the Capitol. "There was some sort of a scramble between two veterans on the sidewalk," Glassford testified later, "and some police officers were taking a hand. . . . I heard a shot and saw Offi-cer [George Shinault] being attacked by a number of civilians. . . . One man had a club and was beating him. Another was choking him. About this time a garbage pail dropped down from above, adding to the confusion, and a few bricks. . . . Shinault, who is rather a powerful man, shook himself free and drew a revolver. As he did so I saw a veteran start toward him, and Shinault fired. I saw the veteran collapse. I heard another shot. I yelled to Shi-nault, 'Put up that gun; stop that shooting.'" More shots rang out, and Glassford kept yelling at the police to cease shooting as more of them closed in on the scene. Glassford told a civilian who had drawn his own gun to put it back in his pocket, which he did.

A passing witness named Bruce Clark corroborated Glassford's account with his own independent testimony. Clark was driving down Pennsylvania Avenue at around 1:45 p.m. when the police directed him to turn down Fourth Street. He parked his car and walked toward Missouri Avenue between Third and Fourth. He saw a commotion in the street there and turned down an alley behind 332 Pennsylvania Avenue. Cops swarmed in and formed a double line as they headed farther along toward the rear of 346 Pennsylvania. A crowd of men were jeering, some shaking their fists, others hoisting bricks over their heads. They were all obvi-ously incensed at the way events had played out. A cordon of police kept the men from advancing up from the bottom of the steps, telling the vets "You cannot come in here."

"The hell we can't!" the vets yelled back.

"All at once," Clark testified, "I saw an officer on the stairs, about eight feet from the bottom, draw his pistol, take aim and fire toward the foot . . . of the stairs. Soon after this shot was fired I heard two or three more in quick succession."

By the time Glassford restored order over the area, one thirty-five-year-old vet named William Hushka, a Lithuanian immigrant who had sold his butcher shop to join the American army, lay dead on the steps with a bullet in his heart, and a second vet named Eric Carlson, thirty-eight, had suffered a bullet wound that claimed his life a few days later. Both men had survived action overseas during the Great War, and they were the only two vets out of the tens of thousands who marched in Washington who would collect their bonuses in full that summer—a benefit paid to their families. Death had its rewards, it appears. The shocking finale to what had been until then a mostly peaceful, carefully orchestrated demonstration in the political heartbeat of the nation pushed the Hoover administration over the edge. Humorist Will Rogers had praised the marchers as the "best behaved of any 15,000 hungry men assembled anywhere in the world." But the president of the United States viewed them differently. If Hoover needed an excuse to take decisive action to rid the city of demonstrating bonus marchers, the tragic developments of July 28 suited him perfectly.

At five feet eleven and 140 pounds, with a ramrod posture, Maj. Gen. Douglas MacArthur gave the appearance of being a taller man. His classmates at West Point invariably referred to him as a six-footer with a military bearing, a natural leader, sometimes aloof and imperious and other times warm and charming, depending on what the occasion called for. He measured himself against the high bar set by his father, Gen. Arthur MacArthur Jr., who distinguished himself as the military governor-general of the Philippines during the American occupation of the islands in 1900.

He and his son Douglas shared the distinction of being the first father and son to receive the Congressional Medal of Honor. Douglas MacArthur's mother Mary Pinkney Hardy MacArthur, known as "Pinky" among her friends in Washington, was the prototypical smother-mother, who took up residence at a hotel near West Point during the four years that Douglas attended the academy. From the beginning Pinky was determined to be the dominant female in his life, a woman who incessantly lobbied the political and military establishment throughout her son's career to promote him to the rank of general.

That said, Douglas MacArthur could not have advanced as quickly as he did without a deep well of talent bordering on genius. His victorious return to the Philippines during World War II reflected an almost preternatural gift on the battlefield against overwhelming odds, while his pacification of Japan epitomized his political skills as well as his military gifts. He was blessed with an eidetic memory and could repeat verbatim long passages from books he had read and speeches he had heard. His sartorial eccentricities matched his brilliance on the battlefield. While many of his colleagues laughed behind his back at his personal dress code, MacArthur's commanding officer Gen. John "Black Jack" Pershing looked the other way and tolerated his peculiarities because of his subordinate's prowess in combat. MacArthur removed the metal support from his hat and wore it squished down at a jaunty angle over his eyes; he would show up on the parade ground with a long raccoon overcoat and a four-foot-long scarf that Pinky had knitted for him; and his aides polished his knee-high riding boots to a point where they glistened in the dark. His unusual regalia was in violation of the military dress code, but MacArthur was able to get away with it because of his value to Pershing.

The one time MacArthur contended with Pershing was when they both set their sights on the same woman, Henrietta Louise Cromwell Brooks, a sexy and wealthy divorcee considered to be one of Washington's most beautiful and attractive women. Pershing got the better of the deal when Louise, as she preferred to be called, chose MacArthur over him. She became MacArthur's first wife and he her second husband of four. Louise blamed her "interfering mother-in-law" for the breakup of her marriage to MacArthur, but in reality she had become bored with life in the Philippines, where MacArthur was stationed, and tried to get him to quit the army and become a stockbroker instead. Louise was a party animal who loved to drink, dance, and stay out late, the opposite of her husband—and Pershing for that matter—who was married first and foremost to the army and practiced the spartan regimen it required.

MacArthur's chief biographer, William Manchester, aptly labeled him an "American Caesar" in his book of that title. Julius Caesar's battlefield skills allowed him to rise as far as he did in his relatively short life, and MacArthur stole a page from the Roman general's memoirs—literally—when he started referring to himself in the third person, as Julius Caesar had done two thousand years earlier. MacArthur had embraced the quirky habit of calling himself "The General," or simply "MacArthur," in his personal correspondence. His military aide, Maj. Dwight D. Eisenhower, was at first amused and later alarmed by his boss's flair for egotistical histrionics. "MacArthur has decided to go into active command in the field," MacArthur told Eisenhower when it was time to evict the vets. "There is incipient revolution in the air." It was as though MacArthur had set himself up on a pedestal that was above the human realm, a demigod in his own mind who was exempt from the rules that governed mere mortals. When asked at a social gathering if he had ever met MacArthur, Eisenhower replied, "Not only have I met him, ma'am; I studied dramatics under him for five years in Washington and four years in the Philippines."

Harold Ickes, who became FDR's secretary of the interior after the 1932 elections, said "MacArthur is the type of man who thinks that when he gets to heaven, God will step down from the great white throne and bow him into His vacated seat."

At age fifty-two MacArthur faced the greatest domestic challenge of his life. Given his opinion of the vets as a motley crew of Communist agitators, he was champing at the bit to take decisive action against them and send them scattering out of town. All he needed was the go-ahead from President Hoover, who had reached the end of his own tether. MacArthur had been in meetings throughout the morning with Maj. Gen. Blanton Winship and others who were in favor of the president declaring martial law, which would turn the matter over to the military under MacArthur's leadership. Eisenhower urged restraint, arguing that quelling a riot was beneath MacArthur's dignity. "The matter could easily become a riot," Eisenhower told his boss. "It is highly inappropriate for the Chief of Staff of the Army to be involved in anything" like this. But MacArthur was determined to carry out Hoover's mandate. "This was a very serious test of the strength of the federal government," he told Eisenhower. He was going to perform his duty, and Eisenhower as his aide was going with him. "They were a bad-looking mob animated by the spirit of revolution," MacArthur said to Ike.

Later that day, U.S. attorney general William D. Mitchell ordered the removal of the veterans, their wives, family members, and friends from all government property. MacArthur girded himself in full battle dress and boots, and he ordered Eisenhower to don his own uniform, which the future president did while cursing quietly to himself. When Glassford rode his motorcycle down to the Ellipse where the troops were gathering, he asked MacArthur what he intended to do. "We are going to break the back of the BEF," MacArthur replied. "Within a short time we will move down Pennsylvania Avenue, sweep through the billets there, and then clean out the other two big camps. The operation will be continuous. It will all be done tonight."

MacArthur intended to clear out the eviction site around the Capitol Building at Third and Pennsylvania Avenues, where the shootings had occurred. Then he wanted to herd the vets southwest and block their access to the White House, clean out the small Communist camp at Thirteenth and B, and finally complete his operation by crossing the bridge and attacking the main encampment in Anacostia.

Glassford asked MacArthur for a ten-minute head start to see if he could get some of the vets to move peacefully before any blood was spilled, and then he roared back along Pennsylvania Avenue to the dilapidated buildings to warn the vets that federal troops were on the way. He managed to clear some of them out of their ramshackle dwelling holes and ushered them across the street where they could observe what was about to take place without a direct confrontation with the troops. "Absolute order prevailed," Glassford said afterward. "Veterans in their billets on the other side of the avenue awaited with eager curiosity the arrival of the soldiers."

The troops were on their way in force. MacArthur ordered Brig. Gen. Perry L. Miles to assemble his forces at Fort Washington, on the Maryland side of the Potomac opposite Mount Vernon, and move them north to the Ellipse. MacArthur telephoned Maj. George S. Patton Jr. at nearby Fort Myer and told him to "saddle up and be prepared to move as soon as possible." At about 4:10 p.m. a battalion of infantry, a squadron of cavalry troops with drawn sabers, a machine-gun unit, and half a dozen tanks under Patton's command—520 soldiers, 35 officers, and numerous horses and trucks in all, with several times that number waiting in reserve if needed—gathered at the Ellipse. It was a frightening display of military power in the homeland, which MacArthur believed would convince the unarmed vets that resistance was hopeless.

If Eisenhower was the voice of reason urging restraint against the vets, George Patton was tailor-made to play MacArthur's alter ego in any kind of military conflict—Mark Antony to MacArthur's Julius Caesar. He was born for combat, and he did not much care who the enemy was. If the federal government identified its own veterans as enemies of the Republic, then so be it. His job was to obliterate them or die on the battlefield, although he later said—not credibly judging by his earlier comments about the attack—that he found MacArthur's assault on the vets "most distasteful." A firm believer in the paranormal, Patton actually believed that he had had at least six past lives, including one as a legionnaire fighting in Northern Gaul under the command of Julius Caesar.

General Miles gave the troops their orders. "Gentlemen, the so-called bonus marchers are occupying certain government properties in Washington and are successfully resisting efforts by the police to evacuate them. This command has been called upon by properly constituted authority to clear those properties. . . . You will use such force as necessary to accomplish your mission. Tear gas will be used. Women and children who may be found in the affected area will be accorded every consideration and kindness."

President Hoover, however, was concerned that an excessive use of military force would not play well in the press, and he got cold feet about giving MacArthur carte blanche to attack the vets and their families in their campsites. Hoover hoped to keep any violence to a minimum, and he informed Secretary of War Patrick Hurley that he wanted to limit the army's role to clearing the vets out of the streets and herding them to Anacostia and other camps where the authorities could surround and investigate them. After he received Hoover's directive Hurley sent two of his own emissaries to deliver the change in plans to MacArthur. "You will maintain contact with the rioters until they have crossed the Anacostia Bridge," MacArthur was informed. "Order them into the veterans' camps in Anacostia and hold all campers, rioters, and marchers until the names of all of them can be tabulated and their fingerprints taken. Those who have incited riot and death will be arrested and then delivered over to civil authorities for prosecution."

Gen. George Van Horn Moseley, one of the men who delivered Hurley's message to MacArthur, later wrote, "Mr. Hurley, the Secretary of War, directed me to inform General MacArthur that the President did not wish the troops to cross the bridge that night, to force the evacuation of the Anacostia Camp. I left my office, contacted General MacArthur, and as we walked away, alone, from the others, I delivered that message to him and discussed it with him. He was very much annoyed in having his plans interfered with in any way until they were executed completely. After assuring myself that he understood the message, I left him. . . . Still later, I was instructed to repeat the message and assure myself that General MacArthur received it before he crossed the Anacostia Bridge. I sent Colonel Clement B. Wright, then Secretary to the General Staff, to repeat the message to MacArthur, and explain the situation as I had it from the White House. Colonel Wright contacted General MacArthur immediately, and explained the situation to him fully. As I now recall, Colonel Wright reported to me that the troops had not crossed the Anacostia Bridge, but were advancing on the bridge."

MacArthur pondered his instructions in his haughty manner. But since he had not received anything in writing, he remained noncommittal about his own strategy for dealing with the bonus marchers. Shortly after 5:00 p.m. MacArthur began his assault on the billets along Pennsylvania Avenue. The vets responded with a barrage of bricks and taunts, telling the troops to get down off their horses and "fight like men. You're yellow, yellow!" they chanted. A sixteen-year-old boy named Fred Blacher happened to be standing on a street corner waiting for a trolley when he looked up Pennsylvania Avenue and took in the startling spectacle.

"By God, all of sudden I see these cavalrymen come up the avenue and then swinging down to the Mall. I thought it was a parade," he said. "I asked a gentleman standing there, I said, 'Do you know what's going on? What holiday is this?' He says, 'It's no parade, bud. The Army is coming in to wipe out all these bonus people down here.'"

After clearing out the camps along Pennsylvania Avenue, MacArthur ordered his troops to start moving from the Ellipse toward the Eleventh Street Bridge, which led to the encampment at Anacostia. Eisenhower had clearly overheard Wright's message, if not Moseley's, since he was all but glued to MacArthur's side throughout most of the encounter, so he was appalled when MacArthur drew closer to the bridge without making any visible effort to slow the advancing troops. Eisenhower later wrote that MacArthur told him "he was too busy and did not want either himself or his staff bothered by people coming down and pretending to bring orders."

MacArthur was determined to carry his own plans forward with or without approval from the president of the United States. "I told that dumb son-of-a-bitch," Eisenhower said in an interview, "that he had no business" defying the president's order and going across the bridge. But MacArthur would not be deterred.

And so the American Caesar took it upon himself to ignore a direct order from the president of the United States, conveyed to him in no uncertain terms by messengers from the country's overlords, and carry out his own plans to deal with the bonus march veterans. Just as Julius Caesar had crossed the Rubicon on his own authority two millennia in the past, MacArthur would replicate the Roman dictator's insubordination by crossing the Anacostia, come hell or high water, in defiance of the highest level of civilian authority. Tanks, troops on horseback, and heavily armed infantry rolled down the streets of the capital on MacArthur's orders. The Republic and the Constitution be damned!

The display of power was truly disconcerting to anyone who stood in the path of the juggernaut. Two hundred mounted cavalry with their sabers drawn and pennants flying rode down Pennsylvania Avenue toward the bridge. Half a dozen tanks and more than three hundred helmeted infantrymen, armed with rifles and fixed bayonets, followed them closely, led by Maj. George S. Patton. The cavalry swept the streets of everyone and everything in its path—pedestrians, curious onlookers, government workers, and veterans and their wives and children. "The last time I saw them bayonets I was going through Marne," one vet said. As they stampeded along, infantrymen with gas masks released hundreds of tear gas grenades into the crowd and set dozens of fires among the veterans' shelters along Pennsylvania Avenue. A seven-year-old boy named Naaman Seigle was in the F. P. May hardware store at Sixth and C Streets with his father when he heard the rumble out on the street. As they emerged from the store a wave of tear gas washed over them.

"I was coughing like hell. So was my father," the boy recalled later.

"Men and women were ridden down indiscriminately," reported the *Baltimore Sun*. "Nothing like this cavalry charge has ever been witnessed in Washington. The mad dash of these armed horsemen against twenty to thirty thousand people who were guilty of nothing more atrocious than standing on private property observing the scene was bitterly commented on by the spectators."

Nothing and no one could stop MacArthur. His determination to follow through with the attack was immutable. George Patton, his all-too-willing subordinate, reflected the general's mindset to the last detail. "Bricks flew, sabers rose and fell with a comforting smack, and the mob ran," Patton recalled gleefully. "We moved on after them, occasionally meeting serious resistance. Once six men in a truck threw a regular barrage of bricks, and several men and horses were hit. Two of us charged at a gallop, and had some nice work at close range with the occupants of the truck, most of them could not sit down for some days." Eisenhower was the odd man out, his objections to the operation so many motes of dust carried off by the indifferent wind. What had transpired so far was only a prelude to the main event. The "Battle of Washington"—as the press called it in its relentless search for a catchy headline—between the active army and the legion of disheartened vets, once active soldiers themselves who had seen combat overseas, was just beginning.

ELEVEN

Flames Light Up the Night

The troops, led by MacArthur in his staff car, crossed the bridge into Anacostia without missing a beat. "These guys got in there and they started waving their sabers, chasing these veterans out," recalled Fred Blacher, who had followed in the wake of the marauding soldiers. "And they started shooting tear gas. There was just so much noise and confusion, hollering, and there was smoke and haze. People couldn't breathe." The gas was laced with adamsite, a riot control agent that induced nausea, dizziness, and even death when used in sufficient doses. It contained arsenic and had been used in chemical warfare during the Great War. MacArthur was resplendent in his starched uniform, with a wall of medals glittering on the left side of his chest. His troops set fire to the smaller campsites on the outskirts of Anacostia, thrashing anyone who got in their way with the flat sides of their sabers. Some of the bolder vets urged their comrades to take up whatever arms they could lay their hands on and fire back at the soldiers, but their situation was hopeless in the face of such overwhelming firepower.

Crowds lined the streets, hurling insults and taunting MacArthur and his forces for turning on the older combatants as the troops pushed on. "Down toward Anacostia the troops went, in a bruising affair all the way, with persons in the streets swinging blows at the soldiers as they swept past, the cavalry wielding sabers and the infantry prodding with bayonets," the *New York Times* reported. Word reached the White House that MacArthur had overstepped his orders, and the frantic president was at a loss about how to rein in his chief of staff. He was caught in a bind. If he criticized MacArthur's actions publicly it would look as though he had lost control of the situation and the military was in charge; if the attack on Anacostia resulted in bloodshed and loss of life the president was the one who would be taken to task. It was already too late, however. As Eisenhower wrote later, "While no troops went more than two or three hundred yards over the bridge" at this point, "that whole encampment started to blaze . . . a pitiful scene." The troops set fire to everything as they moved ahead. The orange glow from the fires lit up the entire sky across the length and breadth of the city.

"Come on! Come on! The soldiers are going to kill us!" yelled the father of seven-year-old twins who had boxed for the vets during the exhibition. The boys were asleep in their tents when their father rousted them from their slumber. Another vet reported that he helped the women and children escape before the army could get to their campsites. Everywhere the vets and their families scampered for cover, some trying to start their jalopies, mothers screaming for their children, all of them racing as fast as they could toward the perimeter of the camp. The soldiers marched in relentlessly, setting fire to wads of rolled-up newspapers, which they used to torch everything in their path. A bystander named Elbridge Purdy remembered the "continuous flames. Veterans were packing and rushing about. Tear gas, which was being used to drive them out, made it difficult to see. . . . It was like riding through the steam of a teakettle. . . . There were pregnant women and some babies. . . . They were grabbing and packing their meager belongings."

In the midst of the assault a veteran's wife miscarried, and a twelve-year-old boy named Bernard Meyer fell victim to the tear gas attack and died later in the hospital. Dozens of vets suffered injuries and many more were arrested. The vets, despite their greater numbers, were no match for the heavily armed, combat-ready soldiers unleashed on them by MacArthur with willing support from Patton and his tanks. Bottles broke against the sides of the tanks, and bricks bounced off without leaving so much as a dent in their thick shells. Onlookers, for the most part, sided with the veterans and hurled a barrage of insults at the young army troops, with no effect. They, too, stood in harm's way if they ventured too close to the action, while many ran off as clouds of tear gas fumes drifted indiscriminately in the warm summer air.

Once he was convinced that his attack was achieving the results he envisioned, MacArthur took a brief break to feed his men. He then ordered them back into action to finish the job and mop up the ungodly mess that lay strewn across the landscape like a vision from the pits of hell. Smoke from the fires and gas fumes polluted the air, and shacks and makeshift shanties erected by the vets lay in ruins as far as the eye could see. Cries from the children and ceaseless weeping by the mothers added grimly to the carnage. MacArthur was jubilant as the assault neared a conclusion with the results he had hoped to achieve. Many of the soldiers, however, were less than proud of their actions as the onlookers taunted them with insults. The *Washington Tribune*, Washington's only African American newspaper at the time, reported, "Many of the soldiers looked scared and most of these mere boys hung their heads as if in shame."

By 10 p.m. the attack was essentially over. MacArthur was euphoric with the smell of his victory wafting in the air along with the tear gas fumes, and he left the operation in the hands of Brigadier General Miles, with instructions to sweep through the camp and clear out any remaining stragglers. MacArthur then hopped in his staff car and offered Eisenhower a lift back to Pennsylvania Avenue, where he planned to meet with Secretary Hurley and President Hoover. Ike warned his boss not to talk to the press that night, since this was a situation best left to the politicians. But Ike may as well have urged a duck not to swim. MacArthur, already preening as his aide rode beside him, appeared oblivious to the notion that Hoover might be furious with him for brazenly disobeying orders from his commander in chief and creating the kind of mayhem in the camps that Hoover had hoped to avoid.

The meeting among the three men lasted about a half hour. If MacArthur expected the president to congratulate him for accomplishing his mission in such short order, he was sorely disappointed with the reception he received. Hoover roundly "upbraided" MacArthur for his insubordination. Hoover later told Assistant Secretary of War F. Trubee Davison that he "bawled MacArthur out" for his act of defiance, knowing at the same time that the president would take "the rap right down the line, when MacArthur was the guy who should have taken the rap." Hoover did not need a crystal ball to warn him about the impending critical coverage of the day's events in the nation's newspapers, while MacArthur seemed to believe that the media and the public would hail him as the conquering hero who had saved the western world from a Communist revolution. In fact that was precisely MacArthur's message when he stepped before the cameras and the microphones at eleven o'clock on the night of July 28.

"The mob was animated by the essence of revolution," MacArthur told the boisterous reporters as he faced them in his starched battle regalia. They were "about to take over in some arbitrary way either direct control of the government or else to control it by indirect methods." They were "insurrectionists. If there was one man in ten in that group today who is a veteran, it would surprise me." MacArthur was enough of a politician himself, however, to understand that he needed to take some pressure off the president, who would suffer most for allowing his chief of staff to ransack the camps and terrorize the vets.

"Had the president not used force he would have been derelict indeed in his judgment regarding the safety of the country because this country is the focal point of the world today," MacArthur added, adroitly shifting blame for the rampage to Hoover, in effect damning him with faint praise. "Had he not acted with force and vigor, which he did, it would have been a bad day for the country tomorrow." Hoover, furious with MacArthur though he was, had little choice but to accept the fait accompli that his chief of staff had created. He was ensnared in a trap with no way to escape other than to play along with MacArthur's version of the day's events.

"I complied with your request for aid from the Army to the police," Hoover wrote in a letter he sent to his commissioners the next day. "It is a matter of satisfaction that, after the arrival of this assistance, the mobs which were defying the municipal government were dissolved without the firing of a shot or the loss of a life." He also repeated the fiction that "a large part" of the demonstrators were not veterans but rather subversives and revolutionaries. Hoover overlooked the fact that shots were indeed fired, and the official tally for the carnage was 3 people killed, 54 injured, and 135 arrested.

At four o'clock in the morning it started to rain, adding to the vets' misery as they roamed through the streets in shock with no clear destination in mind. Troops guarded the bridges leading into Virginia and refused to allow the vets and their families to pass, and state troopers blocked the roads into Maryland, forcing the bonus marchers to wander aimlessly with no way out of the city and no way to turn back. The surrounding states did not want them any more than the federal government did. Finally Mayor Eddie McCloskey of Johnstown, Pennsylvania, a burly former prize fighter and a vet himself, sent word that he would arrange for the vets to seek refuge in his town.

"On to Johnstown!" the vets cried out, and the Maryland state troopers allowed them to pass under the condition that they keep moving as fast as possible toward the Pennsylvania border. McCloskey was shocked, however, when the few hundred vets he expected to accommodate turned into a steady stream of bonus marchers, women, and children numbering close to nine thousand strong. One little boy was suffering from a stab wound in his leg, inflicted by a soldier who bayoneted him when he tried to rush back to his burning shack to rescue his pet rabbit. There was little that McCloskey could provide for all of them except a park to sleep in on the outskirts of town, exposed to the heat and rain, no sanitary facilities, and not enough food to go around. The vets quickly labeled the park Camp McCloskey. When McCloskey ran into resistance from his own constituents about the burden he was imposing on the town's resources, he gruffly replied, "To hell with everybody! Let them come!"

The local newspaper reflected the less-than-sympathetic views of the townspeople, calling the vets and their families "thieves, plug-uglies, and degenerates" who threatened the locals with their presence. The governor of the state, Gifford Pinchot, a Teddy Roosevelt Bull Moose Progressive, sent in the National Guard to ward off any disturbances, but the vets remained peaceful and law-abiding, thankful for a place to rest as they contemplated their next move.

While the mayor's intentions were sound, he was at a loss when it came to dealing effectively with the chaotic conditions he had created, and he appealed to President Hoover to send him some assistance. Water and toilet facilities were in short supply, food supplies were skimpy at best, and housing was nonexistent. Yet most of the vets were reluctant to leave since they had precious few alternatives. Hoover arranged for the Red Cross to send food to the beleaguered town, and then for the Baltimore and Ohio Railroad to provide free transportation from Pennsylvania to Chicago and St. Louis. From there the vets were on their own to travel farther west if they had a place to stay when they got there, or anywhere else where they could find shelter and a way to sustain themselves. It was a tragic ending to a march that had devolved into a domestic diaspora. The vets and their families were, in effect, refugees from their own government.

The following morning, July 29, 1932, dawned hot and steamy in a city that reeked of the wet, charred remains of burned-out campsites, smoldering ashes, and the lingering stench of battle that hovered in the air like a malignant cloud. As the sun broke through the morning mist Waters appeared out of nowhere on the steps of the Capitol, sporting his freshly laundered khaki uniform. He had been nowhere to be found the night before when MacArthur's troops had invaded the camps, so it is likely that he had spent the night in the comfort of the apartment provided by Evalyn Walsh McLean. As the vets trundled their way to the Pennsylvania border Waters announced to the press that he was starting a new movement, which would have its headquarters in Washington, to "clean out the high places of government." His new organization would represent "the inarticulate masses of the country." The *New York Times* ridiculed his performance, reporting that he presented himself in "the role of an American Hitler."

Waters's main problem was that he was positioning himself as the leader of a movement without any followers. The remnants of his army were fleeing northward and westward, seeking a new home in any place that would welcome them. Waters's fifteen minutes of fame had run its course. In the aftermath of the Battle of Washington the very vets whom he had abandoned the day before now abandoned Waters. By August 3 Waters realized that his situation was hopeless. He considered crisscrossing the country on a lecture tour, only to find that the crowds he once attracted had vanished. When he finally returned to Oregon with forty-three members of his original group, a Portland newspaper described them as "dusty, tired, looking somewhat the worse for wear." Waters drifted back into the obscurity he came from. He later renounced his Fascistic views and joined the navy, which sent him overseas during World War II. He died in Washington State in 1959, at age sixty-one, unheralded and forgotten, a footnote in the dustbin of history.

In his home in Hyde Park, New York, Democratic presidential nominee Franklin Delano Roosevelt read an account of the events of July 28 in the *New York Times*. "There's no need to campaign against Hoover now," he said to his aide Rex Tugwell. "The election's all but over. Why didn't Hoover offer the men coffee and sandwiches instead of turning Doug MacArthur loose? They're probably camping on the roads leading out of Washington. They must be in terrible shape." Roosevelt said that MacArthur was "the most dangerous person" in the country. "Did you see the way he strutted in front of the cameras afterward?" Roosevelt regarded MacArthur as "a potential Mussolini. We must tame these fellows and make them useful to us," he said. "Did you ever see anyone more self-satisfied?"

The army spent the early hours of the day cleaning up the mess and clearing out the stragglers who were unable to leave the city the night before. The soldiers came across a group of mothers and their children huddling in a government-owned house, about ninety in all, who had been too shocked and weary to leave without assistance. Charity workers reported that "babies with uncovered heads, no shade, no care or food, were held in the laps of their shocked, suffering mothers." The soldiers hustled them onto trucks and drove them to the edge of the district, where they unloaded them along with a couple of thousand homeless vets and left them to fend for themselves.

Glassford, whose authority in the district had been superseded by the army, was appalled by what had transpired. "I am chief of police," he fumed, "and I intend to enforce the laws here to the best of my ability. By enforcement, however, I do not mean persecution." Glassford said he was speaking as a political nonpartisan, someone who is "neither a Democrat, a Republican, a Socialist, nor a Communist." Glassford, too, had come to the end of the line as far as his tenure in Washington was concerned. He resigned on a high note in October 1932, before the elections, after publishing a series of newspaper articles criticizing Hoover for the way he treated the vets.

His popularity had never been stronger. For ten weeks he had treated the vets with tolerance, respect, and restraint. He had handled many tense situations with grace and common sense, and on several occasions he had dipped into his own pocket to buy food for the legions of hungry and shabby men and their families. He believed that demonstrators were reasonable human beings deserving of a dialogue with the authorities. Glassford mingled with them and sympathized with their plans, hopes, and aspirations. He established himself as an arbiter, an umpire, and a bridge between the vets and the power elite in Washington. On September 17 fifty-five of the capital's most seasoned reporters held a dinner in his honor at the National Press Club and acclaimed him for his honesty, his forbearance, and the relentless pursuit of the truth in his account of what led up to the mayhem of July 28.

Glassford was high on the list for other assignments in the Roosevelt administration. The government considered him for a post as federal relief administrator, chief of the Civilian Conservation Corps, and in New York City Mayor Fiorello La Guardia tried to entice him to take a job as police commissioner; he was also offered the job as commissioner of baseball—none of which came to pass. In 1934 the federal government appointed him federal conciliator for labor disputes in the Imperial Valley of Southern California, a hotbed of union agitation at the time. He served there for a few months, settled several conflicts, and then resigned when he became entangled in bureaucratic infighting. In 1936 Glassford served as police chief of Phoenix, Arizona, where he pushed for legalization of prostitution. He launched an unsuccessful run for a congressional seat as a maverick Democrat. Glassford rejoined the army during World War II and was appointed chief of the Provost Marshal's Office in the Internal Security Division. After the war he took up painting again, supported a local theatrical group in Laguna Beach, California, and was elected president of the town's chamber of commerce. He died there in 1959 at age seventy-six, leaving an estate worth more than $100,000, a considerable legacy at the time.

The most dramatic encounter of all occurred on July 29, the day after the violent evictions. Maj. George Patton was sitting on a bale of hay drinking coffee with a few other officers when a sergeant approached with a small man in tow. The civilian was Joe Angelo, who had been the subject of a couple of articles about his role in saving Patton's life during the Great War. The *New York Times* had headlined its story, "A Cavalry Major Evicts Veteran Who Saved His Life in Battle." Now Angelo had tried to track down Patton the day after the evictions, and when Patton saw the sergeant escorting him in his direction, the tank commander flew into a rage.

"Sergeant, I do not know this man! Take him away!" Patton thundered. "And under no circumstances permit him to return!"

129

While the sergeant was dragging Angelo back where he had found him Patton explained to his fellow officers, "That man was my orderly during the war. When I was wounded, he dragged me from a shell hole under fire. I got him a decoration for it. Since the war, my mother and I have more than supported him. We have given him money. We have set him up in business several times. Can you imagine the headlines if the papers got wind of our meeting here this morning? Of course, we'll take care of him anyway."

TWELVE

Hoover Pays the Price for His Incompetence

Hoover took "the rap" for MacArthur's assault on the vets, as the president knew he would, but he only compounded his problems with his inept handling of public relations in the wake of the battle. He kept insisting that the great majority of veterans were Communist revolutionaries and radicals even when all evidence proved they were not. A grand jury investigation that lasted until August 15 concluded that most of the men arrested were overseas veterans, some holding the Distinguished Service Cross, and that only a handful of them were affiliated with Communist organizations. Yet Hoover went along with his attorney general, William D. Mitchell, who labeled the vets "the largest aggregation of criminals that had ever assembled in the city at one time." Bureau of Investigation (forerunner to the FBI, founded in 1935) chief J. Edgar Hoover maintained that "a very much larger proportion of the Bonus Army than was realized at the time consisted of ex-convicts, persons with criminal records, radicals, and non-servicemen."

The public did not buy it. Instead of putting the matter to rest while he focused instead on the key issues of the campaign—the parlous state of the nation's economy foremost among them—President Hoover kept the treatment of the vets front and center with his stubborn insistence on hammering away on the administration's side of the eviction story. While Roosevelt talked about the main problems facing the nation, particularly what to do about the high rate of unemployment, Hoover opened himself up to media scorn with his faulty profile of the bonus marchers. A leading correspondent of the day—the flamboyant, one-eyed Floyd Gibbons—conducted his own research and concluded, "The proportion of convicts out of forty thousand men that passed through the camps is something like under three percent." He compared that figure with the Harding administration, in which Hoover had been secretary of commerce, which harbored upwards of ten percent with criminal records. "And it wasn't for parking in front of a fire plug either," wrote Gibbons.

Gibbons was not alone in his castigation of Hoover. Hearst reporter Elsie Robinson, normally friendly to Hoover and the Republicans, wrote, "Smugly satisfied, one Government official after another has risen to justify that shameful day. And this week the whole Administration united in an attack on the honor of American ex-soldiers which is unparalleled in heartlessness and arrogance and deliberate misinformation." George R. Brown, a war correspondent with the *Washington Herald*, maintained that he had "personally come in contact with not less than two hundred of the men of the Bonus Army, both before and after the eviction. In nearly all cases, in the course of conversation about the war service of the men," they produced their discharge papers without hesitation.

The great American satirist H. L. Mencken offered his own broadside against Hoover in his inimitable style: "Hoover had to defame the poor idiots he had gassed, and presently there was a sharp reaction. . . . The calm and implacable statesman, bent only on preserving public order, revealed himself overnight as a peevish and unfair partisan, fevered by transparently discreditable fears."

Privately Hoover remained furious with MacArthur for exposing his administration to the crosshairs of the media and the wrath of the public. But by refusing to recall MacArthur—as Harry Truman did nineteen years later for MacArthur's insubordination in Korea—and ask for his resignation, Hoover's only other option was to double down on the propaganda course he had set for himself. Convincing no one, Hoover said it was "obvious that . . . subversive influences obtained control of the men . . . secured repudiation of their elected leaders and inaugurated and organized this attack. . . . Government cannot be coerced by mob rule. . . . There can be no safe harbor in the United States of America for violence." The hole that Hoover had dug for himself grew deeper and deeper with each new utterance.

The voters resoundingly booed and jeered the president at one campaign stop after another. A cluster of posters reading "DOWN WITH HOOVER!" "HOOVER—BALONEY AND APPLESAUCE" visibly rattled Hoover as he staggered farther down the road toward defeat. Some of his advisers urged him to abandon the subject of the bonus army and focus instead on the economic issues about which people cared. "Why don't they make him quit?" one prominent midwestern Republican asked in a state of panic. Hoover's staunchest supporters grew increasingly alarmed as the campaign wore on and the incumbent president appeared to be presiding over his own funeral, which put all Republican candidates at greater risk of losing in November. Even the American Legion, one of the pillars of Republican Party support, was in open revolt against Hoover and refused to print the administration's version of the evictions in its monthly journal.

Predictably Hoover claimed he was "too busy" to meet with a group of prominent American writers, led by Sherwood Anderson, who traveled to Washington to protest the president's harsh criticism of the veterans. Arthur Schlesinger Jr. pointed out that Hoover had plenty of time to host wrestling champions, sorority girls, and beauty contest winners in the White House but not a few spare moments to greet some of the country's leading literary figures. Instead Hoover directed one of his secretaries to lecture the writers about their duty to "spread the truth" about the "radicals and Communists" who started the riots and attacked the police in the nation's capital.

Ironically, Hoover's and Roosevelt's positions on the bonus were not far apart; Roosevelt had gone on record saying he was opposed to paying the bonus now with the economy in turmoil. But Roosevelt would have shown greater compassion in dealing with the vets, and he wisely avoided talking about the subject during the final stretch of the campaign. Not all Democrats were reticent about discussing it, however. Rep. Loring M. Black, running for reelection in New York, called the evictions "the greatest crime in history." Kentucky's Sen. Kenneth D. McKellar called Hoover's use of troops "the highest species of tyranny." Other candidates were equally critical of Hoover's obtuse way of handling the marchers and blamed him for ineptly turning an orderly demonstration into a hideous bloodbath through the blunt force of the military.

November 8, 1932, was cool and dry throughout much of the country as American voters turned out to elect their president and congressional leaders against the backdrop of a grinding economic depression that saw unemployment rise to 24.1 percent. Roosevelt appeared genial and exuded confidence, while Hoover remained unremittingly grim and dour into the final hours of the campaign. The results spoke volumes about the mood of the public, as Roosevelt received close to twenty-three million popular votes, 57.3 percent of the votes cast, to Hoover's nearly sixteen million or 39.6 percent of the total. A little more than 3 percent went to an array of independent party candidates. The electoral vote was 472 to 59, a crushing landslide victory for the challenger. Hoover captured only a handful of New England states plus Pennsylvania and Delaware. Americans also elected substantial Democratic majorities to both houses of Congress in a complete repudiation of Hoover and the Republican Party.

Before Roosevelt was sworn in as the thirty-second president of the United States, an attempt on his life marred his impending tenure in office. The president-elect stepped off the yacht owned by Vincent Astor after it docked in Miami. Not more than twenty-five feet from him an Italian immigrant named Giuseppe Zangara climbed up on a chair to get a clear view of Roosevelt. Zangara was only five-foot-one, and his diminutive stature limited his line of sight. When Roosevelt finished speaking at 9:35 p.m. from the back seat of his light-blue Buick, Zangara fired five rounds from his .32-caliber pistol. A woman in the crowd named Lillian Cross said she pushed the would-be assassin's arm, deflecting his aim, and all five rounds missed Roosevelt and struck other members of his party. Among them was Chicago mayor Anton Cermak, who died two weeks later from the gunshot wound to his stomach.

By the time Roosevelt took the oath of office on March 4, 1933, the entire economy had ground to a halt. The new president, in the beginning at least, sounded like more of a fiscal conservative than his Republican predecessor had. He criticized Hoover for being a "spendthrift" and promised greater economy in government and a balanced budget. "Too often in recent history," FDR had stated innumerable times through the course of his campaign, "liberal governments have been wrecked on rocks of loose fiscal policy." His entire team, including welfare state advocates Rex Tugwell and Harry Hopkins, opposed the immediate payment of the bonus to the vets as an unprincipled raid on the U.S. Treasury. FDR drafted the Economy Act, calling for "sacrifice" and cuts across the board for all government employees and those on public pensions. Passed by the Congress and signed into law by the new president, the legislation cut the salaries of federal workers and reduced benefit payments to veterans in an effort to reduce the federal deficit. While the vets and other affected groups complained bitterly about the president's betrayal, various senators and representatives rose to his defense.

"President Roosevelt is probably the best friend of the ex-service men ever in the White House," said Sen. Harry Ashurst of Arizona. "He has suffered and knows how to sympathize with suffering. Please assure veterans and all others to trust him."

"I do not want any veteran to feel that he and his comrades are being singled out to make sacrifices," Roosevelt explained. On the contrary, he said. He was asking no more from the vets than he was from others whose federal benefits would be trimmed. Suddenly the question of the bonus was no longer a Republican issue; it fell full-square on Roosevelt's shoulders.

Now it was the Republicans' turn to castigate the president for his treatment of the vets. Rep. Hamilton Fish of New York stole a page from William Jennings Bryan's notebook when he accused Roosevelt of crucifying the vets "on a cross of deflation and economy." Democrat Wright Patman responded by blaming the Republicans for failing to adequately tax the incomes and assets of the wealthiest Americans to help pay for the bonus. "If the tax laws are not going to be enforced against the Mellons, Morgans and Mitchells," Patman thundered, "the Federal penitentiary doors at Atlanta, Georgia, should be opened and Al Capone released."

In the end Roosevelt had little choice but to scale back the extent of the cuts called for in his legislation, although he remained opposed to the immediate payment of the bonus. He sought to soften his position by suggesting that all needy Americans, including the vets, could be better served by putting them to work "in reforestation projects" or "on subsistence farms if they had any farming experience." The president also believed that Hoover could have done a lot more to lessen the number of vets that descended on Washington if he had shown more sympathy for their plight and not portrayed them all as Communist rabble-rousers.

The vets had left Washington, but many of them did not stray too far since their homes were in foreclosure and, in any event, they had no jobs to return to. They gravitated instead to shanty-towns in various cities, hammering together makeshift homes from shipping crates, sheets of aluminum, and anything else they could lay their hands on. Miniature villages of displaced vets popped up in Pittsburgh, Philadelphia, Chicago, Detroit, and several towns along the Hudson River where they gathered to shiver through the winter. From time to time rumors circulated that the vets were planning another march on Washington, but most of them turned out to be false alarms, feeble threats to resurrect a movement that had lost its spark. The Communists and a host of right wing radical groups, including the Khaki Shirts and the Silver Shirt Legion, founded by William Dudley Pelley of Massachusetts, failed to generate much interest. The Khaki Shirts were essentially leaderless, with Waters hibernating in Florida after advising against another march on Washington. A fellow from California named Art J. Smith filled the power vacuum created by Waters, and Smith left no doubt about his political leanings when he renamed the BEF the U.S. Fascists.

Harold B. Foulkrod, who had served as the chief lobbyist for the BEF and criticized Waters for his "ignorant and inefficient" leadership, stepped forward with a more credible challenge to the political status quo. He said he could muster as many as fifty thousand vets for a second march on Washington if the new administration failed to agree to his list of demands. He called for the immediate payment of the bonus to as many as two million unemployed vets; preferential treatment for the vets in federal, state, and local jobs that opened up; the dismissal of MacArthur as the president's chief of staff; and the replacement of all married women working for the government with out-of-work veterans. J. Edgar Hoover dug a bit deeper into Foulkrod's background in an effort to discredit him and reported that Foulkrod had a criminal record that included using five different aliases for forgery, passing bad checks, and burglary.

Not to be outdone, the Communists threatened to invade Washington with "many thousands" of disgruntled vets demanding their bonuses. J. Edgar Hoover fed the flames of fear by claiming that a veritable army of radicals, amounting to 473,000 "trained men ready to take action," were on their way to the nation's capital with 116 airplanes and 123 machine guns. A search of the roads leading from the hinterlands and major cities heading into Washington failed to detect an invasion force of any size, let alone the staggering numbers asserted by Hoover. In addition to the Communists a mind-numbing array of other splinter groups also rose up on the left and right with their own agendas. There were the Purple Shirts, the Mystic Multitudes, and representatives of the Oppressed People of the Nation, all maintaining that they could raise thousands of vets under their own banners for a second march on the city.

Roosevelt's primary challenge regarding the vets was to separate the facts from the hyperbole and hysteria emanating from Hoover's reports and the claims of other holdovers from the previous administration. Certainly a second attempt to force the government's hand on the bonus question was more than likely, but not nearly on the scale the alarmists were predicting. With little fanfare FDR had a tent city erected at Fort Hunt in Fairfax County, Virginia, a few miles south of the district, to accommodate up to ten thousand marchers. At the same time he quietly moved an infantry platoon to the site to head off any potential violence. There was considerable tough talk from Foulkrod and the Communists about how they intended to storm the White House "no matter how many police are in front." The *New York Times*, however, described the three thousand vets who did show up as "a bedraggled group of unemployed ex-servicemen, attracted here by the promise of something to eat, a place to sleep," and an opportunity to air their grievances.

Indeed, Roosevelt made sure the vets were treated well once they presented their discharge papers at a check-in center on Pennsylvania Avenue near Sixth Street. Army buses and trucks transported the men to Fort Hunt, where they found neat rows of tents laid out along impromptu "streets," electric lights, sinks with running water, showers and latrines, and field kitchens that were stocked with hearty, adequate food. The men breakfasted on oranges, eggs, potatoes, bread, butter, and coffee. For lunch they were served baked ham, potatoes, peas, rice pudding, bread and butter, and coffee. Dinner consisted of bologna, potato salad, apple butter, bread, and coffee. FDR invited the vets to enroll in his newly created Civilian Conservation Corps, where they would work on various projects in return for food and lodging, a clothing allowance, and a dollar a day for their labor. The Communist contingent denounced these programs as "forced labor camps," an attempt by the government to coopt the downtrodden classes with handouts instead of genuine economic reforms. But the vast majority of vets were only too happy to sign up; more than 2,600 joined the ccc while another 400 took advantage of free transportation back where they came from.

Infighting among the various splinter groups threatened the prevailing peace at Fort Hunt. The new administration had to deal with disturbances on both ends of the political spectrum, with Communists and Fascists fighting each other for dominance over the vets. When Emanuel Levin climbed up on a chair to address the men, shouts of "Kill the Red!" "Lynch Him!" and "Down with Levin!" drowned him out as various right-wing factions attempted to throttle him. The Metropolitan Police, now under a different command with Glassford gone, got to Levin first and hauled him off to safety. FDR was determined not to repeat the mistakes of his predecessor. He knew that his wife Eleanor was one of his best assets in a situation such as this, since she exuded a palpable empathy that was natural to her. On May 15, 1933, President Roosevelt announced that the First Lady would visit Fort Hunt the following day, which she did in the company of his chief secretary, Louis Howe.

"What are we going to do here?" she asked Howe.

"You are going in there and talk to those men," he answered. "Get their gripes, if any, make a tour of the camp and tell them that Franklin sent you out to see about them."

Eleanor was a big hit with the vets, leading them in songs and offering sensible observations on the horrors of war. "I want never to see another war," she told the vets. "I will always be grateful to those who served their country. I hope we will never have to ask such service again, and I hope that you will carry on in peace times as you did in the war days, for that is the duty of every patriotic American." The vets did not receive what they came for, namely the bonus they desperately needed, but the First Lady's genuine compassion for their plight clearly won them over. One vet commented as Eleanor got ready to leave, "Hoover sent the Army. Roosevelt sent his wife."

Thanks in large part to his wife's efforts, Roosevelt had succeeded in defusing a tense situation that could easily have gotten ugly with the political extremes in perpetual conflict. Not everyone was taken in by his good-will initiative, however. A Farmer-Labor congressman from Minnesota, Francis H. Shoemaker, viewed FDR's soft approach in a different light. "You just got what you voted for," he told the vets. "They tell you to come to Washington as often as you please, but don't come inside the city. You fought for democracy, but you got influenza, prohibition, and Hoover. Now you have a new deal, a raw deal I call it."

The second bonus march fizzled out as quickly as it began, with most of the demonstrating vets finding work in the CCC and others taking advantage of free transportation home by the time Congress adjourned for the summer. But Roosevelt had not seen the last of the vets. They would return a third time, although in smaller numbers than previously, with their list of demands, including the payment of the bonus that FDR was as equally opposed to paying as Hoover had been before him.

THIRTEEN

The Vets March Once Again

The struggle on the extremes spilled out into the streets in various cities. In Philadelphia one of the Fascists was killed and their leader, Art Smith, promised to retaliate against the Communists with a well-armed army of millions, as he put it. Rumors circulated that Smith planned to raid the National Guard armory with his followers on Columbus Day and take over Philadelphia, a fanciful notion to be sure. The police took no chances, however. They raided the Khaki Shirts' headquarters beforehand and confiscated a cache of weapons. Smith managed to abscond with about $25,000 of the organization's funds, and his erstwhile followers reinvented themselves, joining up with other right-wing groups to form the Christian Front, an avowedly anti-Semitic and pro-Nazi organization.

The Fascists and Communists were not the only ones causing grief for the new administration. Maj. Gen. Smedley Darlington Butler, a supporter of the BEF in its earliest incarnation, claimed that powerful business leaders had approached him with the possibility of staging a coup d'état against the government at the head of a five-hundred-thousand-man army of veterans. Wealthy Wall Street financiers and other business leaders, including the du Ponts and some conservative Democrats opposed to Roosevelt-, had founded the American Liberty League, and they were anxious to get rid of the president before he made much headway in implementing his plans for revamping the nation's economy.

But Butler was first and foremost a patriotic American who opposed any attempt to overthrow the government. He was a major general in the marine corps, the highest rank authorized at that time, and he would go on to become the most decorated marine in U.S. history. During his thirty-four-year career as a marine he participated in military actions in the Philippines, in China, in France during the Great War, and in the so-called Banana Wars in Central America and the Caribbean. He was openly critical of war and its consequences in general, and he was adamantly against the aptly named "Business Plot," calling for a takeover of the federal government. He presented his case to a congressional committee, detailing the plan to stage a military coup and install him as dictator.

At first the business interests in question ridiculed him and denied the existence of such a plot. The media, too, poked fun at some of Butler's seemingly far-fetched allegations. But a report from a special House of Representatives committee confirmed that much of Butler's testimony was spot on, and it behooved the government to be on guard against any attempt to seize the reins of power by force. Butler's testimony was vindicated, and he became an outspoken critic of international power struggles. A book he wrote in 1935, *War Is a Racket*, criticized the workings of the United States in its foreign actions and wars, including those he participated in, for serving the imperialistic designs of American corporations. After he retired from service Butler became a popular antiwar activist, speaking at meetings organized by veterans, pacifists, and various church groups that harbored a healthy skepticism about the motivation driving international power struggles.

The vets, plot or no plot to overthrow the government, had not given up in their own battle to collect their bonuses. In the spring of 1934 word began to circulate that a large contingent of vets was planning another march on Washington to demonstrate in favor of a new bonus bill. The Communists were especially vocal in this latest effort, "urging a militant action on the part of the veterans for a bonus march." Wright Patman had introduced a new bonus bill at the beginning of the year, but once again it got stalled in committee since there were not enough votes to override Roosevelt's threatened veto. In a letter he wrote to House Speaker Henry T. Rainey, the president promised to veto any bonus legislation—"and I don't care who you tell this to," FDR wrote.

"The government has a responsibility for and toward those who suffered injury or contracted disease while serving in its defense," FDR told the American Legion. "You and I are well aware of the simple fact that as every day passes, the people of this country are less and less willing to tolerate benefits for any one group of citizens which must be paid for by others." Just because someone wore a uniform and served in the defense of his country, however, does not mean that he should be "placed in a special class of beneficiaries over and above all other citizens."

The Congress was not inclined to lie down and play dead. Congressional leaders urged the president to "make public your objections in fairness to approximately three and one half million veterans who believe they have been made victims of discrimination." The House voted Patman's latest bill out of committee on in May 1934 and passed it with a vote of 322 to 98 after a contentious debate, knowing that it would expire in the Senate, which was unlikely to pick a fight with the president over the issue. The Senate responded by voting 54 to 40 in favor, not enough of a margin to overturn Roosevelt's threatened veto. The bonus bill was dead until the next session of Congress took it up. The congressional impasse stirred up the more militant veterans' groups, particularly those in the CCC camps where the major topic of conversation was the immediate payment of the bonus. Wright Patman joined the chorus of those urging the vets not to descend on Washington again, arguing that a march of any kind would be "very detrimental" not only to them but also to the "rights of veterans who do not participate and dependents of those who are dead."

The more radical elements, especially the small but vocal Communist contingent, ignored Patman's advice and proceeded with their plans to prod the political leaders to act in favor of the vets. Only 127 of the 1,500 vets who decided to demonstrate belonged to a Communist-front organization called the Workers' Ex-Serviceman's League (WESL), but they were by far the loudest and most visible. All along they had urged the vets not to join the CCC, claiming that the camps "are the forerunner of Fascism." They included Fort Hunt as a prime example of a Fascist enclave.

The Fascists did not remain silent in the face of the criticism from the left; the latest leader of the Khaki Shirts, R. B. Ellison, called for picketing in favor of the bonus in downtown Washington.

Roosevelt again arranged to house them all at Fort Hunt, where most of the Red leaders smoldered under perceived Fascist domination. They confined their activities to making speeches against "capitalist imperialism" and in favor of a Soviet-style revolution. Since the Fascists were advocating direct political action, the Communists opposed that tactic. "When anyone advocates direct action, look out!" warned Peter Cacchione, an elected New York City councilman with Communist leanings. "Remember, government agents are in our midst. Do nothing that would cause us to lose the respect of those millions back home." Emanuel Levin also adopted a more moderate tone, insisting, "We don't want to provoke a situation. No demonstration just for the sake of a demonstration." Levin remained a devoted Communist until his death in 1959, spending the rest of his life as circulation manager for the *Daily Worker*.

The media largely ignored the latest incarnation of a bonus march on Washington, effectively ensuring that it would suffer a quick death. The encampment at Fort Hunt lasted from May 12 to May 27, 1934, at which time FDR and his advisers hustled the vets off to various camps of the Federal Emergency Relief Administration (FERA)—later renamed the Works Progress Administration (WPA)—around the country. The administration relocated the vets to camps in South Carolina and Florida, where they would undergo a period of "conditioning." At first the government tried to remove them as far away as Fort Jefferson, a big rock in the Dry Tortugas south of the Keys. But that quixotic proposal proved unfeasible, so on October 18, 1934, the government changed the vets' destination to camps in Florida's Upper Keys, where they would be assigned to a road project linking the Upper Keys to Key West.

Before that happy day rolled around, however, Royal Robertson, complete with his neck brace, showed up in June for an encore performance at the head of a new California group he named the Needy Veterans Bonus Association, demanding an immediate bonus for all veterans who failed to earn enough to pay their income taxes. Government officials were shocked to learn that Robertson had managed to arrive in town with a thousand followers unheralded by the press.

"How the group slipped into Washington without attracting attention was something of a mystery," the *New York Times* reported.

Robertson's men had set up a camp in a vacant lot on Pennsylvania Avenue, not far from the White House. They gathered before officials were aware that the veterans had returned, according to a *Wall Street Journal* report. Robertson was less of a threat this time, however. He urged his men to take advantage of the opportunity to find food and shelter at the FERA camps instead of staking out a claim on vacant ground, where their efforts were likely to be unsuccessful. The government shuffled him and his thousand or so followers to the widely scattered FERA locations it was planning. Robertson, like Waters, faded into obscurity afterward. According to Patman FDR eventually relocated as many as eighteen thousand vets who descended on Washington to FERA camps during the first three years of his administration.

The FERA camps proved to be a popular outlet for the administration, scattering not only the disgruntled vets but also as many as five million other destitute, transient Americans to campsites in every state in the country. Most of the work camps were set up on underutilized army bases, which harbored empty barracks and other buildings due to cutbacks in military spending. The soldiers were happy to have the older vets, plus legions of women and children, in their midst to help with basic housekeeping chores and various work projects. The government put them to work for five and a half hours a day, with half of Saturday and all day Sunday off, provided them with food and shelter, and paid them a modest stipend in return for their labor, setting traps for animals with marketable pelts and growing cabbage and other vegetables in gardens they cultivated throughout the camps. The FERA camps succeeded in getting the demonstrators out of Washington, where they had become Roosevelt's problem since he had trounced Hoover in the 1932 election.

In the summer of 1934, a few months before the midterm elections, enough veterans who refused to relocate to FERA camps descended on Washington and assembled in a house at 2626 Pennsylvania Avenue to demand their bonuses. They found a place to sleep there, enough food to go around, and lawyers willing to give them pro bono legal advice in their struggle to collect their bonuses. Their presence only a short walk down Pennsylvania Avenue from the White House was an embarrassment to Roosevelt and his fellow Democrats running in the midterm elections that fall. Roosevelt acted quickly to remove them from the national spotlight, sending them south in October into the Carolinas and all the way down into the Florida Keys. The president found himself entwined in the same dilemma that had bedeviled his predecessor, and he was determined to avoid the mistakes that were largely responsible for Hoover's downfall.

The issue of bonus legislation was never too far off the congressional radar screen. Wright Patman had been patiently waiting for a propitious moment to strike again, and he took advantage of the election results to reintroduce his bonus bill for the sixth time in January 1935. This time he had history and rising militancy among his colleagues on his side. Patman's new bill eventually sailed through the House, after considerable debate, with a vote of 356 to 59, and it passed in the Senate by 74 to 16, enough votes to override Roosevelt's veto.

"My convictions are as impelling today as they were then," FDR offered in defense of his veto. "Therefore I cannot change them." The vets would get their money a year later, nine years ahead of schedule, at a cost of almost $2.5 billion to the already bankrupt government. The vets were elated. They had finally won their personal war against the federal government after years of manning the barricades, thanks to the unflagging efforts of Patman and his congressional allies. But in the meantime they had to live, and FERA was their meal ticket to survival until they actually received their money.

Not everyone was enamored of life in the FERA camps. The Roosevelt administration heralded them as a "war veterans' heaven," but *Time* magazine called them "playgrounds for derelicts" and psychopaths. Many of the men sent there were "shell-shocked, whiskey-shocked and depression-shocked," wrote *New York Times* reporter Charles McLean about camp conditions in South Carolina. Many of the vets were "psychopathic cases and the local police report they have to take a great number of them into custody."

But it was the Florida Keys that would capture the headlines in the coming months. The FERA camps were strung out from the Upper Keys all the way west to Fort Jefferson, basically a rock outcropping in the Dry Tortugas. The major concentration of vets, however, was in the Upper Keys, where the vets were put to work on a road construction project linking them to Key West, at that time a rundown, depression-ravaged town on the remote edge of civilization.

3

The Big Blow

FOURTEEN

The Island of Bones

Cayo Hueso sits 45 miles north of the Tropic of Cancer, 90 miles north of Cuba, and 150 miles south of Miami. Cayo Hueso—Bone Island or Island of Bones. Whose bones the Spanish were referring to when they christened the island remains a mystery. Did bones actually cover the island? If so, whose bones were they? They could have been the remains of the Caloosa Indians who may have buried their dead there. No one knows for sure, but by the 1700s the English translated *Cayo Hueso* into "Key West," and the misnomer has survived the centuries. The local economy had always been marginal, depending on exotic trades like shrimping, fishing, smuggling, and wreck-diving to bring in the money. But by the 1930s even those volatile occupations were gone.

The land itself that Key West rests on is not exactly terra firma. The firma keeps getting rearranged, reconfigured, or wiped away by hurricanes and tropical storms. In 1846 a monster hurricane blasted the Island of Bones and pushed a pile of sand up along the shoreline, so that a small graveyard that had previously been on the water's edge was now a few blocks inland. The lighthouse, too, looked as though it had been physically moved and suddenly became the most landlocked lighthouse in the country. The beacon from the lighthouse, located near Ernest Hemingway's house, guided him home from his late-night drinking sprees at Sloppy Joe's.

"As long as I can see that beacon," Hemingway said, "I'll always be able to find my way home."

Pirates were terrorizing the island in 1822 when an exasperated Spaniard named Juan Salas sold Key West to John Simonton, a businessman from Mobile, Alabama, for $2,000. To celebrate the transfer of the island to an American, Lt. Matthew Perry sailed down to raise the American flag over what is now Mallory Square. He declared before a motley crew of sweating sailors and Cuban fisherman that the new U.S. possession had one of the largest deep-water anchorages in the country. Once the government had established the military significance of Key West, Commodore David Porter followed Perry's wake from the mainland with a squadron of ships to wage war against the pirates. Porter's "Mosquito Fleet," as the natives were quick to call it, took a bit longer to rid the waters of pirates than Porter had anticipated, but by 1830 he had succeeded in chasing them down to Cuba and east over to Puerto Rico.

It did not take the locals long to decide that they preferred the pirates to Porter, who seized the locals' livestock, buildings, and strategic supplies to wage his war. At least they had a fighting chance against the pirates, who made no claims about representing the interests of the federal government. When the government court-martialed Porter for overstepping his authority, he resigned in a huff and joined the Mexican navy as chief of naval operations. The Mexicans didn't like him much either—indeed, General Santa Ana tried to assassinate him twice—so he embarked to Turkey, where he tried to impose his special brand of leadership on the Middle Eastern infidels. Death finally caught up with him in 1843 when he died a bitter old man.

"A retrospect of the history of my life seems a highly-colored romance, which I should be very loath to live over again" was the way he assessed his own life.

Half of Key West did not even exist until real estate developer William Whitehead surveyed the town and carved it up into tiny plots. Ships' carpenters built most of the houses on those plots without paying much attention to architectural style or positioning. The result was a jumble of small ramshackle houses sitting alongside paths and alleys that came in off the main roads at odd angles. Ava Moore Parks described the Key West of the period in her book *The Forgotten Frontier*: "There was nothing else like it;

a city crowded on a small island in the middle of nowhere. . . . This was it—civilization began and ended here."

An anonymous observer summed up Key West as "densely settled, and about as un-American as possible, bearing a strong resemblance to a West Indian town. The houses are of wood, plainly built, and, with few exceptions, painted white. The houses are of all sizes, jumbled up in the oddest way. . . . The interior of each block is filled up with one-story shanties."

Hemingway and other writers found a special charm in the Island of Bones, but Mark Twain was not one of them. Traveling through Key West from Nicaragua in 1867, Twain entered in his diary: "If I have got Key West summed up right, they would receive War, Famine, Pestilence, and Death without a question, call them all by some fancy name and then rope in the survivors and sell them good cigars and brandies at easy prices and horrible dinners at infamous rates. They wouldn't quarantine anybody; they'd say 'come' and say it gladly, if you brought destruction and hell in your wake."

The famous author's vision almost came true when a great fire swept across the island on April Fools' Day 1886. It flared up in the Cuban Patriotic Club on Duval Street and quickly swept across the island. The island's only fire engine had been shipped to New York City for repairs, so there was nothing to contain the conflagration as it roared down Fleming Street from Whitehead to Bahama. The locals tried to fight the inferno by blowing up houses in its path with gunpowder, but the blaze continued to rage for twelve hours straight, wiping out fifty acres of Key West and dozens of its inhabitants.

Finally it spent its fury and died out on its own.

The indomitable locals were not defeated, working around the clock as they cleared out the burnt-out areas. They rebuilt their homes and public buildings quickly. Stubborn to a fault, they replaced what had been incinerated with new houses built of wood. The wealthier among them built new houses larger than the ones they had lost. Key West remained a mostly wooden town, except for a handful of military installations and public facilities made of rusticated stone—concrete blocks formed in a mold. In short order the trees, vines, flowers, and plants grew back, the termites returned and feasted on the wooden porches as they had before, and a casual observer would never know that the look, feel, and pace of the town had gone through a cataclysm just a short time back.

Henry Flagler looked at Key West and formed a different opinion of the place than Mark Twain had. Flagler was a visionary and a businessman first and foremost, and unlike Twain a successful speculator as well. After the turn of the twentieth century he recognized the value of Key West as a port for goods flowing to and from Cuba and South America. Flagler bought 134 acres of land on Trumbo Point to serve as a terminus for a railroad connecting the Keys to the mainland. When his engineers informed him that there was not enough dry land to erect the terminus, Flagler characteristically said, "Then make some."

Times were good once again on the Island of Bones. And they remained so for a while longer. Key West had become the richest town per capita in the United States in the aftermath of the fire, thanks to its deep-water port that made it a center of trade with Cuba and South America. The fishing, sponge, and cigar industries flourished. But, inevitably it seemed, Key West was destined to be plagued by a new blight—this one economic and more difficult to overcome. Prohibition destroyed most of the legitimate commercial activity on the island, and the Crash of '29 drove the final nail into the town's economic coffin. The jobs fled, the population declined by two-thirds, and per capita income sank to the lowest in the nation. Henry Flagler's train from the mainland chugged through the Keys "carrying nothing, nowhere, for nobody," as he put it.

The hard times hit the Island of Bones worse than almost anyplace else in the country. The community found itself $5 million in debt with 80 percent of its twelve thousand inhabitants on welfare. David Sholtz, the governor of Florida, was so distraught that he turned the administration of the town over to the federal government. President Roosevelt responded by appointing an auto-cratic character named Julius F. Stone as the dictator of Key West in all but name. Hemingway and Julius detested each other at first sight. They were both cut from the same mold—haughty, egotis-tical, domineering sons of the Midwest. Hemingway hailed from Oak Park, Illinois, and Julius from Columbus, Ohio. It was incon-ceivable that a town the size of Key West could host two such out-sized egos. The problem for Hemingway was that Julius had the power, the full force and clout of the federal government behind him. Hemingway was not the only writer to take a unique dislike to the imperious Mr. Stone. The eminent American poet Robert Frost was equally disenchanted with him.

"Here in Key West," Frost wrote, "we have a national rehabil-itation project running everything. I am dragged by the house-renting clerk before the Rehabilitator in Chief to see if I will do, that is to say, measure up to his idea of what the new citizenry must look like as it thought, felt and acted under God and the President in Washington. The Rehabilitator is a rich young man in shorts with hairy legs named Stone. . . . It is a very, very dead place because it has died several times. It died as a resort of pirates, then as a house of smugglers and wreckers, then as a cigar man-ufactury. . . . This town has been nationalized to rescue it from its own speculative excesses. The personal interest of Roosevelt in his second coming has been invoked and both mayor and gov-ernor have abdicated till we see what absolute authority can do to restore the prices of the speculators' graveyard plots and make Key West equal to Miami. . . . [Key West] has a million dollars worth of concrete sidewalks with no houses on them."

Hemingway was a literary superstar by the time Julius Stone descended on Key West like a provincial governor on the outskirts of the Roman Empire. Julius cast his gaze wide and far across his domain. He took in the abandoned cigar factories, collapsed piers, and dilapidated houses that had clearly seen better days. His hairy legs, as Frost remarked, were very much on display since he introduced Bermuda shorts to an area that preferred fish-stained trousers or cut-off shorts tied around the waist with a length of rope. The Conchs—or native-born locals—made fun of him walking around in public in what looked like "his underwear." Some took to wearing flowery undershorts themselves, both to spoof him and also to show that they could get away with anything he could. But their taunts were lost on Imperator Stone. Julius was lord and master of all that he surveyed. He had the power as southeastern director of FERA, and they would all knuckle under his rule if they knew what was good for them. Every state had a FERA administrator with almost absolute authority, and in Florida the man whose word was law was Julius Stone.

"Your city is bankrupt," he told the locals, "your streets are littered and filthy, your homes are rundown, and your industry is gone."

Emperor Julius rarely smiled. He stood tall, thin, and unyielding. At first he thought of shutting down the island altogether and moving the inhabitants north, perhaps to Tampa, where they might find work in the cigar factories that had relocated there—whether the locals wanted to go or not. That would have been an early American version of the Pol Pot solution in Cambodia a few decades later: ship an entire population off to an area where they might do something useful with their lives. But that seemed too drastic an option, even for the imperious provincial governor.

Finally Julius hit on a solution that he thought would work. There was one solution to the town's problems, as he saw it, and the ragtag Conchs would have nothing to say about it. The abandoned buildings and houses, the rotting piers, the garbage-strewn streets offended Julius's midwestern sensibilities. He would rip down the homes, such as they were, and rebuild the entire island into a *tourist* Mecca—a new Bermuda in the Gulf Stream. Beyond the blighted wasteland lay dazzling blue-green water teeming with giant fish, some of the most spectacular sunsets on earth, bougainvillea in bloom on the water's edge, great breezes rustling through stately palm trees. Julius literally drafted the town's welfare recipients into the Key West Volunteer Group and put them to work. No work, no relief checks for you. He would feed them and give them shelter in return for their stoop labor. Their options were limited. Slave labor built the pyramids, and what worked for the Egyptians would work for Julius. He intended to transform Key West into a haven for tourists with big boats to tie up in the harbor and pots of legal tender to spend in the island's restaurants, bars, and hotels.

And so began one of the most far-reaching rehabilitation projects in the nation's history. Julius looked on as the locals scurried about, so many dung beetles on a putrefying mound of decay. He permitted some of them to retain title to their houses but charged them rent, which they paid with their relief money until they paid back the cost of renovating their houses. In doing so he overstepped his authority. Nowhere in the federal guidelines did it say that Stone had a right to attach private property and charge the owners rent for it.

"I got away with it because we were so far off no one knew what we were doing," Julius crowed, giddy with absolute power. "With a scratch of my pen I started this work in Key West, and with a scratch of my pen I can stop it—just like that."

Over a whirlwind five-month period in 1935 Stone's four thousand conscripted minions labored long and hard for 1.5 million hours collectively. They fixed up more than two hundred houses; erected cabanas with thatched-roof huts on the beaches; renovated bars, restaurants, and hotels; planted trees along the streets; and put up an aquarium at Mallory Square. And still they were not finished. Their toil was far from over. Stone started a school for maids, enticing the few remaining wealthy dowagers in town to teach the unwashed local girls how to clean, launder, and otherwise serve the needs of the visiting tourists. He drafted unemployed fishermen as guides to teach the moneyed classes how to haul in the giant billfish that lived in the blue-green waters. He conscripted out-of-work musicians into a Hospitality Band to greet wealthy tourists arriving by boat and train. He turned the abandoned submarine base into a private yacht basin. And Emperor Julius admonished the visitors themselves about just how long it would take them to fully appreciate his renovated fiefdom.

"To appreciate Key West with its indigenous architecture, its lanes and byways, its friendly people and general picturesqueness, the visitor must spend at least a few days in the city. . . . Unless a visitor is prepared to spend at least three full days here, the Key West Administration would rather he did not come."

Julius incurred Hemingway's unmitigated fury when he drafted Key West's most celebrated literary icon into serving as a tourist attraction without checking first with the author. There it was—the Whitehead Street house that belonged to Papa, as he started to call himself even in his thirties, listed number eighteen on a list of forty-eight places tourists should plan to visit on the Island of Bones.

It is not clear what infuriated Papa more: being included on the list in the first place, or being placed so far down on Stone's roster of attractions. Shouldn't the Heavyweight Champion of American Writers, the man who had knocked Turgenev, de Maupassant, and Stendhal on their asses in the literary ring, have been number one if he was mentioned at all?

"I started out very quiet and I beat Mr. Turgenev," Hemingway had written. "Then I trained hard and I beat Mr. de Maupassant. I've fought two draws with Mr. Stendhal, and I think I had an edge in the last one. But nobody's going to get me in any ring with Mr. Tolstoy unless I'm crazy or I keep getting better."

Hemingway responded with a characteristic curse and a threat to flatten Julius the next time he saw the dictator, and he even took a shot at Julius's wife: "Anyone would have to be a FERA man to have a wife like that." In a calmer mood, Hemingway had a fence built around his property to keep Julius's nosy tourists from peering at him in his skivvies as he sauntered at dawn across a catwalk to his second-story office in the adjoining tower. Then again, how many rich tourists got up before dawn to see any writer, even one as famous as Hemingway, commuting to his lair to put words on paper?

The *Florida Grower*, a newspaper published in Orlando, also had a dark view of Emperor Julius and his efforts in Key West. "FERA rule is the rule of fear," it claimed. "No American city is more completely ruled by one man than is this small island city."

In a series of articles, United Press reporter Harry Ferguson called Julius "the king of a tight little empire. . . . Call it a 'dictatorship,' a 'kingdom within a republic,' or anything you choose."

Most galling to all of Stone's critics was that his heavy-handed tactics succeeded in creating the tourist Mecca he envisioned. The tourists arrived by boat and train, some by airplane from the mainland. They craved food, drink, shelter, and entertainment to satisfy their desires. The restaurants, bars, hotels, and fishing excursions began to thrive once again. Indeed, many residents turned themselves into entrepreneurs, moving out of their renovated homes to accommodate the invasion and charging exorbitant rents for them. Suddenly all was well on the Island of Bones while the rest of America struggled to free itself from the relentless stranglehold of the Great Depression. The tourists arrived and saved Key West from drowning under the sea that attacked its shoreline on all sides—figuratively if not literally. The Conchs hated the tourists but had no problem turning their houses over to them in return for sorely needed cash. They despised the tourists but welcomed them as benefactors.

The population was sparse throughout the Keys east and north of Key West. They were mostly local Conchs, who fished the waters for whatever they could pull out of the sparkling blue depths, and the ragtag contingent of vets whom Roosevelt had relocated to get them out of the nation's capital, where they were an embarrassment to the administration.

FIFTEEN

Paradise Lost

By the beginning of 1935 the government had enrolled more than eight thousand vets in the "rehabilitation camps," as the media had begun to characterize them, with many of them sent to the Carolinas and Florida. The official count put those assigned to work projects in Florida at 2,724. Their primary job was to work with Florida's state road department to close gaps in the projected overseas highway linking the Florida mainland and Key West, which only a railroad connected at the time. FERA assigned a contingent of about three hundred vets to work under the direction of road department engineers on the construction of four miles of bridges and eight miles of highway to replace twenty-five miles of ferry crossings. The agency charged the vets with adding thirty additional miles to the ninety-mile highway that ran down from Miami to the mobile transient camps where the vets were situated.

The federal government erected eleven work camps in Florida, three of them in the Keys. Camp 1 was put up on Upper Windley Key, the first one to be built. Camp 3 was placed on the lower end of Lower Matecumbe Key, the place from which the unfinished highway would continue. The third work camp, Camp 5, was located on the upper end of Lower Matecumbe Key. The veterans who moved there were a curious mixture of aging, war-torn soldiers who had been damaged by their treatment after the Great War—many of them alcoholics, roustabouts tradesmen when they had any work at all, and poison gas victims. Others had suffered serious wounds, while some had not been incapacitated at all. They were a miserable lot, depressed, battered, and hungry for any work they could get, including building a road for a dollar a day along a godforsaken stretch of sand hundreds of miles off the mainland. They posed a stark contrast to the wealthy tourists flocking down to Key West to check out the sunsets and test their skills hauling giant fish from the surrounding waters.

"The camp is located on the S.E. side of Florida Highway 4-A, 2.5 miles north of the Islamorada Station," wrote assistant regional engineer of FERA F. C. Boyer, "and covers a tract about one thousand feet parallel with the highway and sloping back approximately four hundred feet to the ocean."

The accommodations for the vets consisted of canvas tents sixteen feet long or longer, some with floorboards and siding and some without, capable of housing up to forty men each in the bigger tents. A toilet stood at the edge of the camp, and tank cars transported drinking water from Homestead, about fifty miles north on the mainland. FERA officials viewed the quarters as strictly temporary, an interim arrangement pending the arrival of boxcars to house the vets while the authorities built sturdier facilities. "As tents are claimed not to be satisfactory for all-year use in that locality," wrote Boyer, "the new permanent camps will be of frame construction." The frame buildings, ten by eighteen feet complete with mess halls, recreation facilities, toilets, and showers, were considered better able to withstand the powerful storms that regularly struck the Keys. The federal government, however, dropped the housing issue down to the bottom of its list of concerns because of the extra costs involved. It was clear to all the FERA officials on the site that the government had sent the vets there without adequate preparation for their safety and sanitary needs.

"These camps are in a very unsatisfactory condition," reported Joseph Hyde Pratt, regional engineer for FERA. "Men are arriving . . . at these camps in such large numbers that the camps have not been put in the condition that they should have been before the arrival of the veterans. . . . At present, the sanitary conditions at Camp No. 3 are very bad, as the sewer line has not been constructed nor the toilet houses completed. This camp is not clean."

The response from Washington was a resounding silence. The condition of the vets, how safely they were housed and whether their basic needs were provided for, was totally off the government's radar screen. The administration's main priority in the region was the completion of the overseas bridge project, with little or no regard for the men who were there to do the work. Rubbing salt into already festering wounds, the government hired outside workers to complement the efforts of the vets and provided them priority treatment in the mess hall, clothing allowances, and more spacious living quarters with four men to a tent compared with eight for the vets. The vets responded by staging a strike at the camp on Lower Matecumbe Key. They refused to do any work at all until they received the same pay and other benefits as the contract workers, who were doing the jobs the vets had been assigned to do. When the striking vets threatened to enlist the other vets in nearby camps to join the strike with them, the federal government sent in the National Guard to police the camps and keep the strike from spreading.

Some of the vets complained that they were held prisoner in the camp and denied contact with the outside world.

The government was desperate to keep the vets' side of the story from reaching the public and tried to bar reporters from entering the camps, but its heavy-handed tactics triggered a near riot among the vets. The government relented in order to maintain some semblance of peace, and the vets calmed down when the *Miami Daily News* published a report on their living conditions on March 1, 1935. "The men are quartered in 40 bunkhouses," the paper reported, "holding eight men each, 10 tents with four men each, and one large tent with 40 men. They did not have fresh water for bathing, they said, and must use salt water. They made no complaint of the food, but objected to the civilian workers being waited on while they stood in line and washed their dishes."

Not all the publicity was favorable. The *Washington Post*, a critic of FDR's New Deal and its treatment of the vets as a separate class of citizen, launched its own series of articles about the vets, which stood in stark contrast to the dire conditions that plagued the vets. Reporter Edward T. Folliard wrote about the vets' recovering from a "booze rampage." They were living in "a comparative paradise," according to him, "a palm-dotted strand, washed by the blue-green waters of the Atlantic and the Gulf of Mexico and caressed at this time by a delightful breeze from the East." They feasted on "three whopping meals a day" and received thirty to forty dollars a month for their labor.

But paradise is in the eye of the beholder. Others viewed the area differently. Syndicated columnist Raymond Clapper referred to the Florida sites as "concentration camps far away from the Capital's spotlight." *Time* reported, "If the U.S. had a Devil's Island, the Florida Keys would have been a good place to locate it. A collection of mangrove swamps and low islands of coral sand, they were hot, humid, alive with mosquitoes, and while rattlesnakes coil in the underbrush, sharks, barracudas and poisonous rays infest the milky water."

What Folliard overlooked in his reporting was that paradise has a way of transmogrifying into a hellish nightmare when the sun disappears and high winds and heavy rains churn the ocean into a murky gray force of destruction. Folliard did concede that the vets would willingly abandon their tropical enclave if they got their bonuses. "The food is even better than the army," Folliard quoted some of the vets. He added, "The pay is pretty fair, but none of these things would hold them here if a bonus of $600 or $700 came along."

The threat of hurricanes pummeling the Keys was never far beyond the horizon. "We expect to have between 1,500 and 2,000 veterans encamped on the Keys by the First of July," Fred B. Ghent, the FERA safety director, reported to Joseph Hyde Pratt. "The hurricane season begins July 1st and continues through the last full moon in October. . . . It is our duty to every man employed on the Keys in connection with this program to furnish a safe refuge during a storm." Ghent proposed building a large warehouse on the Keys, sturdy enough to withstand high winds, with facilities for housing the men on the second floor to protect them against flooding. But he received no reply from FERA, which was not inclined to go along with his recommendation because of the expense involved.

So there the matter stood in the waning days of the summer of 1935. It remained at an all-too-familiar impasse, with observers on the scene beseeching Washington to arrange for adequate housing and better living conditions for the vets, and the administration turning a blind eye toward the problem that loomed just a few hundred miles to the east, turning the sunny skies into an ominous sea of churning wind and rain.

On August 20 an advisory reached Key West, warning that a tropical storm was now roiling the ocean just east of Bermuda. On September 1, Sunday of the Labor Day weekend, the *Miami Herald* published a story about tropical storms threatening the coast of Florida as they veered westward from Bermuda. At that time forecasting weather patterns was pretty much a guessing game, since the monitoring services available today did not yet exist. Forecasters relied on reports from weather bureaus about conditions in diverse locations, which they passed along to other weather stations and to anyone else with short-wave radios. Ships and planes at sea also reported on the conditions they encountered. Hurricanes might grow in intensity or suddenly change direction without being detected for long periods. Everyone who stood a chance of being affected by violent weather took whatever precautions they deemed necessary until the threat had passed.

On September 2 the *Miami Herald* advised that the storm's latest trajectory would carry it over Cuba, and Cuban authorities prepared to evacuate Havana and other vulnerable areas along the northern coastline. Cuba's proximity to the United States put the Florida Keys at risk. The camps were situated on land virtually flush with sea level, with no trees or other obstacles to deflect the wind-driven waves that routinely washed ashore when the storms blew in. The tents and flimsy shacks that housed the vets offered scant protection against the hostile elements in this slice of paradise. Walter J. Bennett, the senior meteorologist in Jacksonville, stated later that even if a hurricane had bypassed the Keys on its way through the Florida Straits it "would have caused high tides and strong gales on the Florida Keys with tides possibly as high . . . as ten feet above mean low tide, and winds between gale and hurricane force."

Even the fringes of the approaching storm would have posed

a major threat to the men and their housing in the FERA camps. Compounding the already ominous predicament in which the vets found themselves was the timing: the hurricane, without concern for holidays, threatened to strike sometime over the Labor Day weekend, when many workers were off and only skeleton crews were available to man trains and participate in rescue operations.

As late as Saturday night the Key West Weather Bureau reported that conditions did not appear alarming, but by two o'clock Sunday morning it had begun to look as though the situation had grown worse. Meteorologists informed Fred Ghent that "it was impossible to say just where the storm would strike and just how hard it would strike, but being familiar with hurricanes I thought it would be advisable to take every precaution in advance." In Key West merchants and homeowners boarded up their premises when it became apparent that a direct hit was possible.

The confusion over the course of the storm, and the effects it would likely have on the camps, dictated greater precautions than were taken if even the fringes brushed the region. On the Sunday morning of the Labor Day weekend a train should have been en route to the vets' camps capable of carrying five hundred men to safer ground in Homestead. Yet no one made any effort to evacuate the camps as the heavy winds and rains began to pummel the area. FERA officials in the Keys grew more and more desperate with each passing hour. A near-certain disaster was in the making, and no one in Washington was concerned about taking adequate measures to avert it.

The wind and rain blew in hard off the water and kicked up a chop at the edge of the shore. The weather was relentless—horizontal rain, shuddering wind, dark gray sky—a terrible tempest blasting the people inching down Duval Street toward the dock at the end of the street. The weather was even worse on the islands farther east, particularly on Windley and Matecumbe Keys where the land was flat, the trees spindly, and the structures unfit to withstand little more than a stiff tropical breeze. The fragile lines of communication, relying as they did back then on wireless reports from shipping stations scattered throughout the islands, added to the confusion. The news was getting worse by the hour, and as the Labor Day weekend wore on, the tropical storm evolved into a full-scale hurricane making a serious run toward the Florida Keys—even though the *Miami Herald* still identified it as a "tropical disturbance."

Hemingway studied his charts showing the paths of forty September hurricanes since the turn of the century. Always the meticulous researcher and chronicler of important data—including daily readings on his weight, temperature, and blood pressure—Hemingway estimated that the hurricane would roar into Key West around noon on Monday. On Monday morning Hemingway walked over to the marina at the navy base where he kept *Pilar*, only to find a line of boat-owners ahead of him waiting to have their own boats hauled out of the water onto dry dock. He had to settle for a heavy hawser to secure *Pilar* in an area that he thought would provide the greatest safety during the storm. He returned home to bring in outdoor furniture and board up the windows on his house, then went back to the boatyard where he discovered that the Coast Guard had tied up a confiscated "rum boat" with contraband booze right next to *Pilar*.

"For Christ's sake!" he yelled at the sailor on duty. "You know those lousy ringbolts will pull out of her stern and then she'll come down on us. What's the use of letting a piece of junk like that sink a good boat?"

The marina—the entire town—was in chaos, with people rushing in all directions to secure their boats, their homes, and everything that was not nailed down from the encroaching hurricane. Hemingway double-checked his barometer reading and recalculated that the hurricane would strike at midnight. Sleep was out of the question as he prepared himself, Pauline, and their staff to gear up for the worst. By midnight the barometric reading had dropped to 29.50 and was sinking rapidly. Hemingway figured the lights would blow as the wind picked up. Soon it was rattling the windows, the shutters, the very walls and foundation of his house. Hemingway was sick to his stomach thinking about *Pilar* and the rum boat berthed next to it. He dressed and went outside to get in his car and drive to the marina, but the windblown rain whipping in hard off the water had saturated the engine wires. He had no choice but to push his way through the howling tempest and go down on foot. On the way the batteries in his flashlight shorted out, and he had to fight his way against the wind in zero visibility. His worst fears materialized when he reached the navy yard and saw the rum boat rocking wildly with the ringbolts pulled out. But this time he was lucky. Before it could slam into his boat a Spanish sailor named Jose Rodriguez had stepped aboard and maneuvered the rum boat away from *Pilar*. Hemingway never loved the Spanish and the Cubans more than he did at that moment.

"You feel like hell," he wrote later. "You figure if we get the hurricane from there . . . you will lose the boat and you will never have enough money to get another."

And then a miracle took place. At two in the morning the wind subsided, the rain let up, and the worst of the hurricane passed. Three hours later the barometer held steady and the pressure began to rise. The hurricane, bad as it was, had struck Key West only a glancing blow. When Hemingway returned to his house later in the morning he noticed only minimal damage. Some branches had fallen and trees were uprooted in his yard, but the house was intact. Hemingway, *Pilar*, and Key West had made it through one of the most powerful hurricanes to slam the Island of Bones in its long, turbulent history.

"We got only the outside edge," Hemingway wrote in a letter to his editor Max Perkins on September 7. "It was due for midnight and I went to bed at ten to get a couple of hours sleep if possible having made everything as safe as possible with the boat. Went with the barometer on a chair by the bed and a flashlight to use when the lights should go. At midnight the barometer had fallen to 29.50 and the wind was coming very high and in gusts of great strength tearing down trees, branches etc. Car drowned out and got down to boat afoot and stood by until 5 a.m. when the wind shifting into the west we knew the storm had crossed to the north and was going away."

SIXTEEN

The Hurricane Makes a Direct Hit on the Camps

The hurricane slammed the Keys to the east where the vets were camped with the full force of its fury. There was no hope for them or anyone else who lived there unless a train could be put together to transport them all to safer ground. The wheels should have been set in motion earlier, as soon as warning signs appeared on the horizon and the slowdown commenced for the Labor Day weekend. But Washington was unresponsive, and Ghent was overly timid about taking action on his own even though he was responsible for safety in the area.

"We discussed the probability of getting at least four (4) coaches . . . Sunday night for movement of the veterans from the Keys," reported J. L. Byrum, chief dispatcher in Miami. "I explained to [Ghent] that a number of his men would be either in Key West or Miami and there should be somewhere between 200 and 250 men to move out in case weather conditions demanded. I explained to him that the only way for me to get the coaches in position would be for me to forward them from Miami . . . that morning, which I would do. To be sure we had ample coach space for the veterans from the Keys in case it was decided to come out. With ten coaches it would have been possible to carry eight hundred men from the veterans' camps in addition to their regular passengers."

Ghent lamely replied that Washington was concerned with the cost. The railroad officials said that they would complete the operation without any charge once they got approval from him. They would be willing to arrange for payment later, but in the midst of the crisis "there would be no collection." They could get a train down there in four hours from Miami, but it would take considerably longer once the storm began to intensify. Once it hit, it would be difficult to move trains beyond Marathon, farther east from where the vets were camped, not close enough to do them any good.

Ghent, who was off in St. Augustine on personal business, finally decided to take action on his own as his superiors continued to drag their feet. On Labor Day, Monday, the railroad offices closed at 2 p.m. Ghent placed a panicky call to the general railroad superintendent at his home in St. Augustine and requested a special train to travel down to the camps to relocate the vets to Hollywood. But it was already too late. Any train they could assemble on such short notice, with so many workers off for the weekend, would be unable to leave until 4:25 p.m. "under the best conditions," two and a half hours after Ghent's call. The vets could have been evacuated safely only if a train had "left Miami about 10:00 a.m.," according to railroad official Scott Loftin.

The *Miami Herald* reported that an "11-car Florida East Coast Railway train left Miami at 4:30 p.m. Monday for Matecumbe to evacuate more than 500 world war veterans encamped there." The trains supposedly would transport the vets to safer ground in Hollywood, north of Miami, far removed from the expected path of the storm. But that train never made it all the way to the veterans' camps once the weather unleashed its full savage fury. *Miami Daily News* reporter William Johns recorded his own account of the trip. "I boarded the train at 7 p.m. Monday at Homestead. . . . We proceeded south, making the first stop, of necessity, opposite a rock quarry near Veterans Camp No. 1. A steel cable attached to a quarry crane caught one of the box cars and threatened to derail the train." After an hour-and-a-half delay, the train continued its journey. "As we neared Islamorada," Johns reported, "the wind and water increased. The cars swayed on the rails. . . . The water was slowing us to a snail's pace. It was dark and we expected momentarily the roadbed would give way."

The train got as far as Islamorada when all hell broke loose. "The water forced a stop," Johns reported. It was then just over the rail bed . . . when a wall of water from 15 to 20 feet high picked up our coaches and swirled them about like straws. We felt them going and I imagine everyone thought it was the end. I knew I did."

The passengers were tossed across seats, against windows, and on top of one another on the walls, which had turned into floors. The wind gusts topped one hundred miles an hour, and they worried most that another tidal wave would inundate them and put an end to their misery. Fortunately, however, for Johns and the other passengers, the tidal wave crashed out to sea and the wind subsided before the monster storm drowned them all like rats trapped in a cage. After midnight they surveyed the damage and were astonished to see that several of the cars, including the one they were riding in, had been tossed up to 150 feet from the tracks. "That same wave must have swept Lower Matecumbe," Johns wrote. "I don't see how any living thing, exposed to that rush of water, could have survived."

Scott Loftin's description of the fateful journey corresponded closely to Johns's account. According to him the train was delayed for ten minutes at the Miami River drawbridge by a stream of holiday boaters passing through the draw, most of them attempting to escape from the area while they had the opportunity. The train continued on its way toward the veterans' camps when it ran into gale-force winds south of Homestead. The winds picked up as the hurricane closed in, but the train was able to inch its way along the keys to Quarry, seventy-two miles south of Miami, where it arrived at 6:50 p.m. At that point the train was delayed for about an hour and a half, as Johns had reported, because of obstructions on the tracks caused by the storm. Once they had cleared the debris from the tracks the train proceeded to Islamorada, chugging in at 8:20 p.m. The winds now topped one hundred miles per hour, and the water rose to the level of the coach floors. "Finally, a tidal wave came and turned over all the coaches, baggage cars, and the three freight cars" Loftin said, "leaving only the engine standing on the track."

Loftin repeated that the authorities could have evacuated the vets safely only if the train had left Miami around 10 a.m. on Monday. That would have been the last opportunity to haul them out of the camps before the killer tidal wave crashed across the camps, obliterating everything in its devastating path.

Sadly, the window of opportunity had slammed shut a good six hours before the rescue train finally got under way.

The hurricane was small in size, only about forty miles in diameter and eight to ten miles across the eye at the center, but it was the most violent ever to hit not only the Keys but the continental United States, with wind gusts soaring to 250 miles an hour. It also moved slowly, taking forty hours to travel from the Bahamas to the Florida Keys. The barometric reading on Windley and Matecumbe Keys, where the vets were housed in their flimsy work camps, plummeted to 26.35, the lowest ever recorded. The hurricane made a direct hit on the work camps, pushing a wall of water more than eighteen feet high across the narrow strip of sand. The vets and Conchs had nowhere to go, nothing to hang onto.

When the monster storm struck, a seventeen-year-old fisherman named Bernard Russell—no relation to Hemingway's friend Josie Russell, the owner of Sloppy Joe's—felt his sister's hand pull out of his grip in the pitch-black night as the ferocious winds and towering waves pummeled their bodies.

"You went wherever the waves pushed you and wherever the winds pushed you," he said after the storm. "It was so dark you couldn't see what was going on and maybe that was good."

He never saw his sister again, nor his mother and two other sisters. They were somewhere out there, lost in the sea. He survived when he was tossed on top of a trash pile. "There were sixty-one in the Russell family and fifty of them died that night," he said. The official death toll came to 423; 259 were veterans whose camps had been torn away and flung out into the Gulf as though they never existed.

"There were so many dead people and no place to take them," Russell elaborated. "They stacked them up and burned them." The ones they could find in the horrific aftermath, that is.

Another survivor recalled, "There was a big wall of water—fifteen feet high, twenty maybe. It swept over those shacks and messed them up like they were match boxes."

Someone else remembered that the roof of the canteen was ripped away. "We all started away in the same direction and the roof came down on us. It must have hit every one of us. After the roof fell all I could hear was the grunting and groaning of the boys. I never saw any of them after that."

"Bodies were lying all over the roadway and lumber piled on them and some of them had holes in their heads," read another account. "I saw bodies with tree stumps smashed through their chests—heads blown off—twisted arms and legs torn off by flying timber that cut like big knives."

The 1935 storm was a Category Five hurricane, the first of two to hammer the United States since the government had started to keep records. It took out thirty-five miles of Henry Flagler's railroad and wiped every tree and every structure off Windley and Matecumbe Keys. With *Pilar* now seaworthy once again Hemingway set out a couple of days later to survey the carnage.

"All the next day the winds were too high to get out and there was no communication with the keys," he wrote to Max Perkins. "Telephone, cable and telegraph all down, too rough for boats to leave. The next day we got across and found things in a terrible shape. . . . The foliage absolutely stripped as though by fire for forty miles and the land looking like the abandoned bed of a river. Not a building of any sort standing. . . . Max, you can't imagine it, two women, naked, tossed up into trees by the water, swollen and stinking, their breasts as big as balloons, flies between their legs. Then, by figuring, you locate where it is and recognize them as the two very nice girls who ran a sandwich place and a filling station three miles from the ferry. . . . Harry Hopkins and Roosevelt who sent those poor bonus march guys down here to get rid of them got rid of them all right."

Up to this point Hemingway had not been overtly political. His politics, such as he had thought about politics at all, could best be described as passively anarchistic. He distrusted authority of any sort and was instinctively individualistic. He wanted to be left alone to do his writing the way he saw fit and not have his language censored by bureaucrats always on the hunt for obscenities. And he preferred to keep most of the money he earned and not turn big chunks of it over to tax collectors. But the plight of the vets on the Keys pushed him into a more revolutionary frame of mind. He was no fan of the New Deal and viewed the intrusions of civil authorities as a misguided attempt to improve the lot of working people. Leave people alone and they will find a way to make things better on their own, he believed. In some ways he wandered further to the left of New Deal administrators, but a later generation might have put him further to the right of traditional conservatives into the realm of individual anarchism. Hemingway had become a rebel. He was so infuriated by the death of the vets that he took time out from his regular writing to pen a diatribe, which he called "Who Murdered the Vets?" *New Masses*, a publication of the American Communist Party, asked him to write his version of what happened. Hemingway had no use for Communists or their literature, but he was happy to have an outlet for his fury. The article was published on September 17, 1935.

He described a scene that could have been painted by Hieronymus Bosch: a barren landscape shorn of all foliage and living things, ripped-up railroad tracks, dead men lying face-down and face-up in the formerly green but now brown mangroves, bodies strewn out like logs alongside water tanks. Then, farther along where a tall palmetto tree survived the wreckage, dead veterans high up in the tree where the water had swept them.

"Whom did they annoy and to whom was their possible presence a political danger?" he wrote. "Who sent them down to live in frame shacks on the Florida Keys and left them there in hurricane months? Who is responsible for their deaths?" Many of them were husky and hardworking and simply down on their luck, others had been reduced to near-pathological cases. And why were they not evacuated on Sunday or Monday morning at the latest? Hemingway answered his own questions at the end of the piece and put the blame squarely in the lap of the Roosevelt administration.

"Who sent them down there? I hope he reads this—and how does he feel? He will die too, himself, perhaps even without a hurricane warning, but maybe it will be an easy death, that's the best you get, so that you do not have to hang onto something until you can't hang on, until your fingers won't hang on, and it is dark. . . . You're dead now, brother, but who left you there in the hurricane months on the Keys where a thousand men died before you when they were building the road that's now washed out? Who left you there? And what's the punishment for manslaughter now?"

Thanks to the efforts of local residents who had lived through countless hurricanes that periodically battered the Keys, FERA officials fared better than the vets whose lives and safety they were entrusted to protect. The owner of the Matecumbe Hotel, which FERA officials leased for their own protection, knew enough about the danger the storms unleashed to take adequate precautions in advance. By Sunday night he and his father had boarded up the hotel, a far sturdier structure than the flimsy tents erected for the vets, in anticipation of the encroaching hurricane. The FERA officials ensconced there rode out the howling winds and tidal wave with their lives intact. Other locals advised FERA that the vets were in danger and the government needed to take action to get them out of the area. The falling barometer readings were a sure sign to the locals that the hurricane would strike over the weekend. They had started to worry two weeks earlier that high tides would put the campsites under water, since they were approaching the time of year when even normal tides were at their peak.

R. W. Craig, the owner of a boating supply business, spent all day Sunday fortifying his buildings for the heavy winds he expected. Despite his precautions his store was leveled, and he and a couple of friends sought refuge on the embankment near the railroad tracks, about fourteen feet above sea level as tidal surges washed over them, eventually driving his friends out to sea. The experience turned into a "horrible, pain-throbbing night-mare," he recalled later. "Shivering there in the dark, holding on for dear life, alternatively praying and sobbing." As if the power of the storm had not been enough to result in death and injury, said Craig, "hundreds of ugly crabs descended upon us." They could do nothing about the crabs except to let them explore their bodies freely, crawling inside their clothing as they sought the warmth of the men's bodies. If they had let go for one second to brush them away, they would have lost their grip on the only thing that kept all of them from being carried off into the ocean. Craig said he could understand how many men lost their minds when trapped in such horrifying situations.

After the hurricane blew through, one of the local residents commented that he "saw the [tents] blown to pieces with a common north wind." When asked by federal investigators whether it was "safe to maintain a camp for veterans during the months of September and October," he replied that he did not believe so and he had said as much to FERA officials weeks before the hurricane struck.

Albert Buck, a vet serving as foreman of Camp 5 on the upper end of Lower Matecumbe Key, said that the FERA employees head-quartered in the Matecumbe Hotel seemed unaware that the wind and rain had reached such dangerous levels since the windows were boarded up and the walls were thick enough to cushion the intensity of the advancing storm. The top FERA leaders were not immediately available when they were most needed. One of them was honeymooning in Key West, and Ghent was off taking care of other business out of the danger zone. They had left a minor factotum named Sam Cutler temporarily in charge, with no real authority to act on his own without Ghent's approval.

As for the vets exposed to the elements in their tents, Fred Bon-ner, a watchman at Camp 1 on Upper Windley Key, said that none of the men had any experience with the risk posed by hurricanes and were hoping that the stiff winds "would blow the mosquitoes away and cool things off." Most of the men figured that if they were going to be subjected to a life-threatening situation Ghent would have taken steps to get them all out of there in time. The vets who were alarmed enough to try to move out on their own were told by a FERA official in Ghent's absence that they "would be stopped by the Florida National Guard" for attempting to leave without permission. It was a classic bureaucratic mishmash in the making—no help from the authorities, no proper lines of communications, and even feeble attempts at self-preservation thwarted by clueless functionaries.

Typically, in the wake of what should have been an avoidable calamity, several government officials attempted to shift the blame onto the victims, claiming that most of them were too drunk to be transported out of the danger zone. There is little question that the vets were a hard-drinking group, buying beer at the camp store and whisky from rum runners who had a thriving business smuggling booze in all along the coast. "Friday was payday in the camps," said the manager of the canteen where beer was available, "and Monday being Labor Day was a holiday; there had always been considerable drunkenness in these camps on payday." Sloppy Joe's in Key West was one of their favorite destinations, and Hemingway often treated several of them to drinks when he ran into them. But others in the region disagreed with the notion that the vets were too intoxicated to leave. "Every man was in condition where he could have saved himself," said Thomas Harrell, a camp foreman. "I don't think there was any of the men down where they couldn't have taken care of themselves."

Eugene A. Pattison, a field engineer at the camps, wondered why FERA did not transport the men out in trucks that sat there idly as the hurricane built up momentum. There were "eight or ten pickup trucks and about ten or twelve stake-body trucks, also dump trucks" there—enough to evacuate all the vets safely farther up the Keys. Drunk or sober, the men could have been loaded into them as easily as they could have been shuttled onto a train and moved from ground zero. But no attempt was made to use the trucks as they all waited for the train to make its way down from Miami. None of the FERA officials suggested taking advantage of the trucks. "We thought we was being looked out for by the officials higher up," said Pattison, "and when we saw that we was not, why it was too late to make any preparations."

"We had plenty of gasoline, dump, and stake body trucks at Camp 3 and at the quarry at Snake Creek," said Joseph Hipolito Huau, a camp recreational director. "They were all in good condition and I saw them at the quarry when I got gasoline for my car between 12:00 and 1:00 p.m. to return back to Miami, Monday. . . . There were several civilians connected with our office who were not drunk and could drive cars." John F. Daniels, a survivor at Camp 5, maintained, "We had trucks of the ton or more type and lighter ones to move both men and their clothes." Frank R. Tischenbach, a Camp 3 survivor, said, "If the boys had keys to the trucks down there, there would have been more lives saved than there was. They should have loaded them on there and drove the hell out of there." Herbert S. Wilshire, another Camp 3 vet, said, "Everyone had all their things, including beds, ready to go. It seems as though . . . we could have gotten out of there with trucks. There were trucks enough in camp to take us all out."

Paul Pugh, a top sergeant at Camp 3 who was injured during the hurricane, testified later from his hospital bed that he "began calling [FERA official Ray W.] Sheldon's noon on Sunday when things looked like the blow was coming." Sheldon reported directly to Ghent. "I kept on going to Sheldon's house every few hours as the men were showing signs of unrest, but each time Sheldon said there was no danger. . . . When I went to Sheldon's house on Sunday at about 9 o'clock, I was told there would be no danger for at least forty-eight hours, if there was to be any at all. I couldn't believe it because things just didn't look right to me or any of the other men. I went back again Monday at 10:00 a.m. and was told there was nothing to worry about, and later in the day C. G. Sain, a civilian timekeeper, said there was going to be a train at 5:30."

Earlier Monday afternoon Pugh had asked E. H. Sheeran, superintendent of construction of the Overseas Bridge Project, about the possibility of taking the men out on trucks. Sheeran informed him that FERA had already locked up the keys to the trucks, so that option was off the table. "We had quite a few trucks down there," Sheeran said. But after about 2 p.m. the "road was too slippery, and it was too squally, and there was nothing to protect [the men], and water was over the roads." Therefore, it would have been impossible to use truck transportation once the train failed to arrive. The trucks had been oiled and gassed as early as 8:30 that morning and were in condition to roll. Ray Lester, a Camp I survivor on Upper Windley, testified that he had asked for the key to one of the trucks to "take some women and children out," but Sheldon had issued orders not to turn over any of the truck keys until Ghent or someone else up the command chain gave him further instructions.

With the key decision-makers away, and their FERA underlings playing poker or standing around idly in the relative safety of their hotel, the hours ticked by slowly as the hurricane blew a path across open water, destined to strike directly at the camps with the precision of a laser-guided bomb, delivering its tragic consequences.

SEVENTEEN

The Struggle for Survival

G hent's actions—or, more precisely, his lack of competent leadership—guaranteed that a life-threatening situation would degenerate into a tragedy bordering on criminality: manslaughter, as Hemingway would have it. He was hundreds of miles away in the northeast corner of the state where the hurricane was not a threat, with no way to be reached despite several attempts to contact him by phone. He was negligent in not leaving someone in charge who could act on his own authority. A civilian construction worker named W. Z. Burrus said, "Somebody should have been placed in charge. . . . If it had been construction camp solely we could have carried them up the road to safety. The men had never been through a hurricane before. The officials in charge of the camp did not know anything about it and were not informed that it was as serious as it was. . . . If you go through two or three of them you will take it seriously."

The veterans of the war were left stranded to fight one last battle on their own, thousands of miles away from, and a decade and a half later than, the war they risked their lives in on the battlefields of Europe. Camp I survivor J. R. Combs, who sustained broken ribs, a serious back injury, a crushed foot, and several lacerations and bruises, said, "About five o'clock in the afternoon [Monday, September 2] the captain came into the mess hall and told us to hurry as the train was due any minute. It was already blowing hard then and we piled out as fast as we could. As we came out of the door the corners of the mess hall started breaking off and it began blowing harder each minute. . . . The canteen blew down and wood started flying in all directions."

As the hurricane's fury intensified, Combs and his comrades

were thrown to the ground, searching frantically for something to hold onto to keep from getting blown out to sea. Combs and one of his buddies found a large rock and hung on for their lives. When the tidal wave crashed over them they lost their grip and were sure they were going to drown. Combs, however, was tossed against a telephone pole that anchored him onto the land. He heard innumerable vets shouting, one's voice rising above the others, "Give me a hand, buddy. Save me, I'm drowning." The shouts were mingled with groans of resignation from dozens of others who gave up all hope of saving themselves or being rescued. Combs managed to remove his belt and lash himself to a different telephone pole when the water ripped him away from the first one. Then the roof of the barracks flew off and crushed him beneath its weight, followed by stones propelled through the air like cannon balls that struck different parts of his body. Finally he lost consciousness and lay there through the night. When he woke at daybreak he looked around and saw the bodies of his fellow veterans strewn across the wreckage, some piled on top of others, all of them as lifeless as sodden cordwood.

The medical officer at Camp 1, Earle L. Fox, who also was injured badly during the hurricane, said, "The storm started in fury at 8:00 p.m. . . . Every building was razed and at one time the tide rose entirely over the island. I was at Snake Creek Hotel, which was used as a hospital. This collapsed about 10:00 p.m., with many persons under the ruins. There were about forty patients in this building, about half women and children. Out of this number there were only seven men and three or four of the women and children saved." When the makeshift hospital began to topple Fox was able to walk through a hole in one wall into three or four feet of water filled with floating wood and other debris. The strength of the wind and the rushing water carried heavy timber, rocks, and other materials along at a great speed, causing many casualties as they struck everyone in their path. Fox headed for the railroad grade, the highest point on the island just barely above sea level, and he stumbled along until he reached a rock wall about four feet high where a bunch of men held on with all the strength they had. Flying debris hammered them mercilessly as the water level rose and the winds kicked higher.

Badly battered, Fox and a few others made their way onto the railroad track and positioned themselves on the grade on the far side, which gave them some protection from flying projectiles. They dug down into the mud with their hands and hunkered down into the shallow holes in an effort to keep the debris from bashing in their heads. The survivors clung to their handholds until about three o'clock in the morning, when the wind and rain began to let up. As the storm subsided and the darkness cleared in the eastern sky at dawn, Fox and the other surviving vets found a large water tank, which gave them some protection from the remaining gusts of wind. Miraculously they were able to get a fire going and boiled some coffee they found for the injured men. There they stayed until Tuesday afternoon, when rescue workers were able to reach them and haul them off to safer ground.

Gus Linawik was one of the other vets who sheltered behind the water tank with Fox. "During the storm I was in a cabin, which didn't last twenty minutes," he recounted. "The shack went to sea and I and my friends with it. Four of us kicked out the windows and began swimming in open water. Fortunately, a shift in the wind brought us back to shore. We spent the night clinging to a coral reef. Later we took refuge behind a water tank, which was heavy enough to withstand the wind." Fox, Linawik, and the handful of others with them were among the fortunate few who were able to survive the hurricane with injuries but with their lives intact. Many others were blown and washed away, unable to find anything solid on which to cling. "I'd a whole lot rather be on the battlefield amid the machine-gun fire than go through such a storm again," Linawik said. "In a battle there's always the chance the enemy has bad aim. Anyway, a person can shoot back. In a situation like the one I have just gone through, a man could do little or nothing for himself."

"When dawn broke," said survivor Oliver Griswold, "crushed and dying survivors, some gibbering, some stern-faced and dumb-tongued, saw the incredible horror of bodies lying in windrows, bodies rolling midst sunken boats, bodies hanging from trees, bodies protruding from the sand. Some had no clothes, save belts and shoes, and no skin. They had been literally sand-blasted to death."

Another Camp 1 survivor endured a smashed chest, bruised legs, and lacerations along his neck. He said he and his buddies got word after noon that a serious hurricane was closing in on them. "We were told the train would get there about 4:00 p.m., and told to get ready to leave. We waited—and the storm got worse and worse. There was timber flying through the air and the water got higher. . . . There was a big wall of water, fifteen feet high, twenty maybe. It swept over those shacks and messed them up like they were match boxes. We hung on the best way we could, to railroad ties and trees, but most of us got washed against the reefs." One of the men crushed against the reefs suffered broken bones and countless lacerations. He tried to swim against the pounding surf when a building washed on top of him, knocking one of his drowning comrades out to sea while he himself scrambled to keep his own head above water. A visitor who observed the wreckage afterward said he saw bodies with tree stumps smashed through their chests, their heads blown off, arms and legs bent in terrifying positions by debris that sliced through them like giant knives. Some of the dead looked as though mortar shells had crushed their bodies during the war. It was a vision from the nethermost pits of hell, surreal, brutal, nauseating to see up close.

The howling wind and pounding water were bad enough, but flying roofs torn off buildings, heavy timber, and other projectiles hurtling through the air claimed many of the veterans' lives and caused most of the injuries. There was no escape from flying debris, nothing to deflect the relentless onslaught of heavy objects ripping across the island like a steady barrage of cannon balls. If the churning water failed to wash the men away to their deaths, the steady flight of wood, rocks, and other material transformed into lethal weapons was enough to do the job. The lucky few survived to tell their stories, but they invariably paid a stiff price with broken bones and in many cases permanent, disfiguring injuries. In one instance the ripped-off roof of a shed served to save a vet's life. It bobbed up and down in the tumultuous sea, and he grabbed onto it like a raft. It eventually washed up on some brush along the shore, where he waited for rescuers to come to his aid around 6 p.m. on Tuesday, unable to move since he had suffered broken bones when two heavy beams crushed his legs before he found the roof.

The conditions at Camp 3 on the lower end of Lower Matecumbe Key were much the same. But a heavy tank car filled with ten thousand gallons of water, which had arrived just before the worst of the storm struck, alleviated the situation to some extent—just as a water tank at Camp 1 had provided some protection for the men there. F. L. Meyers, a Camp 3 survivor, went to see construction supervisor Sheeran just after noon on Monday to tell him the tank car had just arrived, and Sheeran advised him not to pump the water into smaller storage tanks. If the hurricane proved to be deadly, the heavy weight in the tank car would prevent it from being blown away, and the men would be assured of a sufficient supply of water. Sheeran's decision not "to pump this car resulted in the saving of some fifty lives," Meyers said. "At least fifty men were saved by clinging to this car during the storm."

Paul Pugh, the top sergeant at Camp 3 whom FERA official Ray Sheldon had informed that the vets were in no immediate danger, owed his own life to the tank car. "At 5:00 p.m. Monday," he said, "we noticed the first stiffening of the winds. The men ran for the mess hall, which rocked and tottered as the wind increased. The wind roared so we could barely hear each other speak." Then, around 7 p.m., the roof of the mess hall flew off across the island, sending men scattering toward the railroad embankment, which sat on a rise of land. "About seventy men grabbed a water tank car," Pugh recalled. "The wind gained in fury and it seemed seven thousand hells had broken loose. At the same time, the water started rising. We could see it creeping up the bank. It was hell to just hang on and not be able to do anything." In France during the war, Pugh said, at least they had an enemy to fight against. Down there in the Keys at the mercy of a monster hurricane, there was no way to fight back; they were only able to hang on in terror and wait for death to strike.

When the tidal wave washed over, the tank car held fast even as the wave ripped away sections of the railroad track. The vets hung on to the tank car with all their strength, but the surge propelled many of them into the mangrove swamp where they were battered to death among trees and rocks. The wave rose high above the land and covered the entire tank car, and the men's hands became raw from the strain of hanging on to keep from being propelled to certain death. Mercifully the wind ceased blowing as abruptly as it had roared in, the water level subsided, and the vets who had been able to cling to life looked up and saw the stars poking through the heavens. The lull lasted about forty minutes, encouraging the men with the feeling that the worst was now over. But then, without warning, the wind kicked up again and blew several of the men to their deaths. Around dawn the hurricane ended for good this time—the eastern sky glimmered orange, the wind ceased, and the water level fell. About seventy vets who had managed to hang onto the tank car through the hellish night looked around at their battered but living comrades. The rest were dead.

"There's one thing we'll always remember," Pugh said, "that's good old tank car No. 3390. If it hadn't been full of water it would have blown over too. But when the tracks on each side blew up it just sank a bit and held fast. We held fast too and we love it like a mother. I'll never see a tank car without wanting to pat it lovingly."

Other Camp 3 survivors had similar stories to tell. Camp supervisor B. E. Davis knew that the lull in the storm described by Pugh was not the end of the danger. "Having been in a hurricane before," he noted, "I knew that the storm was not over and would return from the opposite direction." The eye of the storm was deceiving. As it passed through, granting a temporary respite from wind and rain, it unleashed its full fury as it continued its counterclockwise momentum. The water tank car, plus a beer boat, a ferryboat, and dredge boat located at the camp were the only places to find some semblance of refuge. "I told the men that it was every man for himself," Davis continued. "I was going to the water tank below the camp and the men who chose to go with me to follow." The storm came in with a deafening roar. Davis watched the wall of water approach from the top of the tank car. "It was at least twenty-five feet high and completely submerged us. . . . We survivors were helpless to help one another." At daybreak it was all over, and Davis and the others who had made it through the night were able to tend to the injured vets.

The local fishermen had been through innumerable hurricanes in the past, and they provided the vets with better information than they received from the FERA officials. Thomas F. Lannon, a kitchen worker at Camp 3, said that about 8:00 a.m. on Monday "a fisherman came in, and he says that the barometer is falling; he says, 'We are going to have a hurricane here sometime today.' . . . And somebody else says 'When is the storm going to land here?' 'Well,' he says, 'I don't know, but it will be some time tonight.' So that is the first time I heard there was anything about a storm or a hurricane coming." Lannon was one of the lucky few who had made it through the night safely with Davis by clinging to the tank car when the tidal wave inundated their camp. "There was about seventy of us got on," he recalled. "And the railroad tracks alongside of it started over and went up against this tank. It stood there, didn't move no farther than the tank, or didn't knock the tank off the track. . . . And we stayed there until morning."

Camp 5 was located at the upper end of Lower Matecumbe Key. The vets living there were not quite as fortunate since there was no heavy tank car offering refuge from the worst that the hurricane threw at them. Of the 185 men billeted there only 12 survived the storm: 4 who managed to wander down to Camp 3 before the storm hit hard, and another 8 who saved themselves by clinging to a tree. Others were blown hundreds of yards out into the ocean, and many died when flying timber impaled them like spears hurled through the air. When the hurricane spent its fury at daybreak, there was "not so much as a piece of two-by-four timber left," according to one of the few survivors. "There isn't a whole piece of timber left at No. 5. Everything is twisted and torn beyond recognition."

"We were in a trap, where the camps were placed, and it was pretty bad," said another survivor. "The Gulf on one side and about thirty-five feet to the railroad tracks and the camps were in between." One of the vets who saved himself when he went down to Camp 3 said, "I stayed in [Camp 5] until it was 4:15, and I seen that there was no protection." The structures in Camp 5 were tents with canvas roofs laid on top of them with no support to withstand heavy winds, let alone a massive hurricane. It was literally a death trap for those who remained in Camp 5. He and a few of his fellow vets headed down and "made for the tank car in No. 3. And there was a little supply sergeant out of 3, had a chest of cigarettes he brought up; he says, 'If it does come, we will have cigarettes.'" When the tidal wave washed across the island, the supply sergeant lost his grip on the tank car, along with others who could not hang on. "I had hold of the running board of the tank car," said the survivor who came down from Camp 5, "and I had another buddy alongside of me, in the hair by my left hand, and I threw the guy on top of my car, pulling him on my right arm, and holding him until they pulled on me and got us up."

The unfortunate vets who stayed behind in Camp 5 were blown and washed away to their deaths, except for the handful who managed to cling to trees when the wind and tidal wave roared in. They sought shelter at first in the flimsy shacks waiting for the promised train to arrive and haul them away. But "there was no train and so we just naturally could not do anything but stand in the shanties," recalled Gus Linawik, one of the survivors. "Just like summer tents, screened in and just piling driven in for foundations." None of them had experienced a hurricane before, and they anticipated heavy wind and rain, but nothing serious enough to threaten their lives. But then the rain and wind kicked up, howling like a chorus of demons from the pit of hell, drowning out the men's voices so that they could not even hear themselves speaking.

"All our tents just shook and cracked and pulled out of the nails and pilings," said Linawik.

They ran at first to a cement cesspool to hide from the storm's wrath. They stayed inside as long as they could, until the rising water level overwhelmed the sewer pipe and threatened to drown them all inside. At that point they scurried out through the trap holes of the cesspool into the fury of the hurricane, which was raging across the island. A palmetto tree twenty to twenty-five feet high stood nearby, the only sturdy structure between the men and the churning ocean just a hundred yards away. The vets who managed to reach it scrambled as high up as they could to escape the rising water level, but the height put them more at the mercy of the howling winds. From their perches in the tree the vets could see their tents speeding by as the waves carried them out to sea. The men who remained below tried to hide behind the far bank of the railroad track, thinking they would be safe there. "But in about two minutes a big wave came," said Linawik. The men started to yell, their laments penetrating the roar of the storm. "That was the last of the hollering I heard. It washed them across the railroad and there was no protection for them on the other side—no tree or ground, just rain and sea on that side and canal on the other and the highway and railroad in the middle. That is the last time I saw about thirty of the men."

Hours later, as calm returned to the Keys, the eastern sky turned pink with the first glow of dawn, and the rescue and the clean-up work began. The hurricane had exacted its horrendous toll on the vets who had originally gathered in the nation's capital to demand the payment of the bonus that had been promised them for their service in the war. The hurricane was past, and all that remained now was the disposal of the bodies and the cover-up that followed.

EIGHTEEN

The Cover-Up

The regional and national press descended on the wreckage of human lives and property as soon as they could navigate their way to the demolished camps. "Matecumbe" the Indians who originally settled the region named the Keys that endured most of the damage. Appropriately the word was long believed to mean "place of sorrows," though that interpretation has fallen out of favor. It was there that the local Indians made their last stand against the Europeans, who eventually exterminated them. The vets met a similar fate, wiped out by a devastating force of nature rather than marauding, hostile belligerents. "Snake Creek Hotel, serving as a hospital near Veterans Camp No.1, crumbled as when a heavy-footed man steps on an eggshell," reported *Literary Digest*. "Forty or fifty people were inside. A handful escaped."

Time magazine observed, "When the Red Cross, the American Legion, the National Guard and the Coast Guard finally got into the devastated Keys over the broken bridges and wrecked roads, they found signs of slaughter worse than war. Bodies were in the trees, floating in the creeks, bogged in the mud." *Newsweek* theorized, "If a child built a tiny village of matches and paper and then aimed an electric fan and garden hose at his toy town, we would approximate the effect of last week's disaster on Upper and Lower Matecumbe Keys." *Miami Daily News* staff writer Henry G. Frampton wrote, "When a *Daily News* rescue expedition in the speed yacht *Byronic* docked at the splintered, debris-strewn wreckage of the ferry slip, it seemed impossible a living thing could have survived the cause of this sight. Yet dazed men, in tatters and blood-stained bandages, limped about, still displaying the spirit that carried them through the days of Belleau Wood and the Argonne."

Jack Bell, also writing in the *Miami Daily News*, reported, "The foliage literally has vanished, and the stubborn underbrush everywhere has been whipped to shreds. Sand filled the air, as well as rain and wind, taking the bark off all trees." Arthur Dunn, another reporter for the newspaper, opined, "An aeroplane dropping a bomb on what was this village, and on each of the three groups of veterans encamped on the keys a few miles below, would have caused just as much havoc as the recent hurricane. It is pretty much like the scenes behind the line after battle." The Red Cross did a quick survey and estimated the death toll at 446, at least 327 of them vets, and the rest civilian workers at the camps, plus wives, children, and a few grandchildren. The Florida National Guard reported that within the first few days after the hurricane struck, it had boxed and shipped 108 bodies and cremated 68, all of them identified as vets. It was impossible to come up with an exact count, but a spokesman for the Florida State Board of Health estimated that the "death toll would probably be five hundred" if it had a definitive way of checking all the details.

Factotums in the Roosevelt administration lost little time in attempting to minimize the precise numbers of dead and injured. They classified only 121 vets as officially dead, 90 as missing, and 45 as tentatively dead—presumably compared with those who were *permanently* dead. Only a bureaucratic spinmeister could conceive of such a mind-numbing category. Despite Washington's macabre distortion of facts and its attempt to whitewash the grim reality, its figures were clearly at odds with those put forth by more objective observers who witnessed the devastation in the days following the Labor Day weekend. The *Miami Herald* editorialized, "The aging veterans were shunted down to shacks. Washington was glad to be rid of their presence. . . . Now they are remembered. Now they are lauded. After they have been cremated like so much cordwood." *Newsweek* asked, "What were the veterans doing in the whirlwind's path? . . . Why didn't the FERA move them from the islands after the first hurricane warning? Why was the rescue train so late?"

The moon and sun lit up the sky over the Keys once the storm passed through. The waves calmed down again, lapping against a shore strewn with the debris of demolished shacks and tents and ripped-up foliage. Some bodies made their final journeys home, their funeral services attended by family, friends, and representatives of various veterans' organizations. On September 8 the remains of 112 vets were buried at Miami's Woodlawn Cemetery with full military honors. Twenty thousand observers congregated at Riverfront Park, where a would-be assassin had attempted to end FDR's life three years earlier, and watched navy planes drop rose petals over the ceremony. But many of the dead had been reduced to unrecognizable body parts, and these were put to the torch. While arguments raged in Washington about the precise numbers of those killed, maimed, or missing, funeral pyres glowed eerily over what was left of the Matecumbe Keys.

Washington DC assembled its heaviest guns and swung into action. FERA administrator Harry Hopkins claimed that the weather reports had been so confusing that it was impossible to predict where the hurricane would strike land. Therefore FERA officials in Florida were not at fault for any failure to get the vets out of the Keys on time. Meteorologists from the Weather Bureau, however, took issue with Hopkins' assessment, saying that the information they disseminated contained details about the intensity and direction of the hurricane three days before it hit. Red Cross admiral Cary Grayson agreed and said that the forecasts had been accurate enough to allow his organization plenty of time to prepare for any necessary rescue operations. Hopkins was chagrined enough to dispatch two of his functionaries, Aubrey Williams and Col. George E. Ijams with the Veterans Administration, to Florida to conduct their own investigation.

There was little doubt in their minds about the motivation for the task assigned to them. As Williams's assistant John J. Abt wrote afterward, "We were on a political mission to defend the administration against charges of negligence." Hopkins's main concern, of course, was to deflect any charge of responsibility for the tragic event from the organization he headed—and from the administration in general. Col. Lawrence Westbrook, who reported directly to Hopkins, telephoned Ghent and demanded to know, "What was our justification for putting the camps there? Could we be criticized for putting camps on the Keys?"

"Yes and no. It is a debatable question," Ghent replied.

One can almost see Westbrook squirming for something a bit more definitive than that. "If it is debatable, we could be criticized?"

"Yes."

"On what grounds?"

"Isolation," Ghent answered, a bit cryptically.

"You have no communication with the camps?"

"We have one telegraph office out of there but the facilities are not good."

"What kind of work were they doing?" Westbrook sounded more and more exasperated. "Work that would stand up and be a credit to the administration?"

"I wouldn't like to pass [comment] on that. That is a difference of opinion," said Ghent, who offered no explanation why his subordinates could not reach him by telephone during the most critical period of the weekend. Ghent's fallback excuse was that no one knew for sure until 1:00 or 1:30 p.m. Monday that the hurricane was closing in so rapidly, with reports indicating it was still a couple of hundred miles away. When he finally ordered a train down to the Keys he fully believed it would arrive in time to haul the vets out of harm's way.

Westbrook was in the hot seat as he scrambled to come up with a viable story that the administration could offer to the public. Marvin McIntyre, one of Roosevelt's secretaries, telephoned Westbrook on September 4, just two days after the hurricane hit the Keys. McIntyre was in full damage-control mode as he told Westbrook that the administration was sending Gen. Frank T. Hines, VA administrator, and another aide, Steven Early, "to the camps down there, about taking care of the injured and arranging about funeral services and all that. You don't mind, do you?" he asked Westbrook.

"No, not at all. I will talk to our man down there and tell him to report to whoever the General sends down there. . . . He said he believed three hundred, at least, were lost. Another hundred were injured, the remainder surviving. They are evacuating these people rapidly."

The numbers put McIntyre into a panic. They were far higher than those released by the administration and still fell short of those reported by the various rescue organizations.

"My God!" McIntyre exploded. "Between us, Colonel, there is no blame that can be attached to our administration or to your office, is there?"

"No, it is just a catastrophe."

"Nobody suggested there was any undue risk or anything?"

"No," Westbrook replied glumly, without conviction.

Westbrook got the imperious Julius Stone on the phone, the virtual dictator of Key West whom Hemingway wanted to throttle, but Stone offered no help whatsoever. "The fact of the matter is those fellows had a very bad name," Westbrook said to Stone.

"Who had a bad name?"

"The veterans. There will be some remarks made at headquarters that we would not want to repeat over the telephone."

"What are they?" asked Stone.

"If the thing had to happen, it might just as well take them," Westbrook replied, callously suggesting that the vets were a seedy lot who deserved the fate they suffered. But Stone refused to take the bait.

"Who would say that?"

"Everyone I have heard talk about the accident." Westbrook was twisting in the wind, now reducing the most horrendous natural disaster in recent American history, and its tragic consequences, to a mere "accident."

Westbrook was at a loss about where to turn next. The administration was determined to come up with an accurate body count that would not portray the government as blatantly attempting to whitewash its role in the affair. Two of Roosevelt's secretaries phoned Charles R. Forbes, director of the Veterans Bureau who had been found guilty of pilfering funds from the bureau during the Harding administration, to get a precise reading on the figures. How many have we lost, they wanted to know. The latest estimate was a minimum of three hundred vets, possibly as many as five hundred. "Are they getting more bodies?" they asked Forbes.

"Yes. That condition is terrible," he said.

"Are we being blamed a lot?"

"No," Forbes said. So far, the press had been focusing on the train situation rather than the government's negligence in not taking appropriate action sooner.

But the press coverage changed drastically overnight, as it turned out, when the *Washington Post* blasted the administration in a scathing editorial on September 7. "There is considerable evidence to support [the] conclusion that 'gross negligence somewhere' was responsible. Indeed, the negligence seems to trace far back of the hurricane to the casual policy of assembling 'bonus marchers' in isolated and semi-secret concentration camps. . . . Contrary to its usual practice, the FERA has not publicized this enterprise. Veterans who came to Washington demanding immediate payment of the bonus have been quietly shipped to remote localities under conditions which approximate paying them not to create disturbances. . . . Apparently, the only reason for creating these special 'rehabilitation camps' in the South was to avoid the political embarrassment of further mass lobbying for the bonus." The editorial concluded with the statement that a policy that intended to hide the issue from public view "is one in which we can find nothing to admire."

Six days after the editorial appeared, Williams and Ijams released the report of their own investigation. The bulk of it was a recital of the known facts about the timing of the hurricane's arrival, and the request for a train to make the journey to the Keys in time to evacuate the men from their camps. Regarding the issue of using trucks to get them out earlier, the report stated that such an alternative plan would have been "extremely dangerous" given the condition of the equipment and the difficulty in locating "available driving personnel." Therefore "no one was at fault for the tragedy. There had been no negligence or mistaken judgment. It was rather, the result of an 'act of God.'"

No sooner was the report released when an organization of Florida ministers professed outrage that the government would blame God for its own incompetence. The government was engaging in "a deliberate attempt to whitewash known facts, ignore the inefficiency and irresponsibility of those in charge," according to the Miami Ministerial Association. Secular forces also weighed in against the report issued by Williams and Ijams. The Veterans of Foreign Wars accused the government of whitewashing its own "negligence and poor judgment." The Florida state commander of the vfw called upon Roosevelt "to direct an immediate, thorough and impartial investigation to fix the responsibility for apparent negligence of those in authority, and that the negligent parties, if any, be suitably punished."

But FDR wasn't about to fall into that trap. He instead directed Harry Hopkins to shift the blame for the disaster to another responsible party than the federal government. Hopkins complied by claiming that since the vets were sent there to work on the Overseas Bridge Project, they were technically in the care of Florida Emergency Relief Administration, not FERA. And so the cover-up and whitewash continued, with the federal government refusing to assume responsibility under any circumstances, and other organizations that the government pointed to demanding that Washington own up to a tragedy of its own making. Finally the government responded in a way that only it can, by throwing some money at it. After months and years of refusing to allocate a single dime to alleviate the plight of the vets, Hopkins released a special FERA grant of $200,000 for hurricane relief work, implicitly acknowledging that FERA had some sort of an obligation to take responsibility for the catastrophe in the Keys.

The *Miami Herald* caustically commented: "They were shifted around. They marched on Washington. They asked for the bonus and were given the 'bums' rush.'" The government had billions for boondoggling, aesthetic dancing, art, culture, worthless canals, and schemes without end, the paper maintained, but it had no money for those who defended the nation in combat. "When $200,000 can be thrust out in a moment, after it is too late to help the dead, it ought to be able to do something for the living." The national commander of the vfw, James E. Van Zandt, noted that the bonuses would now have to be paid to the families of the men who were killed in the Keys. He found it "ironic" that those who had lost their lives in the hurricane had made their own bonus certificates immediately payable by the mere fact of their deaths.

The jockeying for credibility spurred the politicians out of their stupor and into action. fera announced that it would discontinue the practice of sending vets to isolated locations like the Keys. And several congressmen announced at a vfw convention in New Orleans that they would reconsider new legislation to pay the bonuses when Congress reconvened in January 1936. Left unsaid was that 1936 was an election year, with FDR running for reelection and scores of representatives and senators scurrying out on the campaign trails to reassure their constituencies that they deserved to retain their seats.

At the same time fera continued its insistence that the blame for the disastrous situation in the Keys belonged elsewhere, presumably with the Florida Emergency Relief Administration rather than with its own officials on the scene. But that position was untenable. Even Ijams dissented, writing later, "Colonel Sheeran's actions, along with other evidence of danger, should have caused the responsible officials to make definite arrangements to be ready to move the men in the event the danger became imminent. The evidence is clear that definite arrangements should have been made for the evacuation immediately after the 10:00 a.m. advisory, Sunday, September 1st." Sheeran was the superintendent of construction of the Overseas Bridge Project, who had complained about fera locking up the keys to the trucks that could have transported the vets out earlier, before the roads became impassable.

In the end fera succumbed to reality and accepted the incontrovertible facts that were now visible for everyone to see. It accepted the conclusion reached by D. W. Kennamer of the va, which put the bulk of the blame on Ghent and Ray Sheldon, who was in charge of the camps in Ghent's absence. Kennamer concluded, "Mr. Ghent and Mr. Sheldon failed to do many things prudent persons would have done. . . . Mr. Ghent and Mr. Sheldon did not communicate with each other from 4:50 p.m. Sunday afternoon until 1:37 p.m. Monday afternoon. . . . Mr. Ghent did not keep long-distance advised as to where he could be reached at all times Monday morning, September 2nd, and it took an hour and fifty-five minutes to get him on the phone when he was much needed."

An American Legion report that National Commander Ray Murphy sent to President Roosevelt said much the same thing as Kennamer's statement. When it hit FDR's desk on November 2, 1935, the president delivered a note to Hopkins asking, "Will you and General Hines talk this over and let me know what you think we should reply to Ray Murphy?" Gen. Frank T. Hines was the VA administrator whom the administration had dispatched to the Keys in the days following the hurricane. Hines recommended that the president acknowledge receipt of the American Legion report without commenting in detail on it. Hines was nothing if not a team player, whose main interest was protecting the president from any embarrassment over the disaster. The 1936 election would swing into full gear in a matter of months, and Hines put on a full-court press with the American Legion to convey FDR's "wishes in the matter," namely that the president would appreciate it if the Legion let the matter drop quietly until the election was over. Afterward the administration would resolve the bonus issue in a way that would benefit the veterans and the Legion, which supported them.

NINETEEN

The Vets Finally Get Their Money

B ut the American Legion and the other veterans' organizations, including the VFW and the Disabled American Veterans, were not inclined to wait a full year until after the 1936 elections to press for a new bonus bill for the vets. The American Legion published the report of its own investigation in the January 1936 issue of *American Legion Magazine*, castigating FERA officials for their negligence in the Keys as the hurricane gathered its forces. The veterans' groups worked together for the first time since the end of the war to draft a bill acceptable to the vets and their organizations. They received the support of Father Charles E. Coughlin, whose widely heard radio program had great influence across the country. He had long championed the vets by urging the government to pay the bonuses, and on January 5, 1936, he told his listeners, "My friends, I have no fear of being a false prophet when I tell you that, without doubt, this so-called soldiers' bonus bill will be paid in the immediate future. Our long battle, in which I am happy to have played a part, is won. Victory is ours!"

The House passed a new bill called the Adjusted Compensation Payment Act by a lopsided margin of 346 to 59 on January 10, and the Senate followed suit on January 20 with a vote of 74 to 16. The new version differed from the original legislation put forward by Patman through its various incarnations. It offered to pay the bonus in the form of fifty-dollar bonds that the vets could redeem on June 15, or else hold to maturity on June 15, 1945, carrying an interest rate of 3 percent, a higher rate than was available from the banks. Naturally the administration hoped that most of the vets would opt for the latter alternative rather than raid the treasury by demanding immediate cash payments.

Roosevelt did not want to appear as though he were caving in to pressure and changing course in midstream, so he vetoed the bill without ceremony, knowing that Congress had enough votes to override him, which both houses did by January 27. "My convictions are as impelling today as they were then. Therefore I cannot change them," FDR said as the bill became law. The issue finally was off the table for good now, he hoped—although the extra cash in the pockets of the vets benefited him more than anyone—allowing him to discuss other weighty and less emotional matters as he campaigned for reelection. As it turned out the great majority of veterans decided to cash their bonds in early, despite recommendations from the veterans' organizations that they hold the certificates to maturity—something they told Roosevelt they would do when Congress passed the bill. The vets redeemed 80 percent of the outstanding bonds within the next twelve months—more than half of them during the first two weeks—costing the federal government more than $1.5 billion.

Each vet received an average of $583, roughly 33 percent of the typical Depression-era income of about $1,500 a year. The highest payment to any single vet amounted to $1,585, while others who had borrowed against their certificates received smaller payments. This came at a time when working-class Americans could cover their expenses on $30 a month. Hearst worked in tandem with the veterans' organizations in setting up bonus payment centers at Hearst newspaper offices and VFW and American Legion posts throughout the country, where the vets could receive help in filling out the forms to collect their bonuses. Employees of the VA, the Treasury Department, and the Post Office worked overtime to get the forms printed and distributed in order to put the issue to rest, and keep it off the headlines, before the campaign entered the homestretch. The government had rarely worked at such speed and so efficiently. Vets who had their forms verified on Tuesday, June 16, had checks to deposit or cash in at the banks two days later. Their mood and that of the country at large was nothing less than euphoric.

"They're really DOUGHboys today!" blared a headline in the

Bridgeport Post. Not to be outdone, the *New York Times* had a little fun with the story when it reported that a bunch of vets in Sing Sing prison would receive $50,000 in bonus payments. Merchants and shopkeepers across the nation prepared for a temporary bonanza, opening their doors to welcome vets who were in the market to buy everything from underwear to automobiles as soon as they got their cash. The vets spent about 80 percent of the face value of their bonds during the first few months after they cashed them in and collected the 3 percent interest on the remainder. The interest rate was a half percent higher than the banks paid, and it could only be collected if the vets hung on to them for at least the next twelve months.

The economy experienced a temporary boost as a result, especially in 1936 when the vets collected their bonuses and again in 1937 when they cashed in most of the remaining 20 percent. The vets needed all the money they could lay their hands on for necessities after years of deprivation, but most of them were careful not to cash in more than they needed since the interest on the balance was attractive at the time. But the lift it gave to the economy was short-lived. The Great Depression ground on relentlessly, with millions of Americans out of work and the prospects of finding employment diminishing every day. The bonus represented a respite for the veterans of the Great War, but it would take another war on a larger scale to spur the government into passing a bill that provided a long-term safety net for veterans returning home to a shaky economy after the ravages of World War II.

For Patman the passage of the bonus bill was especially sweet. He had been the veterans' principal ally in Congress, and he had fought long and hard for its passage and expended a great amount of political capital in the struggle. "Mr. Speaker," he addressed his colleagues the day the bill became law, "today ends a seven-year fight that commenced May 28, 1929." Patman was not a one-issue representative, however. The self-styled populist served in Congress from 1929 until 1976, fighting many battles along the way. He attacked the big banks before it became popular to do so, and he was a leading critic of the Federal Reserve system and its control of monetary policy. One of his more memorable encounters took place in 1972, when he bludgeoned Federal Reserve chairman Arthur Burns with the loaded question, "Can you give me any reason why you should not be in the penitentiary?"

That same year he sponsored a committee to investigate the Watergate scandal that toppled President Richard M. Nixon from his paranoid regency. Mortality finally caught up with Patman on March 7, 1976, when a losing bout with pneumonia claimed the life of the eighty-two-year-old firebrand in Bethesda, Maryland. His remains were interred in Hillcrest Cemetery in Texarkana, Texas, his home state.

Work continued feverishly down in the Keys to rebuild the road connecting the span across Matecumbe Key all the way to Key West, which the construction crews completed on March 29, 1937, using materials salvaged from the wreckage. Henry Flagler's railroad tracks lay twisted in ruins for some time after the hurricane ripped them from their beds; the engineers considered it unwise to restore them considering the ferocity of the storms that Mother Nature launched at will across the Keys whenever the mood struck her. Several piers remained after the storm, visible from the Gulf of Mexico side of the island, squatting there like gray coffins jutting over the water. A structure that remained upright was a stone angel with a broken wing. The hurricane-force winds lifted it from its mooring in Pioneer Cemetery and dropped it on an old highway that no longer exists. Local residents transported it to a plot of land around Cheeka Lodge, near a monument marking a mass grave. Close by is a large stone with an engraving of a palm tree swaying in the wind, which stands guard over the ashes of many of the hurricane's victims. On November 17, 1937, the WPA designed and erected a memorial crypt off the main road in Islamorada containing the remains of an estimated 189 hurricane victims, 128 of them veterans. President Roosevelt sent a telegram to be read at the memorial service.

The Upper Keys Historical Society presided over the monument and accepted the ashes of survivors that family members had sent down during the next forty years. But gradually over the decades developers built commercial structures and homes on the spit of land surrounding the memorial crypt, obscuring the memorial and relegating it to little more than a curiosity on the side of the road for those interested enough to visit it. Disaster struck again in 1960 when another hurricane, this one called Donna, came roaring across the Keys, causing significant property damage and loss of life. Still the development continued in Donna's wake as commercial interests took priority over common sense. "In the 25 years between Key disasters," reported Stephen Trumbull in the *Miami Herald*, "the few feeble voices for restrictions have been shouted down by the builders of shoddy if sometimes showy houses—and the fillers of tidal mangrove swamps for sponge-like subdivisions barely above normal high tides."

As the nation geared up for a new war in Europe the Roosevelt administration worked overtime in rebuilding the country's military might, which had deteriorated considerably since the First World War. FDR at first dragged his feet about being drawn into another foreign conflict, caught in the middle between forces calling for the country to come to the assistance of European allies besieged by Nazi and Fascist aggression in Europe and Asia on one hand, and isolationist sentiment spearheaded by Charles Lindbergh's America First movement on the other. Public opinion was also on the side of neutrality at the time, with a pre-war Gallup poll showing that 88 percent of Americans opposed U.S. involvement in the European war. American citizens, for the most part, realized that U.S. participation in World War I had not resulted in a better world, and in a 1940 off-year election speech Roosevelt stated, "I have said this before, but I shall say it again and again and again: Your boys are not going to be sent into any foreign wars."

Shortly after the November elections, however, in January 1941, the president dispatched his closest advisor, Harry Hopkins, to meet British prime minister Winston Churchill in London. Hopkins allegedly told Churchill that FDR was determined to enter the war if England could not go it alone. "Make no mistake about it," Hopkins said to Churchill. "He has sent me here to tell you that at all costs and by all means he will carry you through, no matter what happens to him—there is nothing he will not do so far as he has human power." William Stevenson noted in *A Man Called Intrepid* that American-British military staff talks began that same month under "utmost secrecy." Robert Sherwood, a biographer friendly to the Roosevelt administration, wrote, "If the isolationists had known the full extent of the secret alliance between the United States and Britain, their demands for impeachment would have rumbled like thunder throughout the land." But by this time Lindbergh had already discredited his America First movement by refusing to recant vitriolic antisemitic statements he had made as he toured the country to bolster support for isolationism. He had long been suspected of harboring pro-Nazi sympathies, and his latest utterances only reinforced his true political views.

Tyler Kent, a code clerk at the U.S. embassy in London, discovered secret dispatches between Roosevelt and Churchill revealing that FDR was determined to engage America in the war on Britain's behalf to keep it from falling to the Nazis. Kent smuggled some of the documents out of the embassy, hoping to alert the American public, but when he was caught with his hand in the proverbial cookie jar he was tried in a British court and confined to prison until the end of the war. The Japanese sneak attack— later softened to "surprise attack" for the sake of diplomacy—on Pearl Harbor, however, decisively ended the impasse. There was no possibility of remaining neutral after the destruction of our naval forces in Hawaii on December 7, 1941. The government set up the machinery for drafting millions of American youth into the armed forces, retooled the country's factories to churn out airplanes, tanks, bombs, and other materiel, and prepared to launch its renewed military strength onto the battlefields of Europe, North Africa, and Asia.

Roosevelt had learned his lesson well about how to treat veterans when they returned from active duty after a war. He embraced the views expressed in a congressional report released in February 1944: "Handled with competence, our adjustment, after the war is won, should be an adventure in prosperity. Our soldiers will not be let down. They are our chief concern. No pressure group of self-seekers will take our thoughts from them." Before the soldiers who fought in World War II returned home, Washington politicians and various groups across the nation started to beat the drums for new legislation designed to assure that veterans would not suffer the same fate as the vets did a generation earlier. But it was not all clear sailing. Several institutions and a coterie of racist politicians expressed their opposition to any such legislation even before it assumed its final form.

Dixiecrat and avowed white supremacist Rep. John Elliott Rankin, chairman of the powerful House Committee on World War Veterans' Legislation, opposed any bill that gave black troops separation bonuses equal to those paid to white veterans. The extra cash, he maintained, would only encourage them to avoid working until the money ran out. *The Nation* magazine lambasted Rankin's racist views as "a rancorous expression of all that is most vicious in our national life." The National Association of Manufacturers, which had opposed the bonus payment to the vets of the last war, came out in favor of a "separation payment" of $550 for each vet, payable in six monthly installments, plus a one-hundred-dollar clothing allowance. Several politicians, including Rep. Lawrence H. Smith of Wisconsin and Rep. Edith Nourse Rogers of Massachusetts, did not think any bonus would be enough to address the needs of vets returning to a post-war economy, and they agitated instead for an array of benefits including free college tuition and vocational training.

The war put eleven million Americans in uniform. More than four hundred thousand were killed, most of them in action; others died as prisoners of war and from an assortment of diseases. Tens of thousands of others were maimed, and thousands more were listed as missing in action. The great fear was that several million young men would be entering a bloated labor force at the end of the war, driving the unemployment rate above its already high level. A bill that gave them free tuition would divert a million or more of them onto college campuses and keep them off the labor market for a year or more while the economy returned to a peacetime footing. Some educational institutions opposed any such legislation, fearing that their campuses would be inundated with returning vets, but the government alleviated their concerns when it said it would revamp military bases as campuses for the vets as part of its program to stave off a new depression and create a latter-day class of leaders for the country.

Congress entertained 243 separate bills in 1943, ranging from a flat bonus payment for the vets to a comprehensive assortment of educational and vocational training benefits. The total cost for accommodating so many former infantrymen, sailors, and airmen as they transitioned to civilian life would be enormous, but it would be more productive and no more costly than simply supplying them with welfare checks. The Department of Labor estimated that as many as fifteen million more Americans would be on the dole unless something was done to prevent it from happening beforehand. Our veterans "must not be demobilized into an environment of inflation and unemployment, to a place on a breadline or on a corner selling apples," FDR told the country on July 28, 1943. "We must, this time, have plans ready."

The American Legion entered the breach on December 15, 1943, with a program to consolidate all the proposals before Congress and draft its own version of a new veterans' bill. Harry W. Colmery, a former national commander of the American Legion and former Republican national chairman, wrote the first draft, jotting down ideas on stationery and a napkin at Washington's Mayflower Hotel. Edith Nourse Rogers also pitched in, earning her the soubriquet "the Mother of the GI Bill."

It served as a blueprint for the legislation that eventually worked its way through the political sausage grinder. The proposed law called for six basic benefits: education and vocational training; low-cost loans to buy a home, a farm, or a business; unemployment insurance guaranteeing twenty dollars a month for a year; job-search assistance; construction of new VA hospitals; and a military review of dishonorable discharges. Initially labeled the

American Legion Omnibus Bill, the final version passed by Congress carried the official name Servicemen's Readjustment Act of 1944, commonly known as the GI Bill of Rights. The Senate voted in favor unanimously 50 to 0 on March 24, and the House (after much wrangling from Rankin, who eventually caved in to pressure from the press, which called him "G.I. Enemy No. 1") passed it with its own lopsided vote of 387 to 0 on May 18.

But the struggle wasn't over. When a conference committee debated the differences between the Senate and House versions, the bill almost died. The Senate members agreed on one particular provision, but the House delegation split 3–3 and the committee chairman refused to vote a sick member's authorized proxy. The politicos finally saved the bill when House members rushed Rep. John Gibson from Georgia to cast a tie-breaking vote. The Senate approved the final form of the bill on June 12, and the House followed on June 13. President Roosevelt signed it into law on June 22, surrounded by five American Legionnaires and several members of Congress, including a smiling Edith Nourse Rogers and a grim-faced John Elliott Rankin, with his arms crossed over his chest as he stood behind Roosevelt.

TWENTY

The Battle Continues

Benefits became available to veterans who had been on active duty during the war years for at least 120 days as long as they had not received dishonorable discharges. Even those who had not been in combat were included. By most accounts the bill proved to be a huge success on several fronts. An estimated eleven million homes of thirteen million built in the 1950s were financed with GI Bill loans. Peter Drucker claimed, "The GI Bill of Rights—and the enthusiastic response to it on the part of America's veterans—signaled the shift to the knowledge society. Future historians may consider it the most important event of the 20th century."

Tom Brokaw regarded it as "a brilliant and enduring commitment to the nation's future." Michael J. Bennett sounded the most ominous alarm of all when he commented, "After World War I, virtually every belligerent nation other than Britain and the United States had its government overthrown by its veterans." It didn't happen in the United States after World War II, according to Bennett, because the GI Bill of Rights enabled "more than one-fourth of the civilian work force" to make a successful transition to a peacetime economy. The implication was that the country got lucky in the years following the First World War. With revolution erupting on the left and right throughout much of Europe, American vets demonstrated peacefully for a redress of their own grievances—only to be routed from their campsites by the megalomaniac Gen. Douglas MacArthur and his hyperactive subordinate, Maj. George Patton, acting at the behest of the ill-fated Hoover administration.

By 1956, 2.2 million veterans had used the GI Bill's education benefits to attend colleges or universities, and an additional 5.6 million took advantage of training programs for various trades. The bill became a model for others established in several countries, including Canada, which achieved similar postwar economic results. But, as is the case with any new programs implemented by the government, the bill gave birth to scam artists looking to fleece the beneficiaries out of their grant money. New "colleges," "universities," and "vocational training schools" sprouted overnight, offering useless certificates and diplomas to vets for lower tuition than they would pay at bona fide institutions. The government is notoriously lax about oversight and protecting honest citizens against fraud. The situation has not improved over the decades. As late as April 27, 2012, President Barack Obama signed an executive order to ensure that predatory merchants did not target vets with shoddy products and bogus educational benefits.

For the most part, however, the GI Bill and its offshoots have benefited millions of American veterans. A returning World War II vet named Don A. Balfour was the first to take advantage of the 1944 GI Bill when he became a student at George Washington University. The government imposed a military draft in 1940, which remained in effect until 1973 when President Richard M. Nixon rescinded it. As a result about one-third of the population encompassing veterans and their dependents became eligible for benefits. The GI Bill spawned new versions of the original legislation in the years following the war, as the government thought it necessary to make the draft more palatable to those who were opposed to serving in the military. During the presidential election of 1952, which swept Dwight D. Eisenhower into the White House, Congress passed the Veterans' Adjustment Act of 1952, which Truman signed into law on July 16, 1952. The clone of the GI Bill offered benefits to veterans of the Korean War who had served for more than ninety days and received honorable discharges.

For Korean War vets returning home following combat duty in a hostile environment halfway around the globe, the new legislation granted unemployment compensation amounting to $26 a week for twenty-six weeks, with the states administering the disbursement of benefits. The federal government sweetened the pot by providing the vets of the Korean War with state and federal benefits, the latter kicking in when the state benefits had run their course. A notable difference between the 1944 GI Bill and the 1952 Veterans' Adjustment Act was that tuition fees were no longer paid directly to the educational institutions but rather to the veterans, who each received a fixed monthly sum of $110 to pay for tuition, fees, books, and living expenses. A House Select Committee on Veterans' Affairs made the change after it uncovered numerous instances of institutions overcharging the government on tuition rates, which amounted to defrauding of the government under the original GI Bill.

In its effort to eliminate the abuses, however, the federal government created a new set of complications. By the time the program expired in January 1965 only half of the Korean vets used their stipends for educational purposes. The rest used the money for ordinary living expenses, or else to buy homes, cars, and other big-ticket items. Again the government's oversight procedure proved to be woefully inadequate. President Eisenhower had been opposed to continuing the expensive array of veterans' benefits during peacetime once he had successfully ended the war in Korea after taking office in 1953. But he was unable to get the Congress to go along with dismantling the latest version of the GI Bill, since it was enormously popular with their constituents back home.

In the 1960s, however, with a new war erupting in Vietnam and Lyndon B. Johnson in command of the White House, the president and the Congress decided to rejigger the GI Bill of Rights yet again. LBJ had originally opposed a separate bill for the vets, figuring that the various "Great Society" programs he had rapidly rushed into law would take care of them. However, he too had to confront political reality and go along with yet a new reincarnation of a veterans' bill, the Veterans' Readjustment Benefits Act of 1966, which he signed with great fanfare on March 3, 1966.

"The Congress has passed this legislation," LBJ said as he faced the cameras with a coterie of political allies lined up behind him. "It passed it without a single dissenting vote. In doing so, it said:

We will support these men who are defending our freedom to debate, who are joining in a most historic protest for their country—a protest against tyranny, a protest against aggression, and a protest against misery."

Almost immediately some dissenting voices on Capitol Hill charged that the bill did not go far enough. At first single veterans who had served more than 180 days and received an honorable discharge got only $100 a month, which had to cover their tuition and all of their expenses. Most analysts found this amount enough to pay for books and minor fees but not enough to live on or attend college full time. In particular, veterans of the Vietnam War objected to the idea that the bill did not provide them with the same educational opportunities as their World War II predecessors. As a result, during the early years of the program only about 25 percent of Vietnam veterans took advantage of their education benefits.

Over the next few years Congress made several successful attempts to raise veterans' benefits. It increased the monthly stipend to $130 in 1967, then lifted it in stages to $175 in 1970, $220 in 1972, $270 in 1974, $292 in 1976, and $311 in 1977. As the monthly checks went up the vets responded by taking advantage of the educational benefits in increasing numbers. In 1976, ten years after the first veterans became eligible under the latest bill, a growing number of Vietnam-era veterans enrolled in colleges and universities. By the end of the program 6.8 million out of 10.3 million eligible vets—roughly two-thirds of them—were using their monthly checks for higher education, more than any previous generation of veterans.

When Nixon ended the military draft in 1973 and moved to an all-volunteer force, the benefits remained in effect, partly as an inducement for the youth of America to sign up for military duty under the so-called Veterans Educational Assistance Program, or veap when the acronym entered the language. veap was popular mostly with working-class Americans, since it departed from previous veterans' bills in that the government contributed to the money the vets spent on higher education at a two-to-one rate.

Vets could contribute up to $100 a month to a limit of $2,700, with the government kicking in double that amount for three years. To qualify for VEAP a veteran had to serve for more than 180 days and receive an honorable discharge, an inducement that persuaded about seven hundred thousand of the nation's youth to put their lives and limbs on the line to fight their country's endless wars on foreign soil.

VEAP turned out to be a prelude to a new bill ushered into existence by Mississippi Democratic congressman Gillespie V. "Sonny" Montgomery in 1985, which essentially expanded on the legislation that came before it. Montgomery had seen action as a second lieutenant in World War II and then in Korea, after rising to the rank of major general in his state's National Guard. Popular with voters in his district, he was elected to a seat in the House which he occupied from 1967 through 1997. He not only sponsored the Montgomery GI Bill, but he also played a key role in establishing the Department of Veterans Affairs as a cabinet-level position.

Montgomery's bill replaced VEAP for vets who served in the military after July 1, 1985. It gave vets the option of forfeiting $100 per month from their first year of pay in return for greater tuition allowances, on-the-job training, Internet education, and a host of other benefits. One of Montgomery's goals, which he shared with President George W. Bush with whom he played paddleball, was to elevate the quality of volunteers who signed up for military duty. They were both concerned that the number of volunteers had begun to tail off, and many of those who did sign up seemed to have little appetite for educational pursuits, which left them unprepared for the evolving technology- and information-based economy. A return home to vanishing manufacturing jobs in industries that were falling by the wayside only insured that the vets would become wards of the government down the road.

Finally the government secured the rights of American servicemen and servicewomen following a struggle that spanned the better part of a century. But the battle was not yet over. With the United States in a permanent state of war since the events of

September 11, 2001, veterans returning from battle zones today with their limbs blasted away are still fighting for adequate health care and job training. The American Empire faces challenges as never before in its 240-year history, much as the Roman Empire did when it began to crumble 1,600 years ago, unable to pay its far-flung legions for their service in protecting Rome against the barbarian onslaught from the northern wilderness.

Even today the media remind us of examples of the shoddy treatment an obtuse government inflicts on veterans who return home following years of combat in the Middle East and other global hot spots. In an age in which top financial executives are allowed to keep their $100 million compensation packages after bringing the global economy to its knees, as they did in 2007 and 2008, the Pentagon has attempted to "claw back" fifteen to twenty thousand bonus dollars from veterans. The government paid the money to entice the vets to reenlist and go back into the war zones when it found itself short of troops to fight the ongoing wars in Afghanistan and Iraq. About ten thousand soldiers, many of whom had already served several combat tours, had received the reenlistment bonuses if they agreed to return to action. Suddenly, in 2016, the Pentagon claimed that it had paid the bonuses erroneously, and if the vets refused to give back the money voluntarily it would pile fines, interest charges, tax liens, wage garnishments, and other penalties on top of the bonuses they had received.

"This is a national issue and affects all states," said Andreas Mueller, the chief of federal policy for the California National Guard. Supposedly the government would earmark the bonuses for soldiers in high-demand assignments like intelligence operations and for noncommissioned officers who were needed in units about to be deployed to Iraq and Afghanistan. But a lack of proper oversight resulted in bonuses paid upfront to many troops recruited by National Guard officials under pressure to meet enlistment targets.

"We say 'government' because it is unclear which branch of that hydra-headed beast is guilty of executing, or not taking the necessary steps to remedy, the fundamental injustice," the *Pitts-*

burgh Post-Gazette editorialized on October 27, 2016. "Parties involved include the Department of Defense, the Department of the Army, the National Guard Bureau, the California National Guard, and, ultimately, the only body probably able to clean up the affair definitely, the U.S. Congress."

Susan Haley, a former army master sergeant who fought in Afghanistan in 2008, was just one of thousands of troops ensnared in the bureaucratic nightmare. She sent the government $650 a month—a quarter of her family's total income—to pay off $20,500 in bonus money the Pentagon claimed she received fraudulently.

"I feel totally betrayed," she said. She had served in the army, along with her husband and son, for twenty-six years. The money the Pentagon was clawing back from her amounted to less than one-tenth of one percent of the $30 million departure package Jamie Dimon received when Sandy Weill fired him at Citigroup in 2000. Dimon and Weill were the two banking executives most responsible for engineering the dismantling of Glass-Steagall, the law that had been in place for sixty years separating various banking functions.

"At the end of the day, the soldiers ended up paying the highest price," said Maj. Gen. Matthew Beevers. To billionaires like Weill and Dimon, $20,000 is little more than pocket lint. To vets like Haley and thousands more like her that sum is a crushing burden to pay back. By the end of 2016 the Pentagon had succeeded in recapturing a grand total of $22 million from the beleaguered vets, a year's pay for Dimon and many of his cohorts.

During the bizarre 2016 presidential race both major party candidates promised to rectify the bonus situation shortly after one of them took the oath of office in January 2017. The greater likelihood is that the new administration will do what previous regimes have done before them: relegate the issue to the bottom of its laundry list of priorities as it grapples with tax and healthcare reform and other headline-grabbing topics. Throughout human history nations have dangled promising enticements before able-bodied youths whom they need to serve as fodder for their military adventures in strange new lands. Once their governments no longer need their services, the general citizenry would just as soon avert its collective gaze from the blasted limbs and body bags, unpleasant reminders of just how horrific the inhumanity of war truly is. And the governments that send them off to fight the latest battles are all too eager to oblige their constituents, all too anxious to bury the promises they made to the vets along with the bits and pieces of their wrecked lives.

ACKNOWLEDGMENTS

I am indebted to the authors who tackled this subject before me and stimulated my own interest in it as we approach the hundredth anniversary of the armistice that ended the First World War. The primary works cited here include *The Bonus Army: An American Epic* by Paul Dickson and Thomas B. Allen; *The President and Protest: Hoover, Conspiracy, and the Bonus Riot* by Donald J. Lisio; *The Bonus March: An Episode of the Great Depression* by Roger Daniels; *FDR and the Bonus Marchers, 1933–1935* by Gary Dean Best; and *B.E.F.: The Whole Story of the Bonus Army* by W. W. Waters as told to William C. White. Each of these books covers the tragic events from the end of the war until 1935 from a different perspective and serves to shed light on one of the sorriest episodes in American history, which has been all but hidden from public view.

The works mentioned above stimulated me to embark on my own research campaign, which led me down diverse paths for two years as I discovered scores of other books and countless articles that had touched on the subject in some detail over the years. A complete bibliography follows this section. Especially helpful were records archived by the U.S. Department of Veterans Affairs, the National Archives and Records Administration, the Library of Congress, and other institutions. The personnel and administrators I contacted there were invariably cooperative.

Many thanks go to my daughter Christine Tuccille Merry, proprietor of Merryhaus Design, who has been an emissary and surrogate for this project every step along the way. Her efforts in researching photographs and securing the rights for their inclusion in the book, promoting the project on social media and other venues, establishing a title-specific webpage, and helping in other ways have been invaluable to me.

This book would not have seen the light of day were it not for my agent, Linda D. Konner, who encouraged me to move forward with it from the time I first mentioned it to her. No writer has ever had better representation. Many thanks go to my editor Tom Swanson. Ernest Hemingway once said that no good writers would need an editor if they had the leisure to wait five years from the time they finished until they published a book. But deadlines are rarely stretched out quite that far. Tom served me well from the time I submitted the book until it was ready for publication, and I am indebted to him for that. Thanks also to the rest of the dedicated staff at the University of Nebraska Press, who ushered my manuscript from the typed page through the final stages of production and promotion.

I owe a great deal to my wife of more than half a century, Marie Winkler Tuccille, who has supported me in more ways than I can count. Marie put up with my compulsive work schedule during the three or more years I researched and wrote the book. She has been a true partner in every sense of the word. Her patience and understanding mean more to me than I could ever express.

If I have left anyone out who has been helpful to me, I apologize. I truly appreciate all contributions and take full responsibility for any errors that may have found their way into the final printed pages of *The War Against the Vets*.

NOTES

Prologue

1 "white skeletons like those jointed": Vidal, *Point to Point Navigation*, chapter 5.

1 "Who Murdered the Vets?": *New Masses*, September 17, 1935.

2 "tossed up into trees": Mellow, *Hemingway*, 481.

2 "Underwood, Leola, Menden, Avoca": Brennan, *An Autobiography of Jack London*, 109.

3 Coxey switched sides, abandoning: "Coxey Dies at 97," *New York Times*, May 19, 1951.

4 Coxey appointed as his majordomo: "General Coxey's Hunger Marches," *Current History*, January 1932, 550.

5 President Calvin Coolidge vetoed: McCoy, *Calvin Coolidge*, 233.

6 The freshman congressman called: Dickson and Allen, *The Bonus Army*, 5.

6 "The half million Negroes": *Advocate*, January 17, 1920.

7 Friction between black and white: Tuccille, *The Roughest Riders*.

8 Hoover decided to take action: Waters, *B.E.F.*, 179.

1. Making the World Safe

13 "We are provincials no longer": Keillor, *Hjalmar Petersen of Minnesota*, 39.

13 The war had exacted: C. N. Trueman, "First World War Casualties," http://www.historylearningsite.co.uk/world-war-one/world-war-one-and-casualties/first-world-war-casualties/.

14 The economy started to grow: Romer, "World War I and the Postwar Depression."

14 "I thought it was a darn shame": Dickson and Allen, *The Bonus Army*, 20.

15 In support of the pending: "Proceedings of the Board of Aldermen of the City of New York," 1920, 4:87.

15 It was a glorious parade: "Thousands March in Bonus Parade," *New York Times*, October 17, 1920.

15 "To float bonds": *Congressional Record*, May 29, 1920, 63.

16 Many of the returning vets: Tuccille, *The Roughest Riders*, 246.

17 Even if the money: *Cleveland Advocate*, January 17, 1920.

17 "is not in the treasury": *Washington Post*, June 1, 1920.

18 "This country is not broke": Rogers and Day, *The Autobiography of Will Rogers*, 88.

18 Thomas Edison celebrated his seventy-fifth: *New York Times*, February 12, 1922.

18 One scandal after another crippled: "Warren G. Harding's Terrible Tenure," *The Atlantic*, August 14, 2015; Murray, *The Harding Era*, 186–88, 308–14.

19 "Patriotism which is bought": McCoy, *Calvin Coolidge*, 232–34.

20 Media wags quickly labeled: Paul Dickson and Thomas B. Allen, "Marching on History," http://www.smithsonianmag.com/history/marching-on -history-75797769/.

21 He thought of himself: Patman Scrapbook, Lyndon Baines Johnson Presidential Library.

21 "They got only twenty-one dollars": *Congressional Record*, 71st Congress, 3rd session.

22 Senator Smith Wildman Brookhart: *Congressional Record*, 71st Congress, 1st session.

2. From a Roar to a Whimper

23 "Economists still agree that Smoot-Hawley": Former chairman of the Federal Reserve Ben Bernanke, speech delivered at the London School of Economics, March 25, 2013.

24 "Stock prices have reached": Rapp, *Bubbles, Booms, and Busts*, 51.

24 "Sooner or later a crash": Jeff Thomas, "Babson's Warning," http://www .internationalman.com/articles/babsons-warning.

25 "The fundamental business of": Hoover, speech to nation, October 25, 1929.

26 He subscribed to a philosophy: Rodgers, *Atlantic Crossings*.

27 "I was particularly offended": Ferrell, *American Diplomacy in the Great Depression*, 95.

28 "Our loving heavenly Father": Herbert Hoover Presidential Library.

28 "There is nothing inside": Manchester, *The Glory and the Dream*.

29 MacNider, who hoped to become: *The Biographical Dictionary of Iowa*, http://uipress.lib.uiowa.edu/bdi/.

30 The powerful banker Andrew Mellon: Hoover, *The Memoirs of Herbert Hoover*.

30 "the most favored class": Severo and Milford, *The Wages of War*.

31 "without doubt the bravest": *Indiana Evening Gazette*, April 4, 1919.

31 "We had a hundred and fifty": *Indiana Evening Gazette*, April 4, 1919.

32 "We went about thirty yards": "Heroes of Camden, New Jersey: Private First Class Joseph T. Angelo," http://dvrbs.com/camden-heroes/CamdenHeroes -Josephtangelo.htm.

33 "The number of veterans": "Veto of the Emergency Adjusted Compensation Bill," February 26, 1931, http://www.presidency.ucsb.edu/ws/?pid=22997.

3. A Motorcycle Cop

36 **"Well, I've been arrested"**: Olmstead, *Right Out of California*, 136.

36 **He arranged for the federal**: "The Artist Who Became a Cop," *Washington Post*, November 15, 1931.

37 **Benjamin fired up his followers**: "When Reds Invaded Washington," *Washington Post*, December 2, 1956.

37 **He actually became a member**: Obituaries, *New York Times*, May 14, 1983.

38 **President Hoover assured his**: Herbert Hoover Presidential Library.

38 **"Our president is still"**: Heineman, *A Catholic New Deal*, 20, 21.

39 **"an ostrich that sticks"**: Heineman, *A Catholic New Deal*, 24.

39 **Hoover's investigation came to naught**: "Father Cox, Andrew Mellon and a Huge March on Washington," *Bloomberg View*, January 10, 1912.

40 **Mellon had told Hoover**: Hoover, *The Memoirs of Herbert Hoover*.

41 **Hoover resolved his dilemma**: Schmelzer, "Wright Patman and the Impeachment of Andrew Mellon," 38.

41 **"Mr. Mellon has violated more laws"**: Schmelzer, "Wright Patman and the Impeachment of Andrew Mellon," 38.

41 **"The millions released by"**: Lisio, *The President and Protest*, 47.

42 **"Every hotel [in Washington]"**: Waldrop, *Will Rogers Views the News*, 91.

42 **After the stock market crash**: "Turning Points in Detroit History," *Michigan History Magazine*, November/December 2000, 14.

43 **"one of the coldest days"**: "Michigan History: How the Great Depression Changed Detroit," *Detroit Times*, March 4, 1999.

44 **"I would guess that hundreds"**: "Michigan History: How the Great Depression Changed Detroit," *Detroit Times*, March 4, 1999.

45 **Indeed, the Communist Party**: "The Unemployed Workers' Movement," https://libcom.org/history/1930-1939-unemployed-workers-movement.

4. American-Style Fascism

47 **He experienced his first**: Waters, *B.E.F.*, 4.

48 **Hoping that a change**: "The Bonus Army," http://mlhpresentationone.blogspot.com/p/walter-w-waters-bonus-army-commander-in.html.

48 **He wrote out a speech**: Waters, *B.E.F.*, 11.

49 **"My interest in all this"**: Waters, *B.E.F.*, 12.

50 **Stevens told President Hoover**: Parker, "The Bonus March of 1932."

51 **Even such stalwart defenders**: Mann, *La Guardia*, 308.

51 **"Soup is cheaper than"**: Mann, *La Guardia*, 308.

51 **He announced the formation**: Waters, *B.E.F.*, 1.

53 **He pulled a gun**: Douglas, *Veterans on the March*, 28.

53 **"A few of us realized"**: Waters, *B.E.F.*, 23.

54 **Waters lost no time**: Waters, *B.E.F.*, 30.

55 **The newspapers headlined the incident**: Paul Dickson and Thomas B. Allen, "Marching on History," http://www.smithsonianmag.com/history /marching-on-history-75797769/.

55 **"I don't know when"**: Severo and Milford, *The Wages of War*.

56 **The Hoover administration lived**: *Time*, January 18, 1932, 17.

5. An Unholy Alliance

57 **"The federal government could not"**: Severo and Milford, *The Wages of War*.

57 **"Intensive investigations of the past months"**: Bendersky, *The Jewish Threat*, 202.

58 **"If you feed and house"**: Glassford Papers, box 5, folder 16.

58 **"The president has taken"**: Hennessy, "The Bonus Army," 252.

58 **"He was friendly, courteous"**: Waters, *B.E.F.*, 63.

59 **"There will be twenty thousand"**: Waters, *B.E.F.*, 64.

60 **Civil rights activist Roy**: "The Bonuseers Ban Jim Crow," *Crisis*, October 1932.

60 **"We fought the last war"**: Schlesinger, *The Crisis of the Old Order*, 519.

60 **After studying the clash**: Schlesinger, *The Crisis of the Old Order*, 519.

61 **"Generally speaking, there were"**: Dickson and Allen, *The Bonus Army*, 82.

61 **Glassford had no way**: "Waters Acts to Drill Vets into Mobile Shock Troops," *Times-Herald*, June 30, 1932.

63 **Further complicating the issue**: Joslin, *Hoover Off the Record*, 265.

63 **"You're welcome here"**: *Washington Star*, May 30, 1932.

65 **"I chose one Oregon man"**: Waters, *B.E.F.*, 66.

6. The Smell of Revolution

67 **"Many of the members"**: Waters, *B.E.F.*, 72.

67 **The *New York Times***: "Walter W. Waters: Leader of the Bonus Army," http:// voiceseducation.org/content/walter-w-waters-leader-bonus-army.

68 **Party leader Emanuel Levin**: *Herald*, June 1, 1932.

68 **He threatened to organize**: *Evening Star*, June 2, 1932.

69 **Addressing the veterans from**: *Washington Post*, June 1, 1932.

70 **"I saw the unshaven"**: McLean, *Father Struck It Rich*, 303.

70 **Waters denied that he**: Waters, *B.E.F.*, 174.

71 **Some of the men maintained**: Daniels, *The Bonus March*, 105.

72 **"When we get in here"**: *Washington Post*, June 30, 1932.

72 **"The Communist Party is not"**: Wyatt Kingseed, "The 'Bonus Army' War in Washington," http://www.historynet.com/the-bonus-army-war-in -washington.htm.

72 **"I want your cooperation"**: "Army Will Not Leave Capital," *Pittsburgh Post-Dispatch*, June 9, 1932.

74 **"Clark, how would you like"**: *Washington Post*, June 8, 1932.

74 **"Men from New York"**: Waters, *B.E.F.*, 83.

7. Glassford's Frankenstein Monster

76 **"Further reductions would be"**: Lisio, *The President and Protest*, 91.

77 **On June 8, during**: *New York Times*, June 9, 1932.

77 **"There is going to be"**: Glassford memorandum, June 15, 1932, Glassford Papers.

78 **"We ought to provide"**: *Congressional Record*, 72nd Congress, June 16, 1932.

79 **Rep. James Frear of Wisconsin**: *Biographical Directory of the U.S. Congress*, http://bioguide.congress.gov/biosearch/biosearch.asp.

79 **"There is the same goulash"**: "The Veterans Come Home to Roost," *New Republic*, June 29, 1932.

79 **"New streets with their"**: "Health Threat to Army Grows," *Evening Star*, June 12, 1932.

80 **One supporter, Rep. Edward Eslick**: *Washington Post*, June 9,1932.

80 **"Those men ought not"**: Letter from Hiram Johnson to son Jack, June 18, 1932, Bancroft Library.

81 **She started to sing**: Lisio, *The President and Protest*, 113.

82 **"Waters swore to us"**: Daniels, *The Bonus March*, 127.

82 **Sen. Elmer Thomas of Oklahoma**: *Congressional Record*, 72nd Congress, 1st session, 1932.

83 **Privately Glassford was miffed**: "Gen. Glassford's Answer," *Washington Daily News*, July 1, 1932.

83 **"It is a fact that these"**: Glassford to commissioners, June 25, 1932, Glassford Papers.

84 **"I have made many mistakes"**: *Washington Star*, June 23, 1932.

84 **Waters created a subgroup**: *B.E.F. News*, July 23, 1932.

85 **The BEF's chief lobbyist**: *Evening Star*, July 12, 1932.

8. The Death March

87 **Robertson wore an elaborate**: *Washington Post*, June 21, 1932.

88 **By the middle of June**: Daniels, *The Bonus March*, 86.

88 **Robertson's response was less**: "A March of Death," *Evening Star*, July 14, 1932.

89 **"Well, I'm going to wait"**: Waters, *B.E.F.*, 165.

89 **"My men will refuse"**: *B.E.F. News*, July 23, 1932.

89 **Glassford and Gnash had**: Daniels, *The Bonus March*, 130.

90 **"When I see him"**: *New York Times*, July 16, 1932.

90 **"I do not see how"**: *New York Times*, October 19, 1932.

90 **After observing Robertson**: "A March of Death," *Evening Star*, July 14, 1932.

91 **The vets' "supreme dramatic gesture"**: *Literary Digest*, June 18, 1932.

92 **When he returned to Washington**: *Milwaukee Journal*, June 28, 1932.

92 **"These men are in"**: McLean, *Father Struck It Rich*, 304.

93 **The plight of the vets**: Dickson and Allen, *The Bonus Army*, 142.

93 **"There is not to be"**: Military Intelligence Division report, July 7, 1932.

94 Glassford flew into a rage: *Washington Daily News*, July 16, 1932.

94 "When I was ten feet": Waters, *B.E.F.*, 168.

95 "It looked for a moment": Furman, *Washington By-Line*, 122.

9. Khaki Shirts Take on the Reds

96 "We are not marching": *New York Times*, June 20, 1932.

97 "Hoover Locks Self in": Dickson and Allen, *The Bonus Army*, 157.

97 The president directed: Herbert Hoover Presidential Library.

98 "They can issue orders": *Washington Post*, July 22, 1932.

98 But new directives passed: Glassford Papers, July 2, 1932.

99 Glassford consulted with Washington's: Glassford Papers, July 2, 1932.

100 "I, as your commander": *Baltimore Sun*, July 23, 1932.

100 Defying Waters, he staged: Sneller, "Bonus March of 1932," 196.

101 At that point a Pace: Sneller, "Bonus March of 1932," 198.

101 The army had secretly: Letter from General Hof to commanding officer at Aberdeen Proving Ground, June 4, 1932.

101 Also present at the: Lisio, *The President and Protest*, 150.

102 Whitney never was able: Whitney, *MacArthur*, 513.

102 Secretary of War Patrick J. Hurley: Lohbeck, *Patrick J. Hurley*, 102.

103 Instead they treated him: Waters, *B.E.F.*, 203.

104 A police officer assigned: Daniels, *The Bonus March*, 149.

104 An increasingly rattled Waters: Sneller, "Bonus March of 1932," 208.

105 The situation took a turn: *New York Times*, July 29, 1932.

106 "It is the opinion of": Daniels, *The Bonus March*, 151.

10. An American Caesar

111 "There was some sort of": *New York Times*, July 29, 1932.

111 A passing witness named: Clark's eyewitness report to Glassford, August 1, 1932.

112 By the time Glassford: Lisio, *The President and Protest*, 185.

112 At five feet eleven: Manchester, *American Caesar*.

113 The one time MacArthur: "Gen. MacArthur Weds Mrs. Brooks," *New York Times*, February 15, 1922.

114 His military aide: Eisenhower, *At Ease*, 215.

114 Harold Ickes, who became: Perry, *The Most Dangerous Man in America*, 3.

115 "It is highly inappropriate": Eisenhower interview by Raymond Henley, July 13, 1967.

115 Later that day, U.S. attorney general: Mitchell memorandum, July 28, 1932.

116 MacArthur ordered: Miles, "Report of Operations Against Bonus Marchers," August 4, 1932.

116 Patton actually believed that: Daniel, *21st Century Patton*, 61.

117 After he received Hoover's: Sneller, "The Bonus March of 1932," 243.

118 **A sixteen-year-old boy:** "The Bonus Army: How a Protest Led to the GI Bill," NPR, November 11, 2011.

118 **Eisenhower later wrote that:** Eisenhower, *At Ease*, 217.

119 **"I told that dumb":** Wukovits, *Eisenhower*, 43.

119 **"I was coughing like hell":** "Troops Burn Anacostia," *Baltimore Sun*, July 29, 1932.

120 **"Bricks flew, sabers rose":** Weaver, "Bonus March," 94.

11. Flames Light Up the Night

121 **"These guys got in":** "The Bonus Army: How a Protest Led to the GI Bill," NPR, November 11, 2011.

122 **"While no troops went":** Eisenhower, *At Ease*, 216.

122 **A bystander named Elbridge Purdy:** *Evening Star*, July 29, 1932.

122 **In the midst of the:** *New York Times*, August 9, 1932.

123 **"Many of the soldiers":** Dickson and Allen, *The Bonus Army*, 179.

124 **Hoover roundly "upbraided" MacArthur:** Davison interview, Oral History Collection, Herbert Hoover Presidential Library.

124 **"The mob was animated":** Lisio, *The President and Protest*, 219.

125 **"I complied with your":** Bernstein, *The Lean Years*, 452.

125 **McCloskey was shocked, however:** *New York Times*, July 29, 30, 1932.

126 **The local newspaper reflected:** *Philadelphia Ledger*, July 31, 1932.

127 **The *New York Times* ridiculed:** *New York Times*, July 30, 1930.

127 **"There's no need to campaign":** Tugwell, *The Brains Trust*, 357.

127 **Roosevelt said that MacArthur:** Tugwell, *The Brains Trust*, 434.

128 **"I am chief of police":** *Washington Daily News*, August 1, 1932.

129 **The *New York Times* had:** *New York Times*, July 30, 1932.

12. Hoover Pays the Price

131 **Yet Hoover went along:** Report of Justice Department investigation of the Bonus Army, September 10, 1932.

131 **A leading correspondent:** Dickon and Allen, *The Bonus Army*, 199.

132 **Hearst reporter Elsie Robinson:** Terkel, *Hard Times*, 31.

132 **The great American satirist:** *American Mercury*, November 1932, 382.

133 **A cluster of posters reading:** "Fifty Ways to Leave the White House," *Washington Post*, November 4, 1992.

133 **Predictably Hoover claimed he:** *Portland Oregonian*, August 11, 1932.

133 **Rep. Loring M. Black:** *Congressional Record*, 72nd Congress, December 12, 14, 1932.

134 **Sen. Kenneth D. McKellar:** *New York Times*, July 30, 1932.

134 **The president-elect stepped:** FBI investigation into assassination attempt on FDR on February 15, 1933.

135 **FDR had stated innumerable times**: "Campaign Address on the Federal Budget," October 14, 1932.

135 **FDR drafted the Economy Act**: Office of the Adjutant General, June 4, 1932.

135 **"President Roosevelt is probably"**: *Congressional Record*, 73rd Congress, March 11, 1933.

135 **Rep. Hamilton Fish of New York**: Roosevelt, *Public Papers and Addresses*, 392.

137 **There were the Purple Shirts**: Hoover, FBI Bonus March Files.

138 **The men breakfasted on**: *New York Times*, May 15,1933.

138 **Infighting among the various**: *Washington Post*, May 14, 1933.

139 **"Hoover sent the Army"**: *New York Times*, May 17, 1933.

139 **A Farmer-Labor congressman**: *New York Times*, May 12, 1933.

13. The Vets March Once Again

141 **Rumors circulated that Smith**: *New York Times*, January 1, 1935.

141 **Maj. Gen. Smedley Darlington Butler**: Wolfskill, *The Revolt of the Conservatives*, 85, 94.

142 **In a letter he wrote**: Daniels, *The Bonus March*, 341.

143 **All along they had**: Schlesinger, *The Crisis of the Old Order*, 519.

144 **The encampment at Fort Hunt**: *New York Times*, September 7, 1935.

145 **Government officials were shocked**: Daniels, *The Bonus March*, 240.

145 **Most of the work camps**: Caton, *Homeless in America*, 10.

146 **This time he had history**: Ickes, *Secret Diary*, 525.

146 **Not everyone was enamored**: *New York Times*, August 11, 1935.

14. The Island of Bones

151 **Cayo Hueso sits 45**: Tuccille, *Hemingway and Gellhorn*.

151 **"As long as I can see that beacon"**: Tuccille, *Hemingway and Gellhorn*.

152 **Porter's "Mosquito Fleet," as the natives**: Tuccille, *Hemingway and Gellhorn*.

152 **"A retrospect of the history"**: Tuccille, *Hemingway and Gellhorn*.

155 **President Roosevelt responded by**: Memorandum, Stone to B. M. Duncan, March 16, 1935.

155 **"Here in Key West"**: Tuccille, *Hemingway and Gellhorn*.

158 **"I started out very"**: "How Do You Like It Now, Gentlemen?" *The New Yorker*, May 13, 1950.

158 **"FERA rule is the rule"**: *Florida Grower*, Summer 1935.

15. Paradise Lost

161 **"The camp is located"**: Boyer memorandum, December 20, 1934.

161 **"These camps are in"**: Joseph Hyde Pratt report on the veterans' camps in the Keys, February 25, 1935.

162 **"The men are quartered"**: *Miami Daily News*, March 1, 1935.

162 **Reporter Edward T. Folliard wrote**: *Washington Post*, March 24, 1935.

163 "concentration camps far away": *Time*, August 26, 1935.

163 "We expect to have between": Ghent testimony, September 19, 1935.

164 On September 1, Sunday: *Miami Herald*, September 1, 1935.

164 "would have caused high tides": *Miami Herald*, September 2, 1935.

165 "it was impossible to say": Statements made by Walter J. Bennett and Gordon E. Dunn with the Jacksonville Weather Bureau.

166 Hemingway studied his charts: Tuccille, *Hemingway and Gellhorn*.

167 "We got only the outside edge": Letter from Hemingway to Maxwell Perkins, September 7, 1935.

16. The Hurricane Makes a Direct Hit

168 "We discussed the probability": Statements made by J. L. Byrum, September 6, 1935, October 1935, National Archives and Records Administration, Record Groups 69 006.1 and 15, 5-3.

169 Ghent, who was off: Statement made by Scott Loftin, National Archives and Records Administration.

169 But that train never: *Miami Herald*, September 3, 1935.

169 "I boarded the train": *Miami Daily News*, September 5, 1935.

170 Scott Loftin's description of: Statement made by Scott Loftin, National Archives and Records Administration.

171 When the monster storm struck: Tuccille, *Hemingway and Gellhorn*.

172 "There was a big wall": Statements from various survivors, National Archives and Records Administration.

172 "All the next day the winds": Hemingway's letters to Max Perkins, September 1935, John F. Kennedy Presidential Library.

173 "Whom did they annoy": *New Masses*, September 17, 1935.

174 Despite his precautions his store: Testimony of R. W. Craig, National Archives and Records Administration.

175 Albert Buck, a vet serving: Testimony of Albert S. Buck, National Archives and Records Administration.

176 But others in the region: Testimony of Thomas Harrell, National Archives and Records Administration.

176 Eugene A. Pattison, a field engineer: Testimony of Eugene A. Pattison, National Archives and Records Administration.

177 "We had plenty of gasoline": Testimony of Joseph Hipolito Huau, National Archives and Records Administration.

177 "If the boys had keys": Statement of Frank R. Tischenbach, National Archives and Records Administration.

177 "began calling [FERA official Ray W.] Sheldon's": *Miami Herald*, September 10, 1935.

177 Sheeran informed him that: Statement of E. H. Sheeran, National Archives and Records Administration.

17. The Struggle for Survival

179 **"Somebody should have been placed"**: Testimony of W. Z. Burrus, National Archives and Records Administration.

179 **"About five o'clock in the"**: Statement of J. R. Combs, National Archives and Records Administration.

180 **"The storm started in fury"**: Statement of Earle E. Fox, National Archives and Records Administration.

181 **"During the storm I was"**: Statement of Gus Linawik, National Archives and Records Administration. (All of the preceding statements and testimonies were printed first in the *Miami Daily News*, September 4, 1935.)

181 **"When dawn broke"**: *Miami Daily News*, September 5, 1935.

182 **"We were told the train"**: Best, *FDR and the Bonus Marchers*, 73.

183 **F. L. Meyers, a Camp 3**: Statement of F. L. Meyers, National Archives and Records Administration.

183 **"At 5:00 p.m. Monday"**: *Miami Daily News*, September 5, 1935.

184 **"Having been in a hurricane"**: Statement of B. E. Davis, September 11, 1935.

185 **Thomas F. Lannon, a kitchen worker**: *Miami Daily News*, September 5, 1935.

185 **Of the 185**: Best, *FDR and the Bonus Marchers*, 94.

186 **"there was no train"**: Statement of Gus Linawik, National Archives and Records Administration.

18. The Cover-Up

188 **"Snake Creek Hotel, serving"**: *Literary Digest*, September 14, 1935.

188 **"When the Red Cross"**: *Time*, September 16, 1935.

188 **"If a child built a tiny"**: *Newsweek*, September 14, 1935.

188 **"When a *Daily News* rescue"**: *Miami Daily News*, September 5, 1935.

189 **"The foliage literally has vanished"**: *Miami Daily News*, September 5, 1935.

189 **"An aeroplane dropping a bomb"**: *Miami Daily News*, September 9, 1935.

189 **The Florida National Guard**: *Miami Daily News*, September 10, 1935.

189 **"What were the veterans doing"**: *Newsweek*, September 14, 1935.

190 **FERA administrator Harry Hopkins**: *Miami Daily News*, September 6, 1935.

190 **As Williams's assistant John J. Abt**: Abt and Myerson, *Advocate and Activist*, 50.

191 **"What kind of work"**: Telephone conversation between Ghent and Westbrook, September 5, 1935.

192 **"My God!" McIntyre exploded**: Telephone conversation between McIntyre and Westbrook, September 4, 1935.

192 **Westbrook got the imperious**: Telephone conversation between Westbrook and Stone, September 5, 1935.

193 **"Are they getting more bodies?"**: Telephone conversation among Milford, Porter, and Forbes, September 6, 1935.

193 **"It was rather, the result"**: Williams and Ijams, "Preliminary Report of Investigation of Key West Hurricane Disaster," September 13, 1935.

194 **"They were shifted around"**: *Miami Herald*, September 15, 1935.

195 **"Colonel Sheeran's actions"**: Ijams's memorandum to Frank T. Hines, January 10, 1936.

196 **An American Legion report**: Report sent by Ray Murphy to FDR, November 2, 1935.

19. The Vets Finally Get Their Money

197 **But the American Legion**: "Battling for the Bonus," vfw *Magazine*, May 1999, 18.

197 **The House passed a new**: Ickes, *Secret Diary*, 525.

198 **Each vet received an average**: *Chicago Tribune*, June 5, 1936.

198 **"They're really DOUGHboys today!"**: *Bridgeport Post*, June 17, 1936

199 **The self-styled populist served**: Cox and McCubbins, *Legislative Leviathan*, 261.

200 **The Upper Keys Historical Society**: Steinberg, *Acts of God*, 79.

201 **Disaster struck again in 1960**: Ralph Higgs, September 2, 1960, San Juan Weather Bureau.

202 **"Make no mistake about it"**: "Churchill and Hopkins: The Main Prop and Animator of Roosevelt Himself," *Finest Hour*, Autumn 2013.

202 **Tyler Kent, a code clerk**: Bearse and Read, *Conspirator*.

203 **"a rancorous expression of all"**: "G.I. Enemy No. 1," *Nation*, May 6, 1944.

203 **Several politicians**: "Veterans Need Help Now," *Boston American*, February 28, 1944.

204 **The Department of Labor estimated**: *Newsweek*, May 29, 1949.

204 **Harry W. Colmery, a former**: *New York Times*, March 9, 1944.

20. The Battle Continues

205 **"The GI Bill of Rights"**: Drucker, *Post-Capitalist Society*, 3.

206 **"a brilliant and enduring commitment"**: Brokaw, *The Greatest Generation*, 372.

206 **Michael J. Bennett sounded**: Dickson and Allen, *The Bonus Army*, 276.

207 **As late as April 27, 2012**: "President Obama Signs Executive Order Supporting Service Members," White House, April 27, 2012.

207 **A returning World War II**: "History and Timeline," U.S. Department of Veterans Affairs.

208 **In the 1960s, however**: Lyndon B. Johnson, March 3, 1966, American Presidency Project, http://www.presidency.ucsb.edu/lyndon_johnson.php.

209 **veap was popular mostly with**: "Veterans Educational Assistance Program," U.S. Department of Veterans Affairs.

210 **veap turned out to be**: Frum, *How We Got Here*, 307.

212 **Susan Haley, a former army**: *Sunday Capital*, October 23, 2016.

BIBLIOGRAPHY

Abt, John, and Michael Myerson. *Advocate and Activist: Memoirs of an American Communist Lawyer*. Champaign: University of Illinois Press, 1993.

Bearse, Ray, and Anthony Read. *Conspirator: The Untold Story of Tyler Kent*. New York: Nan A. Talese, 1991.

Bendersky, Joseph. *The Jewish Threat*. New York: Basic Books, 2000.

Bernstein, Irving. *The Lean Years: A History of the American Worker, 1920–1933*. New York: Houghton Mifflin, 1960.

Best, Gary Dean. *FDR and the Bonus Marchers, 1933–1935*. Westport CT: Praeger, 1992.

Brennan, Stephen, ed. *An Autobiography of Jack London*. New York: Skyhorse Publishing, 2013.

Brokaw, Tom. *The Greatest Generation*. New York: Random House, 1997.

Caton, Carol L. M. *Homeless in America*. Oxford: Oxford University Press, 1990.

Charles River Editors. *The Bonus Army: The History of the Controversial Protests by American World War I Veterans in 1932*. Boston: CreateSpace, 2016.

Cox, Gary W., and Matthew D. McCubbins. *Legislative Leviathan: Party Government in the House*. Oakland: University of California Press, 1993.

Daniel, J. Furman, III. *21st Century Patton: Strategic Insights for the Modern Era*. Annapolis: Naval Institute Press, 2016.

Daniels, Roger. *The Bonus March: An Episode of the Great Depression*. Westport CT: Greenwood Publishing, 1971.

Dickson, Paul, and Thomas B. Allen. *The Bonus Army: An American Epic*. New York: Walker & Company, 2004.

Douglas, Jack. *Veterans on the March*. New York: Workers Library, 1934.

Drucker, Peter F. *Post-Capitalist Society*. New York: HarperBusiness, 1994.

Eisenhower, Dwight D. *At Ease: Stories I Tell to Friends*. New York: Doubleday, 1967.

Ferrell, Robert H. *American Diplomacy in the Great Depression*. New Haven: Yale University Press, 1957.

Frum, David. *How We Got Here: The 70s, the Decade That Brought You Modern Life*. New York: Basic Books, 2000.

Furman, Bess. *Washington By-Line: The Personal History of a Newspaper Woman*. New York: Alfred A. Knopf, 1949.

Gerson, Simon W. *Pete: The Story of Peter V. Cacchione, New York's First Communist Councilman*. New York: International Publishers, 1976.

Heineman, Kenneth J. *A Catholic New Deal: Religion and Reform in Depression Pittsburgh*. University Park: Penn State University Press, 2005.

Hennessy, Arthur L. "The Bonus Army: Its Roots, Growth, and Demise." Doctoral thesis, Georgetown University, 1957.

Hoover, Herbert. *The Memoirs of Herbert Hoover*. Vol. 3. New York: Macmillan, 1952.

Ickes, Harold L. *The Secret Diary of Harold L. Ickes: The Inside Struggle, 1936–1939*. New York: Simon & Schuster, 1954.

Joslin, Theodore B. *Hoover Off the Record*. New York: Doubleday, Doran and Company, 1934.

Keillor, Steven J. *Hjalmar Petersen of Minnesota: The Politics of Provincial Independence*. St. Paul: Minnesota History Society Press, 1987.

Lisio, Donald J. *The President and Protest: Hoover, Conspiracy, and the Bonus Riot*. Columbia: University of Missouri Press, 1974.

Lohbech, Don. *Patrick J. Hurley*. 2nd ed. Chicago: Henry Regnery Company, 1947.

Manchester, William. *American Caesar: Douglas MacArthur*. New York: Little, Brown and Company, 1967.

———. *The Glory and the Dream: A Narrative History of America 1932–1972*. New York: Little, Brown and Company, 1974.

Mann, Arthur. *La Guardia: A Fighter Against His Times*. Chicago: University of Chicago Press, 1959.

McCoy, Donald R. *Calvin Coolidge: The Quiet President*. Newtown CT: American Political Biography Press, 2000.

McLean, Evalyn Walsh. *Father Struck It Rich*. Charleston SC: Nabu Press, 2014.

Mellow, James R. *Hemingway: A Life Without Consequences*. Boston: Houghton Mifflin, 1992.

Murray, Robert K. *The Harding Era: Warren G. Harding and His Administration*. Minneapolis: University of Minnesota Press, 1969.

Olmstead, Kathryn S. *Right Out of California: The 1930s and the Big Business Roots of Modern Conservatism*. New York: The New Press, 2015.

Parker, Robert V. "The Bonus March of 1932: A Unique Experience in North Carolina Political and Social Life." *North Carolina Historical Review* 51, no 1 (January 1974): 64–89.

Perry, Mark. *The Most Dangerous Man in America: The Making of Douglas MacArthur*. New York: Basic Books, 2014.

Rapp, Donald. *Bubbles, Booms, and Busts: The Rise and Fall of Financial Assets*. Gottingen, Germany: Copernicus, 2009.

Rodgers, Daniel T. *Atlantic Crossings: Social Politics in a Progressive Age*. Boston: Harvard University Press, 2000.

Rogers, Will, and Donald Day. *The Autobiography of Will Rogers*. New York: Avon, 1975.

Romer, Christina D. "World War I and the Postwar Depression." *Journal of Monetary Economics* 22, no. 1 (1988): 91–115.

Roosevelt, Franklin D. *The Public Papers and Addresses of Franklin D. Roosevelt.* 13 vols. New York: Random House, 1938–50.

Schlesinger, Arthur M., Jr. *The Crisis of the Old Order: 1919–1933.* New York: Houghton Mifflin, 1957.

Schmelzer, Janet. "Wright Patman and the Impeachment of Andrew Mellon." *East Texas Historical Journal* 23, no. 1 (1985): 33–46.

Severo, Richard, and Milford, Lewis. *The Wages of War: When America's Soldiers Came Home.* New York: Simon and Schuster, 1989.

Sneller, Maurice P., Jr. "The Bonus March of 1932: A Study of Depression Leadership and Its Legacy." PhD diss., University of Virginia, 1960.

Steinberg, Ted. *Acts of God: The Unnatural History of Natural Disaster in America.* Oxford: Oxford University Press, 2006.

Terkel, Studs. *Hard Times: An Oral History of the Great Depression.* New York: Pantheon, 1970.

Tuccille, Jerome. *Hemingway and Gellhorn.* Baltimore: WinklerMedia Books, 2009.

———. *The Roughest Riders: The Untold Story of the Black Soldiers in the Spanish-American War.* Chicago: Chicago Review Press Incorporated, 2015.

Tugwell, R. G. *The Brains Trust.* New York: Viking, 1968. Reprint, New York: Pantheon, 1970.

Vidal, Gore. *Point to Point Navigation: A Memoir.* New York: Doubleday, 2006.

Waldrop, Robert V. *Will Rogers Views the News: Humorist Ponders Current Events.* Bloomington IN: Abbott Press, 2012.

Waters, W. W. *B.E.F.: The Whole Story of the Bonus Army.* As told to William C. White. 1933. Reprint, New York: Arno Press, 1969.

Weaver, John D. "Bonus March." *American Heritage* 14, no. 4 (June 1963).

Webb, Robert N. *The Bonus March on Washington, D.C., May–June 1932.* Danbury CT: Franklin Watts, 1969.

Whitney, Courtney. *MacArthur: His Rendezvous with History.* Westport CT: Praeger, 1977.

Wolfskill, George. *The Revolt of the Conservatives: A History of the American Liberty League 1934–1940.* Westport CT: Greenwood Press, 1962.

Wukovits, John. *Eisenhower: A Biography.* New York: Palgrave Macmillan, 2006.

INDEX

Adjusted Compensation Payment Act, 197
adjusted universal compensation, 5
African American soldiers, 6–7, 16–17, 79
Alman, George, 48–49, 52, 65, 71, 73
"American Caesar." *See* MacArthur, Douglas
American Legion, 29, 133, 143, 198; and Labor Day hurricane of 1935, 188, 196–97; and lobbying for veterans' benefits, 15, 20, 197, 204–5; and opposition to bonus, 50; and Tombstone Bonus, 20
American Liberty League, 141
Anacostia. *See* Camp Marks
Anderson, Sherwood, 133
Angelo, Joseph T., 31–33, 82, 129–30
Ashurst, Harry, 135

Babson, Roger, 24–25
Baltimore Sun, 119
bank failures, 42–43
Battle of Washington, 120–25, 127
big business and veterans' benefits, 18, 19
Blacher, Fred, 118, 121
Black, Loring M., 133
black soldiers. *See* African American soldiers
Black Tuesday, 6, 23
Bolsheviks. *See* Communism
bonus, reenlistment, 211
bonus, World War I, 5–6, 7, 24, 34, 40, 69, 105, 187
bonus bill of 1922, 18
Bonus Expeditionary Force, 47, 53–55, 60, 63, 67, 68, 71, 77, 83, 87–88, 90–97, 102–3, 141; and Battle of East St. Louis, 55; and fight-night fundraiser, 73; and formation, 51–52; and internal dis-

sent, 84–85, 95, 100, 104–5, 136–37; and transformation to U.S. Fascists, 136
Boyer, F. C., 161
Brookhart, Smith Wildman, 22
Brooks, Henrietta Louise Cromwell, 113–14
Brown, George R., 132
Browne, Carl "Old Greasy," 4–5, 33, 38
Buck, Albert, 175
Buffalo Soldiers. *See* African American soldiers
Bundell, Charles M., 93
"Business Plot." *See* Butler, Smedley Darlington
Butler, Smedley Darlington, 141–42
Byrum, J. L., 168

Cacchione, Peter, 144
Camp 1, 160, 165, 171–72, 175–76, 177, 179–83
Camp 3, 160–62, 170, 175, 183–87, 188
Camp 5, 160, 175, 177, 185–87
Camp Bartlett, 64
Camp Glassford, 97
Camp Marks, 64
Camp McCloskey. *See* McCloskey, Eddie
Camp Meigs, 64
Camp Sims, 64
Carlson, Eric, 112
Christian Front, 141
Civilian Conservation Corps, 129, 138, 139, 143
Clapper, Raymond, 163
Clark, Bruce, 111
Cleveland Advocate, 7, 17
Cochran, John J., 31
Combs, J. R., 179–80

Communism, 38, 43, 44–45, 57, 59, 75, 77, 87, 96–107, 115, 131, 136, 137–38, 142, 144, 173; and Emmanuel Levin, 60, 68, 69, 138–39, 144; and Herbert Benjamin, 37; and John T. Pace, 60, 69, 93, 96, 100–101; and march on Washington, 36–37; and marginalization among veterans, 60–61, 63, 66, 68, 72, 93; and revolutionary fervor, 37, 42, 43, 45, 57, 59, 67–68, 72, 81, 124, 131, 144, 206; and Workers' Ex-Servicemen's League, 60, 143
Connery, William, 31
Coolidge, Calvin, 5–6, 19–20, 22, 26
Coughlin, Charles E., 42, 50, 197
Cox, James Renshaw, 38–40
Coxey, Jacob. *See* Coxey's Army
Coxey's Army, 2–5, 33, 38
Craig, R. W., 174–75
Crash of 1929, 22–26, 27, 28, 37, 42, 154
Crosby, Harold B., 58
Curtis, Charles, 89, 92, 94

Davison, F. Trubee, 124
depression of 1920–21, 14
Detroit News, 44
Detroit Times, 43, 44
Disabled American Veterans, 197
Dolan, Mickey, 54, 65, 66
Dos Passos, John, 79
DuPont, Pierre S., 30

Eastman, George, 18
Edison, Thomas, 18
Eicker, Walter, 101
Eisenhower, Dwight, 114–15, 116, 118–19, 120, 122, 123, 207, 208
Ellison, R. B., 144
Eslick, Edward, 80
Ex-Servicemen's Anti-Bonus League, 30

Fascism, 96, 100, 127, 136, 138, 141, 143–44, 201; and Art J. Smith, 136; and Walter W. Waters, 45, 47, 67–68, 83, 96, 127
Federal Emergency Relief Administration (FERA), 144, 156, 158, 160, 161, 163; and Julius F. Stone, 156–58; and "rehabilitation camps," 144–47, 161, 163
First World War. *See* World War I
Fish, Hamilton, III, 20–21, 135

Fisher, Irving, 24
Flagler, Henry, 154, 172, 200
Folliard, Edward T., 162, 163
Ford Massacre, 44
Fort Hunt, 137–39, 143–44
Fort Jefferson, 144, 147
Foulkrod, Harold B., 85, 136–37, 138
Fox, Earle L., 180–81
Frear, James A., 33, 79
Furman, Bess, 95

Garner, John Nance, 95
Ghent, Fred B., 163, 165, 168–69, 175–76, 177, 178, 179, 191, 195–96
Gibbons, Floyd, 131–32
GI Bill, 204, 205, 206–8, 210
Glassford, Pelham Davis, 35–37, 57–66, 67–75, 79, 81–84, 89–91, 93–95, 96, 97–101, 103, 104–7, 111, 112, 139; and Battle of Washington, 115–16, 128–29; and civil liberties, 56, 72, 99, 129; and Communists, 36–37, 38–39, 61, 72, 96; and conflict with the Hoover administration, 36, 58, 72, 75, 94, 98–99, 103, 105, 128; and military experience, 35, 129; and support for veterans, 36, 56, 57–58, 63, 70, 82, 91, 103; and veterans' benefits, 36, 94
Gnash, S. J., 89–90
Grant, Ulysses S., III, 98
Great Depression, 1, 2, 6–8, 14, 31, 36, 39–40, 45, 78, 198; and stock market crash, 23–26; and tax policy, 27; and trade policy, 23, 27; and transformation of Key West, 159; and unemployment, 42, 50, 55, 134, 199
Great Recession of 2008, 23, 41, 211
Great War. *See* World War I

Harding, Warren, 16–19, 26, 92–93, 132, 192
Hazen, Chester A., 51, 53
Headley, Albert, 96
Hearst newspapers, 28, 74, 81, 85, 132, 198
Heath, Ferry K., 97
Hemingway, Ernest, 1–2, 151, 153, 155, 158, 176; and Labor Day hurricane of 1935, 1–2, 166–67, 172–74, 179
Henry, Thomas R., 79, 90–91
Hines, Frank T., 191, 196

Hoover, Herbert, 25–30, 36, 38–41, 44, 45–46, 50, 68, 72, 75, 76, 77, 78, 79, 92–93; and central planning, 26, 27, 78; and federal spending, 27, 40; and response to veteran protests, 8, 45, 51, 55, 57, 58, 59, 61–62, 75, 85–86, 93, 95, 96–97, 98–99, 101, 102, 103, 106–7, 112, 115, 117, 123–26, 127, 128, 131–40, 206; and veterans' benefits, 6, 22, 27, 29, 33–34, 48, 50, 80–81
Hoovervilles, 7–8, 38, 80
Hopkins, Harry, 135, 172, 190–91, 194, 196, 201–2
Houston, David E., 16,
Hurley, Patrick J., 57, 102, 117, 123
Hushka, William, 112

Ickes, Harold, 114
isolationism, 16, 201–2

"Joan of Arc in Overalls," 67
Johns, William, 169–70
Johnson, Hiram, 80
Johnson, Lyndon B., 208–9
Johnson, Royal C., 34

Kelly, Charles T., 3
Kelly's Army, 2, 3
Key West, 2, 144, 147, 151–59, 160, 161, 164, 165–67, 168, 175, 176, 192, 200; and April Fools' Day fire of 1886, 153; and Ava Moore Parks, 152–53; and David Porter, 152; and Henry Flagler, 154, 172, 200. See also Labor Day hurricane of 1935; Stone, Julius, Jr.
Khaki Shirts, 54, 68, 84, 85, 90, 96–107, 136, 141, 144
Korean War, 207–8

Labor Day hurricane of 1935, 1, 8; and Federal Emergency Relief Administration preparations, 168–69, 170–71, 174, 175–76, 177–78; and public responses to veteran casualties, 173–74, 188–90, 193–96, 197; and veteran casualties, 189, 191–92, 193; and veterans' experiences, 169–70, 179–87; and warnings, 164–65, 166, 175
La Guardia, Fiorello, 51, 129
Leffingwell, R. C., 17
Levin, Emanuel, 60, 68, 69, 138–39, 144

Lewis, James Hamilton, 69
Linawik, Gus, 181, 186–87
Loftin, Scott, 169, 170–71
London, Jack, 2–3
Long, Huey "Kingfish," 90
Lower Matecumbe Key. See Camp 3; Camp 5
Lowman, Seymour, 97

MacArthur, Douglas, 76, 101–2, 112–20, 121–24, 126–28, 132, 137, 206; and attitude toward bonus marchers, 76–77, 102, 114, 115; and Battle of Washington, 8, 118–23; and defiance of presidential orders, 117, 118–20, 121–22, 124, 132
MacNider, Hanford "Jack," 29
martial law, 101, 115
McCloskey, Eddie, 125–26
McKellar, Kenneth D., 134
McLean, Charles, 147
McLean, Evalyn Walsh, 70, 92–93, 105, 126
Mellon, Andrew, 30, 39, 40–41, 136
Mencken, H. L., 132
Meyer, Bernard, 122
Meyers, F. L., 183
Miami Daily News, 162, 169, 188–89
Miles, Perry L., 116, 117, 123
Mitchell, William D., 105, 115, 131, 136
Montgomery, Gillespie V. "Sonny," 210
Moseley, George Van Horn, 57, 117, 118
Mystic Multitudes, 137

Needy Veterans Bonus Association, 144–45
New York Daily News, 97
New York Times, 7, 44, 67, 121, 127, 129, 138, 145, 147, 199

Oppressed People of the Nation, 137

Pace, John T., 60, 69, 93, 96, 100–101
Panic of 1893, 2–3
Patman, John William Wright, 6, 7, 21–22, 28–31, 34, 48, 50–51, 77–79, 135–36, 142–43, 145, 146, 197, 199, 200; and Andrew Mellon, 40–41; and Pelham Glassford, 35, 36; and Tombstone Bonus, 21; and veterans' protests, 30, 50, 56, 85
Patton, George S., 31–32, 33, 82, 116, 119, 120, 122, 129–30, 206

Patton, J. O., 104, 106
Pelley, William Dudley, 136
Pinchot, Gifford, 126
Pratt, Joseph Hyde, 161, 163
Pugh, Paul, 177
Purdy, Elbridge, 122
Purple Shirts, 137

Rankin, John Elliott, 203, 205
Reconstruction Finance Corporation, 41–42
Ritchie, Albert C., 61–62
Roaring Twenties, 14, 23
Robertson, Royal W., 87–94, 95, 98, 99, 144–45
Robinson, Elsie, 81, 132
Rogers, Edith Nourse, 203, 204, 205
Rogers, Will, 18, 42, 74, 112
Roosevelt, Eleanor, 139
Roosevelt, Franklin Delano, 8, 28, 39–40, 127–28, 129, 131, 137–38, 139–40, 142–44, 155, 159, 197, 201–3; and assassination attempt, 134; as fiscal conservative, 135–36; and Labor Day hurricane casualties, 2, 172–74, 189–96, 200; and relocation of protesting veterans, 145–47; and veterans' benefits, 90, 133, 135, 136, 140, 142–43, 146, 196–98, 202–3, 205

Shafer, W. Bruce, Jr., 14–15
Sheldon, Ray, 177–78, 183, 195–96
Shinault, George, 111
Shoemaker, Francis H., 139
Sholtz, David L., 154–55
Silver Shirt Legion, 136
Smith, Art J., 136, 141
Smoot, Reed, 78
Smoot-Hawley Tariff, 23, 27, 78
Spanish-American War, 16, 20, 35, 39
Starling, Edmund W., 61
Stevens, Henry L., Jr., 50
Stone, Julius, Jr., 155–59, 192

Thomas, Elmer, 82
Titus, Charles H., 37
Tombstone Bonus, 20–21
Truman, Harry S., 17, 132, 207
Tugwell, Rex, 127, 135

Twain, Mark, 153–54

U.S. Fascists, 136

Veterans Educational Assistance Program (VEAP), 209–10
Veterans of Foreign Wars, 35, 37, 68, 194, 197, 198; and Labor Day hurricane of 1935, 194–95; and lobbying for veterans' benefits, 15, 29, 50–51; and Tombstone Bonus, 20
Vidal, Gore, 1–2
Vietnam War, 208–10
Vinson, Fred, 78

Ward, Herbert S., 101
Washington Star, 82
Washington Tribune, 123
Waters, Walter W., 45–46, 56, 60, 62, 73, 74, 77, 81–83, 84–86, 88–89, 90–93, 94–95, 97–98, 99–100, 102, 136–37; and ambition to lead veterans, 48–50, 51–52, 53–54; as "American Hitler," 67, 127; and Battle of East St. Louis, 55; and Battle of Washington, 126–27; aka Bill Kincaid, 48; and charges of financial misconduct, 70–71; and demand for "complete dictatorial powers," 84; and Fascism, 45, 47, 61, 67–68, 83, 96, 127; and goon squads and shock troops, 65–66, 72, 84, 85, 90; and military experience, 47; and Pelham Glassford, 57, 58–59, 61, 65, 71–72, 81, 82, 84, 95, 98, 101, 103, 104–6
Waters, Wilma, 48, 92–93
Watson, James E., 58
West, W. W., 99
Westbrook, Lawrence, 191–92
Wheeler, Burton K., 78
Whitney, Courtney, 102
Wilkins, Roy, 60
Wilson, Woodrow, 13, 17, 47
Windley Key. See Camp 1
Winship, Blanton, 115
work camps for veterans, 138, 143–44, 145–46, 147, 160–63, 164–65; and Labor Day hurricane of 1935, 168–72, 173–74, 175–78, 179–87, 188–96

Workers' Ex-Servicemen's League (WESL), 60, 143

Works Progress Administration (WPA). *See* Federal Emergency Relief Administration (FERA)

World War I, 31–32, 82, 130; casualties, 13; and postwar isolationism, 16; and postwar recession, 14; and troops' pay, 14, 21, 33; as "war to end all wars," 13

World War II, 201–5. *See also* GI Bill

Wright, Clement B., 117–18

Zangara, Giuseppe, 134

Zelaya, Don, 71